The Juice

The Juice

VINOUS VERITAS

Jay McInerney

ALFRED A. KNOPF NEW YORK 2012

THIS IS A BORZOI BOOK
PUBLISHED BY ALFRED A. KNOPF

Copyright © 2012 by Bright Lights, Big City, Inc.

All rights reserved. Published in the United States by Alfred A. Knopf,
a division of Random House, Inc., New York, and in Canada by
Random House of Canada Limited, Toronto.

www.aaknopf.com

Knopf, Borzoi Books, and the colophon are registered trademarks
of Random House, Inc.

Essays contained in this book were previously published in the following publications:
House & Garden: "Aged Effervescence: 1996 Champagne," "Better Late Than Never:
Ridge," "Big Aussie Monsters," "German Made Simple," "Jacques's Domaine," "Loca-
tion, Location, Location," "Old World Head, New World Body: The Reds of Priorat,"
"Swashbuckling Dandy: Talbott," "A Tuscan in the House: Julian Niccolini and the
Four Seasons," "Way Down South: The Great Whites, and Reds, of Hamilton Russell,"
"The Whole Spice Rack: Old-School Rioja," and "The Woman with All the Toys"; *Men's
Vogue:* "His Magnum Is Bigger Than Yours"; *The New York Times Book Review:* "The
Founding Wine Geek"; *The New Yorker:* "Mondavi on Mondavi"; *The Ritz-Carlton
Magazine:* "Blending Their Way to an Identity: Paso Robles," "Pop Pop, Fizz Fizz!"
(originally titled "Champagne Don't Make Me Crazy"), and "Reasons to Be Cheer-
ful: Barolo and Barbaresco"; *Vanity Fair:* "What to Drink with Thirty-Seven Courses:
El Bulli"; *The Wall Street Journal:* "A Debilitating Pleasure: Tavel," "A Grace Kelly of
Wine: Puligny-Montrachet," "A Towering Red: Château Latour," "Barbera: Piedmont's
Everyday Red," "Becky Wasserman: The American Godmother of Burgundy," "Blood,
Sweat, and Leaps of Faith," "Cold Heaven, Hot Mama," "Does Bordeaux Still Matter?,"
"The Exquisite Sisters of Margaux," "Finally Fashionable: Rosé from Provence to Long
Island," "Is Biodynamics a Hoax?," "Is Cornas Finally Having Its Moment?," "Kiwi Reds
from Craggy Range," "Lean and Fleshy: The Paradox of Santa Rita Hills Chardonnay,"
"The Modigliani of Healdsburg," "My Kind of Cellar: Ted Conklin and the American
Hotel," "The Retro Dudes of Napa," "The Rock Stars of Pinot Noir," "Not Just Mario's
Partner: Joe 'Vino' Bastianich Breaks Out," "The Odd Couple," "Off the Main Drag:
Savigny-lès-Beaune," "Oh No! Not Pinot Grigio!," "Peasants and Plutocrats: La Paulée
de New York," "Rosé Champagne: Not Just for Stage Door Johnnies," "The Salesman
with the Golden Palate," "Secrets of Meursault," "Spanish Olympian," "Starchild and the
Marquis: Earthiness Meets Refinement in Volnay," "White Wine on the Rocks: Chablis,"
"The Wild Wizard of the Loire," "Writer, Importer, Gentleman Spy," and "Zowie!"

Library of Congress Cataloging-in-Publication Data
McInerney, Jay.
The juice : vinous veritas / by Jay McInerney. — First edition.
pages cm
ISBN 978-0-307-95728-3
1. Wine and wine making. I. Title.
TP548.M469 2012   641.2'2—dc23   2011046974

Front-of-jacket photograph by Geoff Spear
Jacket design by Chip Kidd

Manufactured in the United States of America
First Edition

05/2012

Cheers to:

Robert Bohr, Richard Breitkreutz, Lacey Burke, Belinda Chang, Stefane Colling, Thomas Combescot-Lepère, Michel Couvreux, Kenneth Eberle, Dana Farner, Jerusha Frost, Paul Grieco, Daniel Johnnes, Jordan Lari, Richard Luftig, Jean-Luc Le Dû, David Lynch, Michael Madrigale, Greg Majors, Gérard Margeon, Blue Pilkington, Jeffrey Porter, John Ragan, David Ridgway, Carla Rzeszewski, Jordan Salcito, John Slover, Mark Smith, Aldo Sohm, Bernie Sun, Raj Vaidya,

and all the other sommeliers who have educated and indulged me over the years.

What is better than to sit at the table at the end of the day and drink wine with friends, or substitutes for friends?

James Joyce

Contents

The Red and the Black

Heartbreak Hill or, The Golden Slope

Off the Beaten Path

Over the Top

Epilogue

The Juice

Introduction

It all began with Hemingway, as so many things do. Specifically with *The Sun Also Rises,* or, as the Brits call it, *Fiesta.* The latter title being apposite, because part of what I carried away from that book in my youth was the sense that drinking wine was cool and sophisticated. And let's face it, this is one of the reasons we read books, especially in our youth, particularly books by Hemingway and Kerouac and Lawrence Durrell: to find out how to live and how to pose and where to travel and what to eat and drink and smoke along the way. Everybody in Hemingway's first novel is drinking wine. Not long after my vicarious adventures in Pamplona, this sense of wine as an appurtenance of the well-lived life was reinforced by Evelyn Waugh's *Brideshead Revisited,* with Charles Ryder and Sebastian Flyte picturesquely draining the cellar at that estate over the course of a summer. I was so fixated on the wine and the scenery that I don't think I bothered to grasp the nature of their friendship. Not very Hemingwayesque, but again, for some reason I remember the wine . . .

The fact that wine had no place on my parents' suburban dining table seemed to confirm its consumption as a mark of sophistication. They and their friends drank cocktails—martinis, Manhattans, old-fashioneds, and stingers. And when they drank enough of them, they behaved badly, especially when they were in their stingers period, though this didn't strike me as romantic or chic. Much later I realized they were acting like the people in John Cheever's stories, once I finally got around to reading them; in fact it took me years to appreciate his writing, in part because his characters resembled my parents and their friends.

Hemingway was a great fan of Spanish *rosado*, which might be why, on my very first date, at the age of sixteen, I ordered a bottle of Mateus rosé, the spritzy Portuguese pink that came in a Buddha-shaped bottle. Never have I felt quite so worldly as I did that night at the Log Cabin Restaurant in Lenox, Massachusetts, as I sniffed the cork and nodded to the waiter. Many of my college romances were initiated over a bottle of Châteauneuf-du-Pape, the only red wine whose name I could remember, but while lurching toward adulthood, I preferred quicker fixes, partly in the semiconscious belief, suggested by so much of my reading, that the road of excess would lead to the palace of wisdom, that the pursuit of an artistic career as a writer required a strictly Dionysian regimen. Manhattan in the early eighties was a congenial venue for this aesthetic program, especially if your role models included Baudelaire, Dylan Thomas, Keith Richards, and Tom Verlaine. I worked at menial editorial jobs and, briefly, as a fact-checker for *The New Yorker* as I did my best to infiltrate the downtown nightclub scene, which I imagined to be the contemporary equivalent of Isherwood's Berlin or Lautrec's Montmartre.

Not long after I was fired by *The New Yorker,* I was awakened at the crack of 2:00 p.m. by a call from my best friend, who informed me that Raymond Carver was en route to my apartment. You could have knocked me over with a rolled-up twenty-dollar bill, several of which were lying on my bedside table. *Jesus Christ!* Raymond Carver on my doorstep? Granted, there was some context here: my best friend, Gary Fisketjon, a junior editor at Random House, had reviewed a chapbook by Carver for *The Village Voice* and, through his legendary champion Gordon Lish, had gotten to know him. (He would later become Carver's editor, as well as my own.) Some years before, when we were at Williams College, I lent Gary a book called *Will You Please Be Quiet, Please?,* and since then we'd both been passionate Carver fans. Now Gary was returning the favor with interest. They'd had lunch together, and Carver had nothing to do until his reading at Columbia that evening, so Gary volunteered my services as a tour guide for the afternoon, assuming that I would be thrilled. Which I was, despite an apocalyptic headache. The buzzer rang, an indistinct mumble came through the intercom—and then the doorway was filled by this hulking, slouching bear whom I ushered in to a tiny Greenwich Village apartment that showed all the signs of an arduous, recently terminated binge. We never got around to touring the city and instead talked for four or five hours, mostly about writing, until it was well past time to get Carver to his reading. At some point he said, almost apologetically, "I don't know, the life you're living here doesn't seem exactly conducive to writing." While it didn't take a master storyteller to make this observation, from him it sounded like an epiphany. Carver knew whereof he spoke, a devotee of Alcoholics Anonymous who credited that organization with saving his life. Six months later I moved to Syracuse to study with Ray and clean up my act.

Having heard nutritionists distinguish between good fats and bad fats, I would propose a similar dichotomy for intoxicants. Certainly this was the opinion of Thomas Jefferson, the nation's first wine geek. "No nation is drunken where wine is cheap," he declared, "and none sober where the dearness of wine substitutes ardent spirits as the common beverage. It is, in truth, the only antidote to the bane of whiskey." Or vodka, I might add. One can't help but wonder how different Russia's history might have been if the country was warm enough for viticulture. "Wine is one of the most civilized things in the world," Hemingway wrote in *Death in the Afternoon,* "and one of the natural things of the world that has been brought to the greatest perfection, and it offers a greater range for enjoyment and appreciation than, possibly, any other purely sensory thing." Not his greatest prose, perhaps, and like so many encomiums to wine—the earnest Jefferson's springs to mind—it leaves out the buzz factor. Still, it impressed me at the time, especially since I'd discovered that the bane of whiskey and the road of excess hadn't led me to any palaces at all.

But Syracuse was leading me in far more rewarding directions, in large part thanks to Ray and Tobias Wolff demonstrating how to advance from apprenticeship into actual *writing*. To supplement my fellowship—tuition plus four grand a year—I worked as a clerk in the Westcott Cordial Shop, whose Princeton-educated proprietor had an extensive wine library and high hopes for the scabrous neighborhood's eventual gentrification. Here I could oscillate between the stories of Isaac Babel and Hugh Johnson's *World Atlas of Wine,* dip into the stock after finishing my shift, and gradually refine my rudimentary palate.

This is also where I got the call, some two years on, that my novel had been bought by Random House, and a subsequent one from a guy who kept calling me "babe" and wanted to fly me out to Hollywood to meet with his fellow executives at Paramount. "We'll put you up at the Chateau Marmont," he said. "Is that good?" I asked. "It's better than good," he assured me. "John Belushi *died* there." Clearly he'd read *Bright Lights, Big City,* or at least the coverage of the book, and formed an opinion of my bad habits.

A decade later, I was able to merge these double-barreled habits of wine and writing. My friend Dominique Browning, in charge of resurrecting Condé Nast's *House & Garden,* knew of my developing vinous passion, invited me to do a monthly column, and proceeded to send me pretty much any place in the world where I thought there was a good wine story—a master-class education I am profoundly grateful for, and one that would be hard to imagine in this era of editorial budget slashing and what's beginning to look like the mass extinction of general-interest publications. Indeed, somewhat ahead of the curve, *House & Garden* was shut down in 2007. Sad as I was about its demise and my friend's misfortune, I reasoned that it had been a hell of a good run. I'd never intended to write about wine for more than a year or two, and it was time to turn all my energies back to fiction. And so I did until, a couple of years later, *The Wall Street Journal* came calling. A few of the following essays, much revised here, date back to Dominique's magazine, and most from my current gig. One of them, a review of Robert Mondavi's autobiography published in *The New Yorker,* seemed very much worth reprinting here in the wake of his passing. The world of wine would likely look—and taste—very different if not for Mondavi, whom I was fortunate enough to spend time with on several occasions.

Heraclitus tells us you can never step into the same river twice, "for other waters are ever flowing on to you." And likewise, it seems to me, you can never really drink the same wine twice. The appreciation of wine, for all that we might try to quantify it, is in the end a subjective experience. More than a poem or a painting or a concerto, which is problematic enough for the aesthetician, the 1982 La Mission, say, or the 1999 Beaucastel is a moving target. Good wine continues to grow and develop in the glass and in the bottle, to change from one day to the next in response to barometric pressures and other variables; moreover, any given wine— from the same maker, the same vintage, even the same barrel—is subject to our own quirks of receptivity, to the place and the company in which we drink it, to the knowledge we bring with us, and to the food with which we pair it. Even so, in order to develop our appreciation, we agree to a fictional objectivity and attempt to isolate wine from these contextual variables, to treat each and every glass in front of us as if it contained a stable and quantifiable substance. We Americans are often scolded for adhering to this view, and one critic in particular has been accused of reducing wine's infinite variety and complexity to a vulgar game of numbers. On the other hand, the felon in question, Robert Parker, has helped to democratize and demystify something that until very recently was stuffy, arcane, and elitist. His core belief—that wine can be evaluated and graded like any other consumer product—was hugely liberating for those of us on both sides of the Atlantic who wanted to penetrate the mysteries of the great French growths. And it took this middle-class lawyer, who'd grown up drinking *soft drinks* with meals, to begin to clear away the musty, upper-class stench of oenophilia.

I've learned quite a bit in the last fifteen years, and my tastes have shifted accordingly (if sometimes mystifyingly). Burgundy has become something of an obsession, and there are more than a few essays—an entire section, actually—devoted to the fickle, intermittently exhilarating, and heartbreaking wines of that region. But I still love Bordeaux, not only the famous wines, but also the Crus Bourgeois from relatively obscure corners like Fronsac and Lalande-de-Pomerol, which represent tremendous value in the face of the madly escalating prices of the classed growths from the 2009 and 2010 vintages. Just when I think my interest in California is flagging, I taste a new wine like Steve Matthiasson's white blend or an old one like Araujo's 1995 Eisele Vineyard Cabernet Sauvignon and get excited all over again. Italy now accounts for about a third of American wine imports and for me remains a continuing source of wonder and pleasure. Spain might well be the new Italy, a country with a long history of wine making that's finally waking up to its potential. Something similar is happening in South Africa, which has a wine-making tradition extending back to the seventeenth century.

Some of the wines I write about here are costly and hard to find, but I believe it's one of the wine writer's duties, however arduous it might sound, to bring back news of the best and the rarest, just as it's the travel writer's duty to explore exotic and remote destinations. Most readers of automotive magazines won't ever drive a Lamborghini or a Ferrari, and most wine drinkers will never hold a glass of Château Latour, but as an avid reader of *Car and Driver* I'd hate to see it limit its coverage to sensible, affordable rides. No, I want a knowledgeable, badass driver to tell me what it's like to power the new Gallardo Superleggera through the Alps. So, yes, there's some wine porn here. That said, some of the most surprising and exciting moments involve obscure and undervalued wines like the 2007 Movia Pinot Grigio from Slovenia or overachievers like the 2007 Château Jean Faux Bordeaux, which at $25 retail is $1,200 cheaper than the 2010 Latour.

Much as I have ostensibly learned since I started writing about wine, and as lucky as I have been to have tasted some of the renowned vintages, I'm not sure that I've ever enjoyed a bottle of wine more than I did that Mateus rosé back in the Berkshires in 1972. I'd lately acquired my driver's license and was in the company of my first love, with the night and the entire summer stretched out ahead of me like a river full of fat, silvery, pink-fleshed rainbow trout. The wine tasted like summer, and it was about to become the taste of my first real kiss.

Acid Trips

SOME WHITES AND PINKS TO START

White Wine on the Rocks: Chablis

Is it possible to taste minerals in fermented grape juice? Can the roots of the grapevine somehow transmit the unique characteristics of soil and bedrock to the grape itself? Is it a gross abuse of poetic license to detect marine elements in a wine grown on limestone that was once a Jurassic seabed? You might never have asked these questions, but they go to the heart of the French notion of *terroir*—the idea that a wine's qualities are determined by its place of origin. Nowhere do these questions seem more relevant than in Chablis.

"Chablis, oh yeah, that's the stuff my mom used to drink out of a box," a friend told me when I ordered a glass before dinner. "Yeah, right," I said. "And that watch I bought on the street for twenty bucks when I moved to New York was a genuine Rolex."

Like Vuitton or Chanel, Chablis is a world-famous brand that has inspired countless knockoffs and counterfeits over the years. Some of my own earliest encounters with fermented grapes involved something called Almaden California Mountain Chablis, a product that's still on the market. But *le vrai* Chablis, which comes from the northernmost vineyards of Burgundy, is less understood than almost any other major wine type, even though it's made from Chardonnay, the world's favorite white grape. With several terrific vintages currently available on our shores, this is a very good time to come to terms with Chablis.

For hundreds of years tasters have invoked the sea when talking about Chablis, and just as frequently limestone and even flint. Actually, there's a geological basis for these seemingly fanciful associations. The bedrock underlying the region of Chablis is part of what the geologist James Wilson, in his book *Terroir*, calls the Kimmeridgian chain—a huge Cretaceous/Jurassic deposit of chalky marl and limestone riddled with fossil seashells, notably *Exogyra virgule*, a small, comma-shaped oyster. The White Cliffs of Dover are part of this vast formation, which rises and falls beneath north-central France. It crops up in the Loire regions of Sancerre and Pouilly, and then farther west in Chablis. It could be a coincidence that Sancerre and Chablis, though the former is made from the Sauvignon Blanc grape, are traditionally considered perfect wines to accompany oysters. On the other hand, romantics, and certain geologists, think it may have something to do with the prehistoric oyster shells underneath the vineyards. I can't necessarily explain the chemistry of flavor, but I can say if you have never had oysters with Chablis, you should try to rectify this failure immediately.

Chablis is a great food wine, although some true believers seem to hate to mix it up with solids. According to the Beastie Boy Mike Diamond, a serious fan, "It pairs so well with so many foods, yet it's almost an injustice to share a really good Dauvissat or Raveneau with food. I kind of prefer to hog it all to myself, savoring every sip."

Although Chablis is officially part of Burgundy, its unique geology, combined with the fact that it lies almost fifty miles from the northernmost vineyards of the Côte d'Or, makes its whites quite different from those of Meursault or Puligny. According to *The Oxford Companion to Wine:* "There is a unique streak of steely acidity, a firm flintiness, and a mineral quality that is not found elsewhere in Burgundy." And if they're distinct from their Burgundian cousins, they are light-years removed from New World Chardonnays. If you are accustomed to the ripe, tropical-fruit style of old-school Sonoma Chardonnays, like Kistler or Sonoma-Cutrer or Kendall-Jackson Vintner's Reserve, you may have a hard time detecting the family resemblance of Chardonnay grown in chilly Chablis. This is Chardonnay unplugged and stripped down to its essence, like Eric Clapton's acoustic version of "Layla."

Whenever I think about comparing Chablis with Cali Chardonnay, I think of Audrey Hepburn in *Breakfast at Tiffany's*. Truman Capote wanted Marilyn Monroe to play the part; she could have been great, but it would have been a very different movie. And Chardonnay grown in Chablis's Serein River Valley as opposed to the Napa Valley comes out very different indeed. Young Chablis is lean and racy, although with age the best Chablis takes on a dazzling richness.

One of the best things about Chablis is that it's possible to experience its unique character even in the less expensive bottlings. When you spend even $20 on a Village wine from a quality-oriented producer, there is no mistaking where it is from. Chablis shares Burgundy's system of vineyard hierarchy—Grand Cru being the highest designation followed by Premier Cru and finally Village wine, labeled simply "Chablis." The seven Grands Crus all occupy a single contiguous southwest-facing hillside across the valley from town. The Premiers Crus occupy various well-exposed slopes, while the flatter and cooler sites are home to Village Chablis.

The top Grands Crus from the various Montrachet vineyards can cost $400 or $500, while the Grands Crus of Chablis are usually priced in the double digits. Even generic Chablis can be a fine drink, with a citric snap and a touch of minerality, particularly in vintages like 2007 and 2008. The 2009 vintage is a little richer and fleshier, which might make it a good introductory Chablis for those with New World palates. When I first wrote about Chablis, one had to be very choosy with makers, some of whom were lazy and others over-infatuated with new oak barrels, but the level of wine making overall has greatly improved in recent years.

Raveneau and Dauvissat have long been acknowledged as the

top producers, but William Fèvre, under the management of the brilliant Joseph Henriot, has now joined their ranks. Top wines from these domaines develop incredible complexity with age. Domaine Drouhin Vaudon, owned by the Beaune-based negotiant Joseph Drouhin, has made particularly impressive 2008s. (Not to be confused with Droin, which has also made its best wines yet with this vintage.) The local cooperative La Chablisienne turns out surprisingly good Chablis at all levels. Some other favorites: Billaud-Simon, Louis Michel, Christian Moreau, Pinson, Daniel Dampt, Laroche, and Barat.

These and other makers may convince you that it's possible to taste rocks, or even fossils, in your glass. At the very least you will discover the best of all possible matches for an oyster.

Cold Heaven, Hot Mama

Making a name for oneself as a winemaker with a grape that almost no one has ever heard of is a bit like writing pop songs for the cello. "Eleanor Rigby" aside, you're probably starting with a handicap. But Morgan Clendenen had her reasons for choosing Viognier as the focus of her aspirations when she started Cold Heaven in 1996. For one thing, her then husband, Jim Clendenen, cast a long shadow as the godfather of Pinot Noir and Chardonnay in the Santa Barbara region. Starting his winery, Au Bon Climat, in 1982, he'd been instrumental in showing the potential these Burgundian varietals had, which influenced his wife's decision to try something different. That and the fact that she loved Viognier, a passion I happen to share.

Although it seems to be a descendant of the northern Italian Nebbiolo, this grape found a home on the steep slopes of the Rhône River just south of Côte Rôtie in a small appellation called Condrieu. It appeared to be headed for extinction just a few decades ago; in the French agricultural census of 1968 only thirty-five acres remained here and in the tiny adjacent appellation of Château-Grillet. Fortunately, Condrieu was rediscovered in part thanks to the enthusiasm of Robert Parker and to the efforts of Etienne Guigal, the renowned Côte Rôtie winery, which has become the largest producer of Condrieu. Indeed, there was a moment when Condrieu was almost fashionable, at least among wine wonks.

What makes Condrieu irresistible to some of us is its heady aroma and flavors, both of which suggest peaches and apricots and honeysuckle, as well as its rich, viscous texture. The best smell as if they will be sweet, and even start out tasting that way, but finish dry. They are full-bodied, voluptuous whites that stop just short of being floozy. Viognier is low in acid, and if it gets too ripe, it will remind you of the syrup at the bottom of canned fruit salad. In Condrieu, the climate and the soils, not to mention generations of experience, usually seem to keep Viognier from putting on the red light. But there will always be a hint of decadence, something fin de siècle and Oscar Wildeish, about it.

In the past two decades Condrieu fans have planted Viognier around the world, from the Languedoc to Australia, with decidedly mixed results. In California's central coast, pioneers like John Alban and Calera's Josh Jensen made some promising examples; more recently, Greg Brewer has produced racy Viogniers at Melville in the Santa Rita Hills appellation. Morgan Clendenen, who looks in person like a cross between Jodie Foster and Kate Hudson, grew up in rural North Carolina, where her father had a bottled-springwater company. "My dad would set up water tastings. I became attuned to slight variations in flavors and tastes." When she got a job with a local wine importer, she noticed that the Calera Viognier always sold out in advance, and while she never got to taste it, she was intrigued. Moving west to pursue her interest in wine, she spent eighteen months at Sinskey Vineyards in Napa, where she met Jim Clendenen. For an aspiring winemaker, marrying such an icon was a mixed blessing. She needed to find her own niche. When the owner of the Sanford and Benedict Vineyard asked Jim if he had any interest in a batch of Viognier, "Jim said no, but I kicked him under the table," she says. "I was interested." Thus was her Cold Heaven winery born.

"I loved Condrieu but was less than impressed with most of the California Viogniers that started appearing in the nineties. In Condrieu it makes this elegant noble wine, but here in California it was sweet and cloying." In fact, most Golden State microclimates are probably too hot for Viognier, but Clendenen believed that parts of the central coast, with its transverse valleys that funnel cool Pacific air into the interior, could prove congenial. Cool heaven, so to speak. (The winery is actually named after a Yeats poem.) After stumbling on the grapes from Sanford and Benedict in 1996—no one could quite tell her when they were planted or by whom—she decided to plant more at the Le Bon Climat Vineyard in the Santa Ynez Valley in 1998. With her husband she traveled to Condrieu to taste Viognier at the source. She wanted to meet Yves Cuilleron, the rising star of the appellation, but he was away when she first visited, and she subsequently ran into him in her own backyard at the Hospice du Rhône in Paso Robles, an annual event celebrating Rhône Valley wine varietals.

Cuilleron's grandfather had founded the estate, although Yves had little interest in wine when he was growing up. "I thought I would be a mechanic," he told me when I first visited him, as we walked the steep Chaillon vineyard looking down on the silvery Rhône River below. "And then, during my military service, I was sent to Alsace, where I became interested in food and wine." In 1987 he took over the family domaine and helped spark the renaissance of the appellation, taking his place alongside the standard-bearers like Georges Vernay and André Perret.

It's not hard to imagine him being charmed when he met the attractive young American at the Hospice du Rhône. More important, he liked her wine. She traveled again to Condrieu, and together they hatched an improbable plan—to make a Franco-American blend using grapes from both places. In 2002, Cuilleron shipped several barrels of Condrieu to Santa Ynez, where Clendenen blended them with juice from the Sanford and Benedict Vineyard. The wine, called Deux Cs, quickly became a cult item, fought over by sommeliers on both coasts of the United States. The som who first introduced me to it leaned in close and whispered the news, as if he were offering me something illegal. *Jim Clendenen's wife . . . Cuilleron . . . sick juice.* ("Sick juice" is sommelier speak for "great wine.") And indeed it tasted almost criminally decadent.

The duo launched a second wine, Domaine des Deux Mondes, using Sanford and Benedict grapes vinified to Cuilleron's recipe. Ironically, the master of Condrieu favors a richer, deeper, almost New World style, using new oak barrels, which Clendenen normally eschews, and riper grapes. Her natural style is frankly more Old World; she picks early to maintain acidity and ferments in old barrels. The Clendenen-made, Cuilleron-styled Viognier is called Saints and Sinners—"because in France Yves would be considered a sinner for performing this kind of experiment," she explains, "but he's a saint to us Americans." Whatever, the result tastes more sinful than saintly to me, and I mean that as a compliment. Cuilleron recommends trying his wines with Thai and other spicy Asian cuisines; Clendenen concurs, and also suggests Mexican. I'd add lobster to the list.

The Clendenen marriage ended a few years ago, and Morgan had to scramble to find a new home for her winery, formerly housed in the sprawling Au Bon Climat and Qupé quarters Jim shares with the Syrah star Bob Lindquist in the middle of the Bien Nacido Vineyards. But her partnership with Cuilleron continues. Her own Cold Heaven Viogniers are available from the winery, and Cuilleron's Condrieus can be found, intermittently, in most major American markets. The largest producer of Condrieu, Guigal, is easier to find and inevitably excellent, as are the more exclusive bottlings of André Perret and Georges Vernay. Alban, Calera, and Melville are among the most consistent California producers. When you find any of the above, feel free to pop the cork right away. Not particularly benefiting from age, Viognier is a wine of instant gratification. It's a wine for hedonists, for followers of Dionysus rather than of Apollo, for those who secretly like Gauguin more than Cézanne.

Oh No! Not Pinot Grigio!

Oddly enough, the first time I encountered Pinot Grigio was at Elaine's, the legendary Manhattan restaurant, back in the eighties, when the literary lions of the silver age were roaring and preening there. This is what Norman Mailer called his era; Fitzgerald, Hemingway, and Faulkner ruled the golden age, and I was a representative, he informed me cheerfully, of the bronze age. Most of the writers who frequented the place drank scotch mixed with testosterone. Mailer, George Plimpton, William Styron, Peter Maas, Gay Talese, Kurt Vonnegut—these guys were the highball generation, and they seldom bothered with anything as wimpy as white wine. Nevertheless, women were usually present, and I recall a lot of Santa Margherita Pinot Grigio on the tables. Not being much of a scotch fan, I drank gallons of it myself, though I tried not to do so when Mailer was watching. Many others, apparently, were doing the same.

Santa Margherita Pinot Grigio is one of the great marketing success stories of modern times, the reason that Pinot Grigio is virtually a brand name, the second-most-requested wine by the glass in American restaurants. It was pretty much unknown in the United States when Tony Terlato, a young importer, went to Italy in 1979 in search of the next great white varietal. The story goes that at a hotel in Milan he was charmed by a glass of something called Pinot Grigio and promptly drove to Alto Adige, in northeastern Italy, to find it. "Upon arriving," according to the Terlato Wines Web site, "Tony sat down at a small restaurant in a local inn and ordered 18 bottles of Pinot Grigio off of the wine list."

The winner was called Santa Margherita. He promptly set off to visit the winery and secure the rights to import the wine. Thirty years later, Santa Margherita annually exports 600,000 cases to the States, selling at around $30 a bottle retail, while brands like Cavit and Ecco Domani have taken advantage of demand with lower-priced wines. The Australian wine giant Yellow Tail is piling on with its own version. PG has become such a celebrity it has impersonators; according to one industry insider, the price of these grapes in Italy has soared to the point that much of what gets sold as Pinot Grigio is in fact composed of cheaper white grapes like Chardonnay and Garganega.

It's doubtful whether PG would have become famous if it had been called Gray Pinot. The grape originated in France—where it's called Pinot Gris—as a mutation of Pinot Noir, but it never got much recognition under that name. Still, the variety does well elsewhere, and it's interesting that some New World producers call their wines Pinot Gris while others, like Steve Clifton of Palmina, use the Italian moniker. And weirdly enough, in Alsace, where it reaches perhaps its greatest heights, it's sometimes called Tokay. Go figure.

In Oregon, where it has become something of a specialty, most producers use the French name. It was introduced here by the same man who brought Pinot Noir to the Willamette Valley, David Lett of Eyrie Vineyards, and acreage has increased steadily over the years. At its best Oregon Pinot Gris tastes like ripe pears, with smoky highlights. Some makers barrel ferment the grapes, like their counterparts in Alsace, which results in a slightly richer wine than is typical in Italy. "It has a unique spicy style that goes well with Asian and fusion cuisine," says Mark Vlossak of St. Innocent Winery, in Salem, who makes one of the real standouts. Initially, he emulated the Italian model, but after visiting Alsace, he moved toward that region's richer style.

In eastern Long Island, where the climate is similar to that of

Friuli, the source of the best Italian examples, Christopher Tracy of Channing Daughters uses the name Pinot Grigio. He fell in love with the crisp Friulian versions and thinks the grape deserves more respect. "Done with care with moderate to low yields, it can be amazing." He loves the "oilier and weightier" Alsatians but feels his climate is better suited to the style of northeast Italy. "The flavor profile with luck has that elusive minerality. And also a white-flower quality and a tree-fruit character." Tracy makes a crisp, stony tank-fermented version and also a Ramato style, fermented with the skins, which can vary in color from purple to gray. This was the traditional method in Friuli for many centuries. Ramato, which means "copper" in Italian, describes the color of the finished wine, which is much richer than the white versions. "The majority of the flavor compounds are in the first six or seven layers of cells in the skins, and as a result the Ramato is more intensively flavored." In fact it's a very intense, rich dry wine that behaves more like a red than a white, and it does well with anything barbecued and is also great with a cheese plate.

Pinot Grigio found a niche in part because it's more versatile and less assertive than oaky Chardonnay. But popularity comes at a price. (Just ask the members of Coldplay.) Most serious wine drinkers shun PG the way they once shunned Soave, and not entirely without reason. One should never underestimate the power of snobbery, but the fact is, 99 percent of what's called Pinot Grigio from Italy is dilute and flavor challenged, a refreshing, lemonade-like food lubricant and buzz-delivery system.

Like many of my peers, I turned my back on Pinot Grigio early in the nineties and remained slightly embarrassed about my early enthusiasm, much as I did about my earlier reverence for the music of the Monkees. PG seemed like the vinous equivalent of the novels of Paulo Coelho. As its popularity grew and it was planted all over Italy, far beyond its natural home in the northeast, its identity became rather nebulous. Then, about ten years ago, I visited

Friuli, and I drank some very good, in fact some really excellent, Pinot Grigio, and then wondered if a reconsideration was called for. After all, PG is a mutation of Pinot Noir, universally acknowledged to be one of the greatest grapes on the planet.

In Friuli, I had really stunning examples from Lis Neris and Vie di Romans, but of course we all know the syndrome of the little country wine that tastes unbelievably great in context, when one is on vacation, surrounded by scenic ruins and charming rustics. But a few years ago I dined at Gramercy Tavern with Alois Lageder, a fifth-generation winemaker from the Alto Adige region, and I was highly impressed by his Pinot Grigios, notably a single-vineyard bottling called Benefizium Porer. More recently on a visit to the Breslin Bar, a fashionable and calorific Manhattan hot spot, I encountered a Pinot Grigio that blew my mind and encouraged me to reopen the question, can PG possibly be serious? The wine was a 2007 Pinot Grigio from Movia, a winery founded a year before Lageder's in 1823, adjacent to some of the best vineyards of Friuli, just across the border in Slovenia.

I had met Aleš Kristančič, Movia's winemaker and proprietor, in Friuli and again in New York, and he impressed me as one of the most energetic, not to say manic, characters of my acquaintance. In my notes from that first encounter, I quote him as saying: "We are solar men. Our power is not money. We can find solar energy in a dark place." I believe he was speaking about marshaling the sun's energy in the dark recesses of a wine cellar, but who the hell knows. He also makes up a lot of words. At any rate, his wines are incredibly expressive and singular, and already, in his mid-forties, he's legendary. Like almost everything about Aleš, his Pinot Grigio is larger than life, rich and concentrated with a host of exotic fruit and mineral flavors. Was this a one-off, or was it possible that real men could drink Pinot Grigio again? I started buying and tasting as many PGs as I could find, subjecting myself to the derision of sommeliers and wine store clerks.

I consulted Henry Davar, the wine director at the Manhattan restaurant Del Posto, who helped me to organize a tasting. Davar was enthusiastic about this project, though he informed me, somewhat ominously, "We don't serve PG by the glass. We don't want our guests to order something just by default." We stuck mostly to bottles from northeast Italy, to see if we could find regional as well as varietal characteristics. And I'm sorry to say we had more misses than hits, although the latter gave us hope and a few wines to put into rotation on our drinking cards. We were hard-pressed to find any flavor at all in the 2009 Santa Margherita, maybe the merest hint of lemon drop? But flavor abounded in the 2009 Palmina, the winemaker Steve Clifton's Cali-Itali project. Or is that Itali-Cali? Whichever—he grows Italian varietals in Santa Barbara, and his Pinot Grigio is really impressive, especially at $20 a bottle.

"I tasted some great Pinot Grigios in Friuli," he says, "and I wanted to make one that wasn't just a water substitute. It has to be grown on a good site that expresses minerality, but at its best it's a bridge between Sauvignon Blanc and Chardonnay. Pinot Grigio hits the middle for seafood dishes that are too delicate for Chardonnay."

A certain stony element characterized the PGs Davar and I liked the best—and sometimes stone fruits like peaches—most of them from the Collio region of Friuli. The standouts were three successive vintages of Movia's Pinot Grigio, the 2005–2007, the latter being a spectacular wine with a nose suggestive of a young red Burgundy, reminding us that PG is indeed a relative of that noble grape. "You can drink Pinot Grigio as a thirst quencher on a terrace," Davar said afterward. "Then there are a few wines like these, which are on a level with the great whites of France."

Anyone who's ever had a Zind Humbrecht Pinot Gris will believe that nobility is possible with this grape. The best Italian examples come from small, deeply committed producers in Friuli around the Collio region and Alto Adige, and at $20 to $25 they represent real value. I'm going to seek out Pinot Grigios by Schio-petto, Lis Neris, Lageder, Jermann, Vie di Romans, and Long Island's Channing Daughters, the sneers of my peers be damned. But I don't recommend that anyone undertake this course lightly. One of the scents I sometimes imagined in nosing certain Pinot Grigios was hay, which brings to mind the all too apposite maxim about the needle in the you-know-what.

Pop Pop, Fizz Fizz

Champagne don't hurt me baby
Cocaine don't drive me crazy
—Eric von Schmidt

You might imagine that the recession would have killed the Champagne market, especially the superpremium brands, the so-called Têtes des Cuvées, all priced above $100. If so, you'll be surprised to discover that just a year after Lehman tanked, arguably the finest house of all, Krug, released the second vintage of a single-vineyard cuvée at around $3,500 a pop. Fortunately, a lot of great Champagne is available for double digits, and those prices have softened over the past year. In fact, thanks to the explosion of small growers and good weather, there's probably never been a better time to drink Champagne.

Do I need to explain that by Champagne, I mean the sparkling wine from the eponymous region north of Paris? Many places around the world produce good sparkling wines, but they are not Champagne, and you'll have to read about them elsewhere. Champagne is the product of a uniquely marginal climate, which in an average year just barely ripens the grapes, and a set of soils based on limestone. The large houses blend wines from different vineyards and grapes, including Pinot Noir, Pinot Meunier, and Chardonnay, to create a relatively uniform product year in and year out, and you can hardly go wrong with the nonvintage bottlings from Veuve Clicquot, Pol Roger, Bollinger, Moët, and Perrier-

Jouët, although only by tasting will you learn which style most appeals to you. For instance, Bollinger, beloved of the Brits, tends to be heavier and heartier than the more citrusy Perrier-Jouët.

While blending smooths out the deficiencies of inferior vintages and helps maintain a brand's signature, most houses produce single-vintage bottlings in years that are at least theoretically exceptional. These inevitably cost more, and whether they're worth it or not is strictly a matter of taste and budget. At the top of the Champagne hierarchy are the luxury cuvées—vintage bottlings from the best vineyards and the best lots, usually, packaged in exotic-looking bottles, Dom Pérignon being unquestionably the most famous. If you can afford it, it's extraordinarily good, although there is significant vintage variation. Cristal, Dom Ruinart, Veuve Clicquot's La Grande Dame, Pol Roger's Cuvée Sir Winston Churchill, and Taittinger's Comtes de Champagne are all very good and tend to get better with age. They also make a big statement whenever one is required. If you really need to impress somebody, choose DP because it speaks the lingua franca.

For those more interested in quality than image, and whose budgets aren't unlimited, the real excitement these days comes from "grower Champagnes"—what the importer Terry Theise calls "farmer fizz." The grapes that go into the vats of the big houses come largely from thousands of small individually owned vineyards throughout the region. In recent years more and more of these growers have begun to bottle their own wine, and several astute American importers have been scouring the rolling hills around Reims and Épernay to discover the best of them.

Visiting Francis Egly in the village of Ambonnay is a very different experience from visiting the grandee's corporate offices. When Mrs. Egly finally answers the door of the small Tudor house in the middle of a vineyard, she kicks aside baby toys to clear my path into the living room. It takes her some time to locate her husband, Francis, who's out on his tractor, and when I shake his hand, he apologizes for the dirt on his fingers. I tell him dirty hands are a good sign on anybody growing grapes. But his winery, in a new concrete-and-steel barn out back, is spotless, and his wines are among the most distinctive in all of Champagne. You'll find them on some of the best wine lists from Paris to Napa and beyond.

The guru of the grower movement is Anselme Selosse, another proud farmer with dirty hands who studied in Burgundy and brought back to his father's domaine in Avize all kinds of new ideas, including the basic insight that everything begins in the vineyards. In Champagne, however, this was a radical idea—the big houses bought grapes in bulk from growers who had little incentive for meticulous viticulture.

Smaller is not always better, but it's not unlikely that a guy making his own wine with his own grapes is going to take better care of them than someone who sells them by the pound to a corporation. Another argument in their favor is that almost everywhere else, specificity of origin is considered essential to any wine's character. In a (French) word, *terroir:* the concept that wine reflects the weather, soil, geology, and topography of the land on which the grapes are grown, and that the most unique and exceptional wines come from a single exceptional vineyard. In Burgundy, for instance, grapes grown in the vineyard of Romanée-Conti produce the most prized reds in the world, while those grown only a few hundred feet away in different soil and at different elevations sell for thousands less. Not all these Champagnes come from a single vineyard—some growers own different patches of land—but most come from specific villages, and experienced tasters distinguish between one from Mesnil and another from Bouzy. "Single vineyards are the future," says Selosse, whose wines you're likely to find only on the finest restaurant lists.

The $3,500 release from Krug is from a single vineyard called Clos d'Ambonnay. While the virtues of blending are evident in the company's superb multi-vintage Grand Cuvée (it's called "multi" instead of "non" presumably to distinguish it from lesser, cheaper blends), Krug almost single-handedly made the single-vineyard case with its Clos du Mesnil, which it first released in 1979 and which until the release of Clos d'Ambonnay was probably the most expensive Champagne in the world. While Clos du Mesnil is made exclusively from Chardonnay grapes from a medieval vineyard enclosed by stone walls within the very center of the town of Mesnil, Clos d'Ambonnay is made from Pinot Noir grapes from a vineyard that's barely an acre. I was lucky enough to taste the 1996 vintage with Olivier Krug, the managing director of the firm, in the Oak Bar of The Plaza hotel, which seemed like a suitable grand setting for the most expensive Champagne in history. I have to say it was one of the finest I've ever tasted, very pure and precise, a little leaner and more focused than the "regular" 1996, which is itself an awesome wine. If you're an extremely wealthy connoisseur, the kind of guy who owns a yacht *and* a jet, it just might be worth it. The 2005 vintages of Petrus and Romanée-Conti sell for a similar price, so in a sense Krug may be trying to lift the whole category to parity with Burgundy and Bordeaux. There's no question that a ridiculously deep-pocketed market exists; just witness the contemporary art market or real estate prices in London. Olivier told me at the time that all three thousand bottles of the 1996 Clos d'Ambonnay were spoken for.

By comparison, the Armand de Brignac, nowadays the favorite tipple of Jay-Z and A-Rod, is a relative steal at merely $300. It comes in a gold bottle with an ace of spades engraved on it, and while the package is a little gaudy for my taste, the wine itself has won strong reviews from such critics as the esteemed Jancis Robinson and *Fine Champagne Magazine.* You might recall that Cristal was once the rapper's choice, until Roederer's chief, Frédéric Rouzaud, seemed to dis the hip-hop community by telling a reporter, "We can't forbid people from buying it." But, he said, the association "brought unwanted attention to the brand." Sniffing racism, Jay-Z declared a boycott, and the timing couldn't have been better for Cattier, which created Armand de Brignac. The first release, not a single-vintage bottling like Cristal or Dom Pérignon, but a blend like Krug's so-called multi-vintage, appeared in 2006, not long after *l'affaire* Cristal. Jay-Z introduced it to the world in his video "Show Me What You Got" and has continued to promote it, amid much speculation about his financial relationship to Cattier.

For those of us without a recording contract, nonvintage grower Champagnes are a relatively affordable luxury. Because these producers don't spend millions on advertising, their prices tend to be competitive with the big-house blends. Therefore, exemplars like Pierre Peters, Vilmart & Cie, Cédric Bouchard, Marguet, Michel Turgy, José Dhondt, André Clouet, and Gimonnet, just to name a few, are well worth seeking out. My wife, who drinks nothing but Champagne, replaced one of the major brands with Marguet as her regular tipple.

Not all of the two-thousand-odd artisanal vintners make great juice, but most of those imported to the States are the crème de la crème. Just check to see that the initials RM (for Récoltant-Manipulant) are somewhere on the bottle, which means that the grapes were grown and produced by the same guy. Shun bottles with the letters RC (Récoltant-Coopérateur), which indicate that the grower sent his grapes off to be made by a big cooperative.

Far too many people save Champagne for special occasions or drink it strictly as an aperitif, but in fact it's one of the most versatile food wines. As Terry Theise says, "Champagne doesn't require an occasion. Champagne *is* the occasion."

German Made Simple

> A German wine label is one of the things life's too short for, a
> daunting testimony to that peculiar nation's love of detail and
> organization.
>
> —Kingsley Amis, *Everyday Drinking*

Hugh Johnson once remarked that he was surprised that no university had endowed a chair in German wine labeling. For most
English speakers, such is the perceived complexity of the Gothic-
looking labels, with their information overload and terrifying
terminology, that they make Burgundy seem simple by comparison. Graacher Himmelreich Trockenbeerenauslese, anyone? Even
hardened wine wonks ask themselves whether life is long enough
to learn the difference between *Spätlese* and *Auslese*. (Admit it,
you're scared already.) German winemakers have long recognized
this dilemma, without necessarily knowing what the hell to do
about it. "The Germans haven't made it easy for you, me, or anyone else," says the importer Terry Theise, a passionate advocate of
their Rieslings. Lately, though, some of Germany's best Riesling
producers are wooing American consumers with simplified labels.

One technical term that's worth mastering is *Kabinett,* the
lightest of five "predicates" indicating levels of ripeness. For mid-
summer drinking, a low-alcohol, semidry *Kabinett* from the Mosel
region is, to my mind, one of the few beverages that can compete
with a nice dry pilsner and far sprightlier and lighter on its feet
than the average Chilean or Australian Chardonnay. And Riesling
Kabinetts are quite possibly the most versatile food wines in the

world—perfect not only for lighter fish, chicken, and pork preparations but also for sweet and spicy Asian, Mexican, and fusion dishes. They are also, generally, below 10 percent alcohol, which makes them more refreshing, and less punishing, than a 15 percent Chardonnay. Viewed from another angle—you can drink more.

The typical rap against German wines is that they are "too sweet," and many of us are under the impression that sweet is somehow bad. Most *Kabinetts* have some residual sugar, but this is almost always balanced by acidity. I think the German Wine Council should run ads featuring a modified version of the Blue Öyster Cult classic "Don't Fear the Sweetness." There is a trend lately in Germany toward dry, or *trocken,* wines, though the truth is that Riesling without some residual sugar can be shockingly tart. More and more of the wines from the Mosel, the Rheingau, and the Rheinhessen are being made in a style that's drier than Dorothy Parker's wit.

Those of you who won't be able to remember the word *Kabinett* five minutes after reading this essay are not necessarily out of luck. Raimund Prüm, of S. A. Prüm in the Mosel, understands your anxiety about those labels. He owns vines in some of the greatest vineyards in Germany, perched on steep, sun-trapping slopes high above the Moselle River, including Wehlener Sonnenuhr, named after the sundial that his great-great-grandfather Jodocus Prüm constructed in that famous vineyard in 1842. And one of these days, after you've developed an appreciation for great Riesling, you may remember the name of this vineyard, planted on blue slate, which is believed to impart a distinctive stony flavor to the wines. In the meantime, you can probably recall the term "Blue Slate," the name of a semidry *Kabinett*-level Riesling that had its debut in this country with the 2003 vintage, and risk the $15 to give it a try. Prüm also makes a lighter, slightly fruitier $10 bottle called Essence, which is my new default beverage setting for Chinese takeout.

Prüm's roots in the region go deep; he says his family has been in the Mosel for eight hundred years. His roots are also tall—his grandfather, who served in Kaiser Wilhelm's Dragoon Mounted Bodyguard, stood over six feet nine. Prüm himself tops out at a mere six four and is crowned with unruly flaming-red hair that has earned him the nickname *der Specht*—the woodpecker. Appropriately, he bobs his head as he gets excited talking about his wines, which can be pretty damn thrilling at the higher end (the wines, not his head bobbing). Every wine lover should eventually taste a great Eiswein (ice wine) like his 1998 from the Graacher Himmelreich vineyard, the frozen grapes of which were picked the morning of November 26. The grapes are pressed while still frozen and yield precious little juice—but that juice is incredibly concentrated. Freezing concentrates not only the sugar but also the acid and the extract, and the resulting wine is nectar worthy of the Wagnerian gods.

The affable, puckish Raimund has a slew of relatives in the area who are also making Riesling under various, somewhat confusing Prüm-inflected labels, including the great Joh. Jos. Prüm and Dr. F. Weins-Prüm. (They take their doctorates seriously in Germany, and every other winemaker seems to use the title.) Another great Mosel producer is Dr. Ernst Loosen, *Decanter* magazine's 2005 Man of the Year. His Wehlener Sonnenuhrs (he, too, has vines in that vineyard) are brilliant, long-lived wines, but he also bottles another under the name Doctor L. that's made from several vineyards, a good value, and a great, not too serious, summertime quaff. Loosen also produces a very fine Riesling in Washington State in collaboration with Chateau Ste. Michelle called Eroica. Simplified labeling is, of course, no guarantee of quality. It was Blue Nun, after all, that created the stereotype of German whites as the vinous equivalent of Dunkin' Donuts. The most important element on these labels is the maker's name, and in order to experience the transcendent pleasures of these wines, you need to memorize a few. Lingenfelder's Bird label and Selbach's (of Selbach-Oster) Fish label are two entry-level Rieslings from serious makers, and both offer good value at about twelve bucks.

At a slightly more ambitious level are Dragonstone, from Leitz; Erben Riesling, from Joh. Jos. Christoffel; and Jean-Baptiste, from Gunderloch. Robert Weil's top Rieslings from the Rheingau are among the most sought after and expensive in Germany, but he bottles a *Kabinett* and a wine called simply Riesling that should be approached with caution, lest you find yourself developing a serious habit. It's a little like reading *A Portrait of the Artist as a Young Man*. Next thing you know, you're neck deep in *Ulysses* or, God forbid, *Finnegans Wake,* which is, come to think of it, the literary equivalent of *Trockenbeerenauslese*—the highest rung of the German qualitative ranking system, the richest and rarest wines produced from voluptuously ripe grapes afflicted with noble rot. And yes, they're sweet. If that scares you, stick with the *Kabinetts.* No Ph.D. required.

Finally Fashionable:
Rosé from Provence to Long Island

Dining on Shelter Island one recent summer evening, I noticed that many of the wine buckets in the room were filled with bottles of rosé. Sunset Beach is the Hamptons' answer to the beachside restaurants of the Côte d'Azur, and perhaps not so coincidentally more than a few of the tables were occupied by French speakers. Rosé has long been the summer beverage of choice for fashionable diners in Cannes and St. Tropez, but Americans have yet to fully embrace it. Even in the towns on Long Island's South Fork, known collectively as the Hamptons, which serve as summer headquarters for some of America's best-traveled and most trend-conscious consumers, rosé is just starting to get its due. But there are encouraging indications that it's becoming fashionable, and Long Island is beginning to distinguish itself as a source of excellent dry rosé.

Among the unmistakable signs of a rising tide of rosé consciousness is the fact that the hotelier André Balazs, the proprietor of Sunset Beach as well as the Mercer hotel in Manhattan and the Chateau Marmont in Los Angeles, has lent his name to a rosé that is available in his hotels from South Beach to L.A. "I spent summers in St. Tropez growing up, and I associate rosé with long summer lunches on the beach. When we started Sunset Beach fifteen years ago, it was with the desire to bring the warmth and richness of life there to the Hamptons. It was pretty clear then that not many Americans knew what rosé was. Now more than half the wine we sell there is rosé." André Balazs rosé is made from grapes grown in the heart of the Hamptons by Roman Roth, the German-born winemaker for the Wölffer Estate Vineyard, who produced what probably was Long Island's first dry rosé in 1992, the year he arrived on the South Fork.

"It was a terrible year, cold and wet," he says of his first vintage. "We couldn't really get the grapes ripe enough to make great red wines. So I said, let's make a rosé." Founded by the bon vivant and equestrian entrepreneur Christian Wölffer in 1987, the Wölffer Estate Vineyard comprises fifty-five acres of some of the most expensive real estate in America. (He died in 2008 at the age of seventy after being hit by a powerboat while swimming off the coast of Rio de Janeiro.) Since Roth's first vintage, rosé's share of the production has grown larger and larger each year and is now a specialty of the estate. "At first we had to force people to taste it," Roth says. (I can't help imagining Roth and Wölffer, with their German accents, cornering visitors at the vineyard. "Ve must insist you try our rosé.")

"To me," Balazs says, "rosé isn't just a wine but almost a life-style, something which involves friendship and leisure and a specific way to enjoy a meal. It's totally casual but supremely sexy. It's just more robust and fun than white wine." Michael Cinque, the proprietor of Amagansett Wine and Spirits, describes its appeal rather more prosaically. "Most white wines have too much acidity on hot days to reveal much fruit. Rosés have acidity but also berry flavors and cassis." Cinque recently hosted an informal tasting of ten rosés, including bottles from Provence and Long Island, and was pleasantly surprised to discover that the 2009 Channing Daughters Cabernet Franc rosé, also from Long Island, took second place, with the Wölffer Estate in third.

The Wölffer rosé is leaner and racier than those from Provence, which may in part reflect the cooler climate of eastern Long Island. Southern France has a longer, hotter growing season, and the rosés typically have a heavy dose of Grenache, a fleshy, low-acid red grape. For Balazs, who loves the French style, Roth picks the grapes later, creating a riper and more voluptuous wine than the Wölffer rosé, something a little more like Château Minuty or Domaines Ott. The latter is widely regarded as the gold standard of rosé, the rich coppery nectar in the vaguely amphora-shaped bottle that costs as much as a good bottle of Bordeaux. Ott was my introduction to dry rosé. I first recall encountering it at a beach-side restaurant in the Côte d'Azur and downing several bottles with my friends over the course of a very long lunch to wash down the amazing fish soup and langoustines. Our table hung over the beach and extraordinarily good-looking, half-naked people kept walking past, and it's quite possible that I would have appreciated a jar of Night Train in that context, but I can honestly say I have seldom enjoyed a wine more. Domaines Ott has long been the gateway to drinking pink for many visitors to southern France or St. Barts, and for many remains *the* rosé (although in fact it's actually three rosés, made at three different properties). Whether it's worth more than twice the average price—about $40—is an open question, though for some buyers that's part of its appeal. Recently, an even more expensive rosé has appeared on the market, from Château d'Esclans, a relatively new venture created by Sacha Lichine, son of the legendary Alexis Lichine, along with Patrick Leon, the longtime winemaker at Château Mouton Roth-schild. Like Balazs, Sacha drank rosé on the Côte d'Or as a young man while vacationing with his father. After Alexis died in 1989, his son began looking for a project of his own. "I saw an opportunity in rosé," he says. "I spent eight years and visited thirty properties. Everybody thought I was crazy to want to leave Bordeaux for Provence." (Not me, I'd much rather live in the south.) Lichine and Leon decided to treat this wine with the respect of a Burgundy or a Bordeaux—by fermenting in barrels, for instance. Today they make five cuvées of rosé, including a small-production wine called Garrus that retails for a hundred bucks. I've never tasted it, so I can't render a verdict, but I can highly recommend Whispering Angel, their entry-level offering that retails for around twenty.

Rosés are typically made from red grapes, which are removed immediately after pressing from their pigment-bearing skins, although there are as many variations on this basic recipe as there are for bouillabaisse. Roth uses about one-third Chardonnay along with Merlot and Cabernet Sauvignon. And he ferments the wine dry, waiting until all the sugar has been converted to alcohol. One reason rosé has a dubious reputation might be that many drinkers remember the sweet blush wines and so-called white Zinfandels that were so popular in the seventies and eighties. Remember Sutter Home White Zinfandel? Technically a rosé, it was kind of sickly sweet—thanks to residual sugar from an incomplete fermentation—unlike the pink wines of southern France, which are the models most Long Island makers emulate.

Lately, others are following Wölffer's lead, including the Channing Daughters Winery in Bridgehampton, which makes four excellent single-vineyard rosés from single varietals: Merlot, Cabernet Franc, Cabernet Sauvignon, and even Refosco (a red grape from Friuli). "This is a great place for rosé," says Christopher Tracy, a former actor and chef who's now the winemaker there. "We can make great rosé here every year even in a vintage when the red grapes don't get ripe enough to make great reds."

Nearby on the North Fork of Long Island, Paula and Michael Croteau operate what might be the only vineyard in the United States devoted entirely to rosé, creating some six different cuvées from different clones of Merlot. The Manhattan refugees bought their eighteenth-century farm in Southold in the early nineties. "We'd have people coming by our place and saying it feels like Provence," Michael says. "And when we thought about planting vines, rosé seemed like a great fit based on the lifestyle out here on the East End. Culturally, rosé seemed like a great fit."

Fortunately, you don't have to travel to the Hamptons or Provence to experience the incomparable pleasure of a cold rosé on a hot summer day.

Lean and Fleshy:
The Paradox of Santa Rita Hills Chardonnay

The first time I tasted a Chardonnay from the Santa Rita Hills I was baffled; on the one hand it was very ripe and fleshy, and on the other it had a bracing acidic slap that I associated with cool-climate whites and even a mineral note you seldom find in New World wines. It was a little like meeting Jessica Simpson, only to have her start speaking perfect French in Carla Bruni's voice. To say I was disoriented would be an understatement. That was just before the movie *Sideways* made a star out of Santa Barbara Pinot Noir, not to mention Paul Giamatti. (You may remember Merlot in the role of villain.) This region—specifically the Santa Ynez and Santa Maria Valleys—is by now renowned as a source of fine Pinot Noirs. What's less well-known is that it's producing some of California's most compelling Chardonnays.

The hottest area for Chardonnay, the Santa Rita Hills, is an appellation that only came into existence in 2001. (On bottles you will see this abbreviated as Sta. Rita Hills thanks to a legal dispute with the Chilean wine producer Viña Santa Rita.) Actually, it's not so much hot as it is cool, which is what gives these Chards a crispness that's missing from so many California Chards. The wine that impressed and confused me was a 2003 Brewer-Clifton Sweeney Canyon Chardonnay, crafted by the ex-surfer and rock guitarist Steve Clifton and the former French professor Greg Brewer in a prefab metal shed located in an industrial park not far from the Lompoc prison. After tasting their Chards, I knew I had to meet these guys. It's sort of amusing to imagine that their odd-couple chemistry has something to do with the contradictory lean-versus-fleshy quality of their wines: Brewer is a lean, hyperactive ex–competitive cyclist; the Laguna-bred Clifton looks like a younger version of the former *CSI* star William Petersen and still seems much more like a surfer than an oenologist, brawnier and far more laid-back. But both are quick to credit the unique geography of their chosen turf. (They also make excellent Pinot, but it's the whites that first caught my attention.) "This is such an extreme region," Brewer says. "It gives us the material for these really radical Chards."

The cool Alaska current hits the California coast at Point Conception just west of here, and the mountain ranges that frame the Santa Ynez Valley run from west to east, funneling this bracing marine air up the valley. As the temperature in the interior rises over the course of the day, the cold air is drawn inland; a blanket of fog covers much of the valley almost every night. This cooling effect is what makes the Chardonnays so crisp, preserving their natural acidity. Even in summer, the temperature in the Santa Rita Hills rarely tops seventy and in the evening can fall as low as forty-five.

Back in 1970, after falling in love with the wines of Burgundy, a young Vietnam veteran named Richard Sanford was scouring California for a suitable climate to grow the Burgundian varietals of Pinot Noir and Chardonnay. Sanford drove up and down the Santa Ynez Valley in a pickup truck with a thermometer, taking new readings every mile. Eventually, he decided that the cool western part of the valley had exactly the right climate and with a partner bought land and planted the Sanford and Benedict Vineyard. They made Pinots and Chardonnays and also sold grapes to others, including Jim Clendenen of Au Bon Climat, the rock-and-roll Robert Mondavi of Santa Barbara, whose Sanford and Benedict bottlings helped spread the fame of the vineyard. Other vineyards were planted, and Sanford eventually lost control of his own in a legal dispute. He now makes wines under the Alma Rosa label. Clendenen's Au Bon Climat Sanford and Benedict Chardonnay remains the benchmark for this great vineyard.

Wineries like Babcock, Foley, Ojai, and Melville gradually followed Sanford's lead. Greg and Steve apprenticed at several of them before starting Brewer-Clifton in 1996, maxing out credit cards, borrowing from friends, and buying grapes from growers in the valley and nearby Santa Maria, eventually focusing on the Santa Rita Hills. Their Pinots and Chardonnays have achieved cult status and stellar ratings from critics.

I find the Chards particularly compelling, edgy and extreme, sometimes tasting like turbocharged Chablis, and in fact the partners share a passion for Burgundy's northernmost white. After a 2004 visit to the area, including a quasi-religious-experience tasting in the cellar of Domaine Raveneau, Greg was inspired to start a new Chardonnay project called Diatom. "I wanted to push the limits, to make something really pure and extreme." While most winemakers in California and Burgundy use some new oak barrels to help oxygenate and mellow their Chardonnays, and encourage a secondary fermentation to soften the malic acids, Brewer has created a minimalist Chardonnay at Melville that was fermented in stainless steel. The result, called Inox, is lean and crisp, utterly lacking the buttery quality of old-school Cali Chard.

With Diatom, Brewer pushed Santa Rita Chardonnay to a new extreme. "I think of Brewer-Clifton as skiing, Melville Inox as snowboarding and Diatom as the X Games. I wanted to push Chardonnay to an absolute extreme." Extreme, but minimal. He lets the grapes get extremely ripe, which in a hotter area would result in a flabby wine, ferments in stainless steel, and blocks the secondary fermentation. The result is radical indeed, an extreme example of the fat/lean syndrome. "Diatom is so radical it's deviant," Brewer says. I agree. My tasting note on the 2009 Diatom

Huber vineyard reads: "Incredible tension and precision. Great flesh and great acidity. A deconstructed margarita—lime and salt and alcohol and even agave. Wowsah!"

Brewer sees heavily oaked Chardonnays as elaborately cooked and sauced dishes. "Diatom is like a piece of toro, fatty but also pure and minimal." He also believes the minimalist wine-making style lets the characteristics of the vineyards, and the area, shine through. It's unique, and yet it highlights the family traits of the region. I like to pour these Chards for friends who claim they don't like California Chardonnay. Even those who aren't instantly converted tend to be pleasantly surprised.

Rosé Champagne:
Not Just for Stage Door Johnnies

My first experience with a sparkling pink wine took place on a blanket on the lawn at Tanglewood in the company of a girl named Joan Coughlin. The Who were onstage performing *Tommy,* and the warm summer air was perfumed with incense and cannabis. The wine in question, Cold Duck, was popular with the theater crowd at Taconic High School and was, I learned much later, composed of two parts New York state sparkling wine and one part California bulk red wine. I eventually learned to turn up my nose at Cold Duck, but my fond memories of that evening must have something to do with my abiding enthusiasm for rosé Champagne.

Champagne has long been perceived as celebratory. Its pink version, it seems to me, is less declamatory, more romantic; if great Champagne is the vinous equivalent of a white diamond, then rosé is a pink diamond—rarer and yes, I'm afraid, more expensive. Though it represents just a small fraction of the production of France's eponymous Champagne region, rosé has exploded in popularity in recent years. "It used to be for stage door Johnnies," says Beaver Truax of Chambers Street Wines in New York City. "Rosé was fun, but it wasn't serious Champagne. And that's definitely changed." A 2010 tasting with Richard Geoffroy, the winemaker of Dom Pérignon, reminded me of just how great it can be.

If Dom Pérignon is the Porsche 911 Carrera of the wine world, then DP rosé is the 911 Turbo. The inaugural 1921 Dom, released in 1936, was probably the first prestige cuvée—a premium blend of the best vats in the Moët cellars. In 1959, Dom produced its first rosé Champagne, which, weather permitting, has been produced several vintages a decade since. I happened to be present at a rather raucous New York auction in March 2008 when two bottles of the 1959 DP rosé, from the collection of the über-collector Rob Rosania, went for $85,000, astonishing nearly everyone in the room.

DP's rosés are typically held for about ten years; the 2000 vintage hit American store shelves in the spring of 2010, and it appears to be a classic. As if that weren't reason enough to max out one of your credit cards, the 1990 Dom Pérignon Oenothèque rosé was released almost simultaneously. The Oenothèque series is a kind of ultra-premium DP, vintage juice that's been mellowing long after the initial vintage release in the chalk tunnels of the Moët & Chandon cellars deep under the town of Épernay. Until now, there's never been an Oenothèque rosé, and collectors and geeks have been buzzing in anticipation of this one. It really is spectacular, one of the greatest rosés I've ever tasted. Among many pleasant sensations it evoked, I thought of Julianne Moore, whose pink-hued beauty had struck me on the street in the West Village earlier that day—but this is the kind of wine that can call forth a thousand associations.

Curiously enough, 1990 was the first vintage created by Richard Geoffroy, who has been the head winemaker at Dom Pérignon for twenty years. He started on a high note with a great, hotter-than-usual vintage that resulted in richer wines. Geoffroy has had many triumphs since then, and I have to say that the only man I've ever known who seems to enjoy his job as much as he does is Hugh Hefner. Geoffroy's no sybarite, but he is messianic about Champagne in general and DP in particular. Born into a family of Champagne growers, Geoffroy tried to escape his destiny by studying medicine; he completed his degree in 1982 but never practiced. Instead, he went to work for Moët & Chandon, starting his career at the Domaine Chandon in the Napa Valley. While I realize there may be those who feel a doctor ranks higher on the scale of social utility than a winemaker, I'm pretty sure they've never tasted the 1990 Dom Pérignon Oenothèque rosé. I suspect that in his twenty years at DP, Geoffroy has lifted more spirits and ameliorated more malaise than most GPs.

I'm not going to pretend that either the 2000 or the 1990 Oenothèque is inexpensive, but look at it this way: the former costs about the same as the tasting menu at Per Se, without wine; the latter the same as the tasting menu for two. (At $700, the Oenothèque is still cheaper than Krug's 1996 Clos d'Ambonnay, a single-vineyard white Champagne that sells for around three grand.) Fortunately, there are far more more affordable rosé Champagnes out there. Many New Yorkers of my vintage first encountered fine rosé Champagne at Danny Meyer's Union Square Cafe, where Billecart-Salmon has been on offer since 1985. After a wobbly period Billecart is back on form—a dry, relatively rich rosé I like to drink as an aperitif, though it's powerful enough to stand up to salmon or even a mild curry.

Most rosés are made by adding 8 to 10 percent of still Pinot Noir to a Champagne base. A very few are made by leaving the Pinot Noir grapes in contact with their pigment-bearing skins for a short period during fermentation, a trickier process. Of these, Laurent-Perrier is a standout and tends to have a deep, rich coho-salmon tint. Color is one of the great pleasures of rosé Champagnes, which can range from faint onion skin to bright raspberry with every imaginable shade of smoked salmon in between, some more orange than pink.

The big-name Champagne houses have been responding to the increasing demand for rosé with varying degrees of success. Bollinger, Moët, and Pol Roger are, in descending order of power and body, among those I like best. The most exciting development in recent years has been the proliferation of small-grower Champagnes, both white and pink. Rather than selling their grapes to the big houses, these producers vinify and bottle their own, the best of which reflects the individual characteristics of specific regions and soils.

The spiritual leader of this movement is a mad scientist named Anselme Selosse, who studied oenology in Burgundy, where the concept of *terroir* is a religion. "Everything that makes a wine unique is in the ground," Selosse told me on a recent visit to New York. His rich, orange-hued, nonvintage rosé is worth traveling to France to taste, which you may have to do since it's very hard to find here. Look for Egly-Ouriet, Savès, Larmandier-Bernier, and Bruno Paillard. As for me, the next time I open a bottle of rosé Champagne, I'm going to raise a glass to Joan Coughlin, who is no longer among us.

A Debilitating Pleasure: Tavel

During a year at the Sorbonne, very little of it spent in classrooms, A. J. Liebling fell hard for Paris, and for the food and wine of France. Arriving in the City of Light in 1926 and returning often during his life, he would become one of the great gourmands of the era, eventually developing an intimacy with the greatest growths of Burgundy and Bordeaux. But he never lost his affection for the rosés of Tavel, which sustained him during that first year in Paris and which before him had been the favorite beverage of Louis XVI and Honoré de Balzac. When Liebling first landed, Tavel was synonymous with rosé; now that pink wine is produced throughout France and around the world, and is enjoying a period of fashionability, it's worth revisiting the motherland of rosé, as well as the writings of one of its biggest fans.

Situated across the Rhône from Châteauneuf-du-Pape, just north of Avignon, the small village of Tavel and the surrounding commune have been producing rosé for hundreds of years. Originally, the wines were composed of Cinsault and Grenache, although since 1969 Syrah and Mourvèdre have also been permitted under the rules of the appellation. Typically, the juice from these red grapes is briefly macerated with the pigment-bearing skins, then bled off before the pink juice turns red. Unlike other regions, where rosé is an also-ran, a by-product of red wine production, Tavel produces nothing else. For Liebling, it was "the only worthy rosé."

The son of a well-to-do furrier, Liebling had previously been working as a reporter for the Providence, Rhode Island, *Evening*

Bulletin when—always a great storyteller—he invented an engagement with a loose woman in order to convince his father to send him to Paris. "The girl is ten years older than I am," he told him, "and Mother might think she is kind of fast, because she is being kept by a cotton broker from Memphis, Tennessee, who only comes North once in a while. But you are a man of the world, and you understand that a woman can't always help herself." When he claimed he intended to marry the girl, his father immediately agreed to finance the trip.

Liebling's funds arrived monthly, an allowance not so generous as to permit him to indulge his heroic appetite indiscriminately, and he considered this a key aspect of his training as a gourmand. "If," he wrote later in *Between Meals*, his great memoir of Paris, "the first requisite for writing well about food is a good appetite, the second is to put in your apprenticeship as a feeder when you have enough money to pay the check but not enough to produce indifference to the size of the total." A rich man would start at the top of the food chain—the most expensive dishes and the most expensive restaurants—without learning about the basics of *la cuisine française*, while the poor man eats only for subsistence.

The same principles applied to learning about wine: "Our hypothetical rich *client* might even have ordered a Pommard, because it was listed at a higher price than the Tavel, and because he was more likely to be acquainted with it. He would then never have learned that a good Tavel is better than a fair-to-middling Pommard—better than a fair-to-middling almost anything, in my opinion." Pommard, of course, is one of the great communes of Burgundy's famed Côte d'Or, and Liebling was certainly a fan. But his esteem for Tavel was undiminished even after he could afford the good stuff.

At the Maison Teyssedre-Balazuc, a Left Bank restaurant where he did much of his apprentice eating in 1926 and 1927, the Tavel *supérieure* was three and a half francs. The proprietor bought the wine in a barrel and bottled it in his basement. "The taste is warm but dry," Liebling wrote later, "like an enthusiasm held under restraint, and there is a tantalizing suspicion of bitterness when the wine hits the top of the palate." This strikes me still as a fine description of a good Tavel, especially the touch about bitterness, which keeps the wine from being cloying.

Liebling used to torment himself trying to decide between the regular Tavel and the more expensive *supérieure,* but almost inevitably chose the latter. That he hated to deny himself was illustrated by his considerable girth. He once described one of his ideal meals as consisting of "a dozen Gardiners Island oysters, a bowl of clam chowder, a peck of steamers, some bay scallops, three sautéed soft-shelled·crabs, a few ears of fresh-picked corn, a thin swordfish steak of generous area, a pair of lobsters, and a Long Island duck." All of this would presumably be washed down with a bottle of Champagne and at least two or three bottles of Tavel. "No sane man can afford to dispense with debilitating pleasures," he wrote in *Between Meals.* "No ascetic can be considered reliably sane." For Liebling, "Hitler was the archetype of the abstemious man."

He returned to Providence after his year abroad and eventually washed up at *The New Yorker,* with which he remained associated for the rest of his life, returning to France in 1939 to cover the war, only to retreat ahead of the German occupation. He later accompanied the Allied troops who liberated Paris in 1944 and was awarded the Legion of Honor for his war reporting. He wrote about many subjects, including boxing and horse racing, and practically invented modern media criticism, but for me *Between Meals,* his final book, is his most luminous and enduring achievement, a memoir of Paris that bears comparison with Hemingway's *Moveable Feast,* as the great James Salter suggests in his fine introduction to the 1986 reissue of the book.

Only traces of Liebling's Paris remain, but his favorite wine, from the sunny southern Rhône Valley at the edge of Provence, is little changed, although its fame has been diluted by the proliferation of pink wines from other regions. Tavel remains the archetypal rosé, a wine that pairs well with almost anything you might be eating in the summer, from shellfish all the way to grilled lamb. Don't let the color fool you—it's a dry wine, although the Grenache gives a slight impression of sweetness, offset by that mid-palate bitterness that Liebling found so appealing. Like all the wines of the southern Rhône, it's easy to understand and to enjoy, more rock and roll than jazz. "'Subtlety,' that hackneyed wine word, is a cliché seldom employed in writing about Rhone wines," Liebling aptly observed. "Their appeal is totally unambiguous."

The Château d'Aquéria has been making Tavel for more than four hundred years in the southern corner of the appellation. My favorite producer, the Domaine de la Mordorée, is based in nearby Lirac, also a source of fine rosés. It makes three cuvées of Tavel rosé, including the rich and complex Cuvée de la Reine des Bois, which makes the similarly expensive Domaines Ott Château de Selle, from the Côtes de Provence, seem like pinkish plonk by comparison. I like to imagine that it resembles Liebling's beloved Tavel *supérieure.* I recommend drinking it, or any other Tavel you can lay your hands on, while reading *Between Meals.*

Grape Nuts

The Founding Wine Geek

"Life is much more successfully looked at through a single window, after all," says that famous voyeur Nick Carraway in *The Great Gatsby*, a line decanted by John Hailman in his introduction to *Thomas Jefferson on Wine*. Then again, perhaps viewing a life as multifaceted and eventful as Jefferson's through the narrow lens of oenophilia is like training an electron microscope on an orgy; one is apt to miss some of the major events, or to see them from a bizarre perspective (as in the section on the American Revolution, titled: "The Revolutionary War: Gross Inflation in the Wine Market"). And yet, that said, for some of us the question of whether or not Jefferson sired children with Sally Hemings is less urgent than whether he preferred Bordeaux or Burgundy.

In addition to being an architect, archaeologist, astronomer, jurist, musician, natural philosopher, slaveholder, statesman, the author of the Declaration of Independence, and the third president of the United States, Thomas Jefferson was the country's first wine geek. Most of the founding fathers were deeply fond of good claret and Madeira, but none were as passionate or systematic in their appreciation of the grape as Jefferson, who was utterly compulsive on the subject.

Both a connoisseur and a proselytizer, he planted dozens of grape varieties at Monticello and predicted that someday America would compete with France and Italy as a wine-producing nation. Believing that wine was much healthier than the whiskey and brandy that was being consumed in such vast quantities in our young nation, he pushed for lower import duties. "No nation is drunken where wine is cheap," he declared, "and none sober where the dearness of wine substitutes ardent spirits as the common beverage. It is, in truth, the only antidote to the bane of whiskey."

In 1784, Jefferson joined Franklin and Adams as a commissioner in Paris, a position he had long coveted. Though his interest in wine seems to have developed during his student days at William and Mary, it was only after the Revolution, when he went to France, that his oenophilia really metastasized.

"The first thing to be done in Paris," Adams advised, "is always to send for a tailor, a perukemaker and a shoemaker, for this nation has established such a domination over fashion that neither clothes, wigs nor shoes made in any other place will do in Paris." Jefferson seems to have followed this advice. The 1786 Mather Brown portrait, painted in Paris, shows him looking fairly dandy in a powdered wig. Practically the next thing he did was to order twelve cases of Haut-Brion, the great first-growth Bordeaux, which was the first brand-name wine to appear in English literature: Samuel Pepys had mentioned it as having "a good and most perticular taste."

In 1787, after inheriting the title of American minister to the king of France from the ailing Franklin, Jefferson made a trip through France and Italy that he described to Lafayette as "combining public service with private gratification." Officially, he was checking out prospects for American trade, but his itinerary took him through most of the great wine regions of Europe, starting in Burgundy and moving on to the Rhône Valley, making his way down into Italy's Piedmont before looping north again to Bordeaux. Most of Jefferson's widely quoted writing about wine comes from his journal of this journey and a subsequent one to Germany's Rhine and Mosel regions as well as Champagne. He was a keen observer. While in Burgundy he notes that in Volnay they eat "good wheat bread" whereas in nearby Meursault it's rye. "I asked the reason of the difference. They told me that the white wines fail in quality much oftener than the red. . . . The farmer therefore cannot afford to feed his labourers so well."

Much of what he wrote about the character of the countries and wines he encountered could have been written last week, spelling eccentricities aside. "Chambertin, Voujeau, and Veaune are strongest," he says of the red wines of Burgundy's Côte de Nuits; he declares "Diquem" (Château d'Yquem) the best Sauternes—observations that wouldn't seem terribly out of place in the current issue of *Wine Spectator.*

It's hard to imagine any aspect of contemporary life that Jefferson would recognize if he were to suddenly reappear among us, with one exception: he would be very comfortable navigating the wine list of a three-star restaurant in Paris. It is a testament partly to his connoisseurship and partly to the durability and conservatism of European wine traditions that many of the wines Jefferson drank and collected are the same ones that excite the interest of today's grape nuts. Almost a century before the official classification of the great growths of Bordeaux, Jefferson recorded a hierarchy remarkably similar to the present classification. In addition to Haut-Brion, he ordered multiple cases of Lafite, Margaux, and Château d'Yquem for the cellar of his new residence, the Hotel de Langeac on the Champs-Élysées. He also sent many of these wines to President George Washington, who was happy to be the beneficiary of Jefferson's growing expertise. When Jefferson occupied the White House himself, he raised the standard of hospitality considerably, spending lavishly on food and wine—one factor in his later bankruptcy. Afterward, at Monticello, he became a budget drinker, substituting the wines of southern France and Tuscany for the great growths of Bordeaux and Burgundy.

Jefferson is usually assumed to be a Bordeaux man, because he wrote the most about it and perhaps because it seems like the wine that best reflects his character; claret, as the English call it, is an Apollonian wine, a beverage for intellectuals, for men of patience and reason. Austere in its youth, it predictably develops great complexity over the years. There are few surprises in Bordeaux. Burgundy, on the other hand, engages the emotions more than the intellect—a wine for the lunatic, the lover, and the poet. So it comes as a bit of a shock to learn here that during his years in Paris, when he had access to all the great growths of France, the sober sage of Monticello stocked his cellar with more Burgundy than Bordeaux, and his taste in it seems to have been impeccable: he was partial to the reds of Volnay, still a connoisseur's wine; among the whites he liked Montrachet, which remains the most coveted white wine on the planet, though he sometimes chose the less expensive Meursault Goutte d'Or, a robust white Burgundy from a slightly less exalted slope just down the road.

Perhaps Jefferson's apparent preference for Burgundy will eventually lead to one of those reassessments of his character that seem to arrive every decade or two; having presented the evidence, Hailman—who certainly knows his wines—doesn't make much of it, perhaps because he is so engrossed in the commercial and bookkeeping minutiae of Jefferson's correspondence with wine merchants and customs agents, which take up many pages of this volume. True, it was hard work to be a wine lover in those days. "To order wine, Jefferson had to specify in each letter the ship, the captain, the ports of exit and entry, how the wines should be packaged, and how he would get payment across the ocean and determine and pay the customs duties." As someone who can order his Meursault Goutte d'Or online, I feel for the guy, but dozens of pages of this kind of trivia could drive many readers to hard liquor, which is the last thing the father of American oenophilia would have desired.

Writer, Importer, Gentleman Spy

The 2007 Burgundies didn't generate as much advance excitement as the 2002 or 2005 vintages, which benefited from more favorable weather. But in the spring of 2009 a tasting of a very select group of 2007 reds and whites had many New York wine professionals buzzing with admiration—perhaps proving the axiom that in Burgundy, the maker is more important than the year. Included were some of the top names in Burgundy—a group selected more than fifty years ago by Frank Schoonmaker, a writer, importer, and gentleman spy who did as much to educate American wine drinkers as anyone before or since.

The son of a Columbia classics professor and a prominent feminist, he arrived at Princeton in 1923, not long after Scott Fitzgerald departed, and dropped out after two years. He then roamed Europe for several years, eventually distilling his travels into guidebooks including *Through Europe on Two Dollars a Day* and *Come with Me Through France.* Schoonmaker's passion for wine was fueled by his friendship with Raymond Baudoin, editor of *La Revue du Vin de France,* then, as now, the most influential wine publication in the country. The young American traveled the principal regions with Baudoin, tasting and learning, making contacts that would ultimately serve him well as an importer when Prohibition ended in 1933. Burgundy became his special passion.

Unlike Bordeaux, a region of vast estates owned by wealthy families and corporations, the typical Burgundian domaine, then as now, consisted of only a few acres of vines. A family's holdings were generally scattered, thanks to inheritance issues, among different vineyards. Most growers sold their young wine in casks to big negotiants in the town of Beaune, who would blend and bottle them under their own labels. *Au contraire,* said Baudoin and Schoonmaker, encouraging their favorite growers to bottle their own wines, a relatively radical concept at the time.

After the Volstead Act was finally repealed, the seasoned Francophile moved to New York and launched Frank Schoonmaker Selections. The glitch in his business plan was that after fourteen years of Prohibition, few Americans knew anything about French or any other wines. To help rectify this situation, he published a book called *The Complete Wine Book,* based in part on a series of articles he'd written for *The New Yorker.*

Early on, Schoonmaker hired a loquacious young Russian émigré named Alexis Lichine, who'd recently dropped out of Penn, as his national sales manager. Together they traveled to California to scout domestic wines for their portfolio. At the time it was the practice in California to slap French regional names like Chablis and Burgundy on the local bottlings, but they convinced several California estates to label their wines according to grape variety, a practice that has become universal in California and the New World in the years since. Their first success was with Wente Vineyards, which changed the name of its white wine from Graves (a region of Bordeaux) to Sauvignon Blanc—the name of the grape from which it was made—and watched sales soar.

World War II interrupted their partnership; after Pearl Harbor, Schoonmaker joined the OSS, the CIA precursor created by Wild Bill Donovan that drew its ranks from the Ivy League and the Social Register, while Lichine joined army intelligence. Using his wine business as a cover, Schoonmaker went to Madrid. "It was a source of some pride to him," according to his obit in the *Daytona Beach Morning Journal,* "that the then United States Ambassador to Spain complained about how vigorously he pursued some of his underground activities in that country." He made frequent forays into France to aid the resistance, until, according to his friend Frank E. Johnson, "the Spanish police caught on to what was happening. Schoonmaker was arrested, brought back to Madrid and had his head shaved to identify him as a marked man." He subsequently slipped out of Spain and attached himself to the U.S. Seventh Army, which invaded southern France in August 1944. Not far from Lyon, he was hospitalized after his jeep hit a land mine, but he later managed to visit some of his growers in Burgundy and the Rhône. He was ultimately discharged with the rank of colonel, and to this day he is still referred to as Le Colonel by Burgundian old-timers.

Lichine had also distinguished himself in the war and retired as a major, but when he demanded full partnership in the business, he and Schoonmaker parted ways. Lichine made a name for himself as a wine writer and the owner of Château Prieuré-Lichine and Château Lascombes in Bordeaux. In the years after the war, Schoonmaker continued to educate the American drinker with a series of lively and erudite articles about wine in *Gourmet* magazine (you can find them in the archives at Gourmet.com) and eventually published the *Encyclopedia of Wine*, for many years a definitive reference.

In a 1947 *Gourmet* piece about red Burgundy, he makes clear his preference for the wines of that region over Bordeaux. "Heartwarming and *joyeux*, heady, big of body, magnificent and Rabelaisian, this is Burgundy," he writes. (I might question "big of body," but this is his story.) "The most celebrated poet of Bordeaux, Biarnez, wrote of the chateaux and the wines so dear to his heart in cool and measured Alexandrines reminiscent of Racine. Burgundy is celebrated in bawdy tavern songs." No doubt where the man's heart lies. In fact he seems to be saying that Bordeaux has no heart, that it's all head, but of course he was selling Burgundy. He then goes on to give us a detailed tour of the region that remains useful to this day while referencing Thackeray, Alexandre Dumas, Petrarch, Philip the Bold, and many others.

Schoonmaker seems to have had more taste than business acumen. At the age of sixty-seven he sold his business to Pillsbury, staying on as part of a new wine division. The union was not a happy one. After his death in 1976, Seagram took over Schoonmaker's Burgundy portfolio, which was then purchased in 2001 by Diageo. Some seventy-five years after Schoonmaker started his company, the domaines represented at Diageo's 2009 Manhattan tasting are still among the most revered in Burgundy. Ramonet, Niellon, Matrot, d'Angerville, de Courcel, Grivot, and Roumier are among its most consistently excellent producers, as they proved yet again with their 2007 wines. Several growers admitted it was a challenging vintage, given the cool summer, but many of these wines, especially the reds, were surprisingly accessible and attractive at this early stage, unlike, say, the big but backward 2005s, which will require cellar time to mellow out. Though it was probably a stronger year for the whites, the reds are more precocious, providing great drinking from five to ten years of age. The words "pretty" and "charming" kept coming up among growers and tasters with regard to the reds. For those unfamiliar with the fleshy, earthy pleasure of good Burgundy, the relatively inexpensive 2007s could be a good place to start. Tell your wine merchant, or sommelier, that Frank sent you.

The Salesman with the Golden Palate

Even in a life as eventful as Alexis Lichine's, 1951 would count as a very big year. He published *Wines of France,* which would go through many editions and influence several generations of Americans. That same year he realized a lifelong dream and purchased Château Prieuré-Cantenac, a classified Bordeaux château that soon was officially rechristened Château Prieuré-Lichine. His genius as a salesman was inseparable from his gift for self-promotion, and for many years his name was one of the most successful brands in the world of fine wine. Along the way he married a countess and then a movie star, won a Bronze Star and a Croix de Guerre for his service in World War II, bought a vast apartment on Fifth Avenue, and intrepidly barnstormed the heartland, spreading the gospel of fine wine.

Lichine's father, a wealthy businessman, managed to escape Moscow with his family in 1917 shortly after the Bolshevik revolution. After a brief stay in New York, they settled in Paris, where Alexis attended a lycée. After graduating from the University of Pennsylvania, he returned to Paris and landed a job at the *Herald Tribune.* Shortly after the repeal of Prohibition, the paper commissioned Lichine to write a series about French wines for the benefit of newly liberated American palates. He honed his own palate while researching the articles, touring the great wine regions of France.

Though he would continue to write about wine throughout his life, Lichine was a salesman at heart, and in 1934, with Prohibition ending, he moved to New York. After working for several retailers, he teamed up with Frank Schoonmaker, a connoisseur and the author of *The Complete Wine Book* who had established a successful importing business in the wake of repeal. Schoonmaker and Lichine were a potent team, an odd couple who shared the same passion for wine. Together, and then separately, as rivals, they virtually created the American market for French wine.

Their association was highly successful, despite, or perhaps because of, temperamental differences. "Although he respected his palate, Schoonmaker evidently considered Lichine something of an upstart," according to the importer Frank E. Johnson, "and Lichine never had much faith in Schoonmaker's salesmanship." There was also romantic competition, Schoonmaker eventually marrying one of Lichine's girlfriends. The differences might ultimately be summed up by acknowledging that in the end, Schoonmaker was a partisan of Burgundy and Lichine was a Bordeaux man—sort of like the dichotomy between breast men and leg men, or between Mets and Yankees fans. (The first chapter of Lichine's *Wines of France* is titled "Bordeaux: The Greatest Wine District.")

When war broke out in Europe and they were cut off from their French sources, they went to California to seek domestic wines. Eventually, both men enlisted, Lichine with army intelligence and Schoonmaker in the OSS. Although Lichine rose to the rank of major and was decorated for bravery, his wartime service was an extension of his civilian profession. "I was an aide to a very wine-minded general stationed in Corsica," he told an interviewer some thirty years later. He seems to have brought his gift for the good life to war. Landing on Elba, he managed to spend a night in Napoleon's bed. By his own account, he endeared himself to his comrades by slipping through enemy lines in the South of France and returning with several bottles of drinkable rosé. He was subsequently charged with contacting Cognac producers and arranging shipments to troops on leave in southern France. Eventually, he ended up as an aide-de-camp to General Eisenhower, in which capacity he met Winston Churchill. "The prime minister talked war for a while," he recalled, "then started telling me about wines over his claret. I politely intervened, and he finally sat down and said, 'You do the talking and I'll do the listening, young man.'" It's a great story, whether or not it's true; all of these anecdotes of his service were provided by Lichine himself, a true master of self-promotion.

What is indisputable is that on his return to New York, he married the countess Renée de Villeneuve, whom he'd met in Marseilles, though the marriage lasted only a year. Lichine went back to France in 1948, trying to persuade growers to sell their wines in America exclusively through him. These buying trips also formed the basis for his *Wines of France,* which in turn helped to create a market in the States for his wines. Within a few years he'd made enough to purchase the run-down Prieuré-Cantenac—ranked as a fourth growth in the 1855 classification—not that the initial purchase price was high; his son, Sacha, told me he paid about $16,000 for the former priory and some twenty-five neglected acres of vines. Within a year, with a consortium of banker friends, he bought the nearby Château Lascombes, a second growth. He restored and managed both properties in between sales trips to the United States.

Lichine's proselytizing was indefatigable. According to Sacha, "He'd hop on a Greyhound bus, go to Buffalo and Syracuse and Chicago, drop 150, 200 cases." It's difficult to imagine the dashing and impeccably tailored Lichine on a bus, yet he seems to have been able to summon the common touch, speaking to ladies' clubs, going on radio shows, conducting wine tastings. Dining at Galatoire's in New Orleans, he ordered six wines at once, declared three of them undrinkable, and promptly revamped the wine list with the stunned acquiescence of the proprietor. He brought American-style salesmanship to Bordeaux, where the great châteaus had always been closed to the public, by opening a tasting room at the Prieuré and posting billboards on the main road. He gave Georges Duboeuf, the king of Beaujolais, his first job, and at one point owned 25 percent of his company. He also had a flourishing career as a ladies' man, from which he took a brief hiatus when the actress Arlene Dahl became his third wife. (His second wife, Sacha's mother, was Frankfurt-born Giselle Strauss.)

As successful as he was, Lichine was always undercapitalized, according to Sacha, and he had lavish tastes. In the sixties he sold his company to get access to working capital, staying on as president until business disagreements prompted him to walk out after three years. Unfortunately, under the terms of the contract, he was banned from using the name Alexis Lichine Selections. Like Halston, the fashion designer, he'd sold his own name (in fact to the same company, Norton Simon). This clouded his later years, according to Sacha, although he continued to run Prieuré-Lichine and to write about wine, publishing and revising the influential *Alexis Lichine's New Encyclopedia of Wines & Spirits* and *Alexis Lichine's Guide to the Wines and Vineyards of France,* his son serving as designated driver on the research expeditions for the latter. "The image I retain is of him tasting, of us tasting together. He disliked mediocrity, which made him a difficult father, but he taught me how to taste.

"I don't think the American wine market would be nearly as evolved as it is without him," says Sacha, who sold Prieuré in 1999 and is the proprietor of a premium provencal rosé estate called Château d'Esclans. By the time his father died at his beloved Prieuré in 1989, his adoptive country was in the grip of a wine boom that shows no signs of abating to this day. And his inevitable advice, when asked how one learns about wine, remains invaluable: "Buy a corkscrew, and use it."

The Retro Dudes of Napa

Are we still in the Napa Valley? Certainly not the Napa I'm familiar with. We have turned off Highway 29 into a dense housing development, a maze of nearly identical, recently constructed single-family residences. I've spent the day at some of the valley's iconic wineries, touring cellars gleaming with stainless steel tanks, fragrant with new oak barrels, admiring houses featured in *Architectural Digest* and *Wine Spectator*. My driver, Dan Petroski, works by day at Larkmead, one of Napa's premier producers, but he's off duty now. Petroski, who studied wine making in Sicily before moving to Napa, has a personal wine-making project, Massican, named after a mountain range in the southern Italian region of Campania, and produces crisp, intensely flavored white wines from Sauvignon Blanc, Ribolla Gialla, and Viognier. And he has a band of brothers engaged in similarly arcane wine-making ventures.

It seems as if we have been driving past the same houses for ten minutes when we finally spot the number we're looking for and turn in to a driveway that leads us through backyards behind the housing development. Finally we emerge, as if through a time warp, into a sprawling vista of vineyards and orchards stretching all the way to the Mayacamas range to the west, foregrounded by a bright yellow nineteenth-century Queen Anne–style bungalow and an unpainted barn that looks as if it's about to fall over. It's a real through-the-looking-glass transition, and not a bad metaphor for the new world I'm about to discover. I'm about to meet the Retro Dudes of Napa.

Napa is known for big Cabernets bred from big fortunes chasing big scores, but there's another school of wine making here, composed in part of those who work at the big wineries by day and in their spare time pursue their passion for quirky, individualistic, artisanal wines. They produce a few hundred cases, using purchased grapes. And while they have different approaches, they seem to share a common goal of creating wines that express the character of the vineyards of origin and a relative distrust of high technology. The 1903 farmhouse owned by Steve Matthiasson and his wife, Jill Klein Matthiasson, seems like the perfect setting for a gathering of this tribe.

Matthiasson works as a vineyard consultant for top Cabernet producers such as Araujo and Spottswoode. He seems, in alternating sentences, both intensely earnest and offhandedly wry, a combination that makes a little more sense when I learn he was born in Canada. Under his own name he makes a few hundred cases of one of the most interesting California white wines I've ever tasted, a blend of Sauvignon, Sémillon, Tocai Friulano, and Ribolla Gialla, an ancient grape variety from Friuli, as well as a superb red blend. Matthiasson calls his white "our New World conception of a mythical ideal Old World wine." Some of the grapes come from the vineyards that surround the house, although more are purchased from carefully chosen sites that he's found over the years working up and down the Napa Valley. And if the Old World forms part of his inspiration, so does pre-Prohibition-era Napa and the farmers who preceded him here.

Gradually, as the sun declines and cars pull in, I meet the tribe.

Abe Schoener, fifty-two, originally from Kansas, pulls up in a chauffeured town car, a stylish but also sensible strategy. This does not have the hallmarks of a dry evening. Earlier, when I asked Matthiasson how he got into wine making, he cited a "longtime close personal relationship with alcohol" before urging me to try the pâté he made from a wild boar he shot in the Dry Creek Valley last week. Meantime, the aluminum washtub full of ice is also filling with bottles from winemaker guests. It's going to be that kind of night.

A former professor of Greek philosophy, Schoener is the proprietor of the Scholium Project, a winery that makes deeply eccentric (mostly white) wines beloved by sommeliers and geeks. He looks a little alien here in his sharp black suit and his tinted Utopia L.A. glasses, but it's clear that he's part of the gang. He exchanges affectionate greetings with Duncan Arnot Meyers and Nathan Lee Roberts, who grew up together here in Napa. With their similar athletic builds and closely shaved skulls, they are initially hard to tell apart. Together they own Arnot-Roberts, a tiny artisanal winery based in Forestville. In recent years Nathan has worked at top wineries like Acacia, Groth, Caymus, and Pax. Duncan is a second-generation cooper who makes the barrels used in the wine making; he goes to France to choose the wood. The childhood friends don't own a single vineyard acre; they scour Napa and Sonoma looking for hillside vineyards with "intense character," buying fruit from the owners, generally producing no more than a few hundred cases of each wine.

If this were actually a school of wine making, instead of just a loose band of confederates, the headmaster would be George Vare, who arrives by pickup truck bearing an armload of unlabeled bottles. Tall and silver-haired, Vare is a genial patriarch, at least a generation older than most of the company. He is the cofounder of Luna Vineyards, where some of the company, including Abe Schoener, got their start. He's also a kind of unofficial ambassador for the wines of Friuli, the northeastern Italian wine region that serves as inspiration for everyone in the group. For the past decade, Vare has traveled to the region with friends, including Schoener and Matthiasson. At Luna, which made a name for itself with Pinot Grigio, he hired John Kongsgaard, a Napa native who would eventually achieve renown with his eponymous wines, especially his Chardonnays. Kongsgaard is definitely an honorary retro Napa dude.

Vare is the owner of California's only vineyard devoted to Ribolla Gialla, the Friulian white grape, and all of the winemakers assembled here have made wines with grapes purchased from his vineyard. In the hands of such Friulian masters as Stanko Radikon and Josko Gravner, who preside over eponymous wineries in the town of Oslavia, Ribolla produces powerful, age-worthy whites. Early results from Vare and friends have been extremely promising, although as often as not it is in a blend with other grapes—as with Matthiasson's Napa white or Petroski's Annia—that the grape finds its perfect home. In Friuli, grape varietals were traditionally interplanted—in part as insurance against the failure of one variety—and blended together in a cask, a practice that was also common among Napa's Italian-immigrant farmers in the nineteenth century.

Schoener has brought along some teal shot by one of his grape growers, but someone forgets to turn on the oven, and by the time the ducks hit the outdoor picnic table, it's late, and loud, and the searing heat of the day has long dissipated. But in the meantime I've tasted some of the most intriguing and delicious wines in recent memory, some of them bracingly fresh and floral, like Petroski's 2009 Gemina, a Viognier-Chardonnay blend, or the 2009 Arnot-Roberts Trousseau; some incredibly rich and opulent, like Schoener's 2005 Scholium Project Cena Trimalchionis, a honeyed nectar made from Sauvignon Blanc infected with botrytis, or noble rot. (Appropriately enough, the wine was named for the banquet/orgy scene in Petronius's *Satyricon*.)

Whether the inspiration is European or pre-Mondavi Napa Valley, these friends have rejected some of the technological wine making of the modern era in search of wine authenticity (and presumably drinkability). Matthiasson presses his grapes the old-fashioned way, with his feet. The Arnot-Roberts duo often work with grapes that most modern Napa vintners would consider underripe, as earlier generations of Californians did. Schoener leaves his white grapes in their skins till they turn orange and waits for natural yeasts to induce fermentation (as did all wine-makers until recently) rather than introducing artificial yeast, even if it takes years.

It would be hard to pigeonhole these wines, precisely because what distinguishes them is that they don't really taste like one another, or quite like anything else out there. As someone who sometimes fears he's in danger of drowning in an ocean of ripe, fruity, oaky, over-manipulated Frankenwine, I think that's a good thing.

The Rock Stars of Pinot Noir

When I meet the team behind the Anthill Farms label, I have to remind myself several times that I'm writing about wine—and not, as I sometimes do, about music; these guys seem more like members of a garage band on the cusp than like winemakers. Webster Marquez, Anthony Filiberti, and Dave Low are still in their twenties, and they all have day jobs working for other wineries. I spent only a couple of hours with them at their provisional home at Papapietro Perry Winery in the Dry Creek Valley, so I can't be sure, but I think Web, big and bearded and genial, would be the guy who books the gigs and drives the van and plays rhythm; Anthony, the intense, articulate one who sings and gets a lot of girls; and Dave the one tinkering with new sounds and writing songs. No, wait, sorry, they're winemakers. They come from Virginia (Web), Sonoma (Anthony), and Kansas (Dave) and met in 2003, when they all worked as cellar rats at Williams Selyem, the pioneering producer that put Sonoma Pinot Noir on the map. And they are part of a second or possibly third generation that's redefining California Pinot Noir. Most of these winemakers have day jobs at larger wineries and pursue their passion for small-production Pinot Noir on the side. With a few exceptions, they don't own wineries or vineyards. Some of them make big, jammy Zins and Cabs for their employers, but the new Pinot Noir paradigm emphasizes balance and restraint over power and volume.

It may help to go back to the beginning, to the fifties, when Joe Rochioli bought the land in the Russian River Valley that his father had farmed. His son Joe junior, out of some genius intuition, persuaded him to plant some Pinot Noir, a finicky and not very productive or fashionable grape. (Rumor has it Joe senior demanded he plant beans between the vines.) Enter Ed Selyem and Burt Williams, two wine-loving friends who decided to make wine in a two-car garage with purchased grapes. They worked on weekends and fermented in dairy tanks. Williams Selyem acquired a devoted following, and in 1987 its Pinot Noir from the Rochioli Vineyard won the California State Fair, and demand has far outstripped supply ever since. Shortly thereafter, Williams and Selyem helped the Rochiolis, their main grape suppliers, make their own wines, and within a few years the two labels were synonymous with Russian River Pinot Noir. Pinot needs a cooler climate than Cabernet, and the Russian River funneled the cool Pacific air into this picturesque valley, with its highly variable geology.

Certain sectors of the wine world went into mourning when Burt and Ed sold their baby to the New York investor John Dyson in 1998, and many had never heard of Bob Cabral, whom Williams designated as his successor, though in fact Cabral was a veteran winemaker who'd been on the Williams Selyem mailing list since 1985, becoming customer number 576 when he was studying oenology at Fresno State. Under Dyson, Williams Selyem has indeed expanded; in 2010 it unveiled a stunning new winery designed by the D.arc Group, on Westside Road south of Healdsburg, at a raucous party that embraced much of Sonoma's wine-making community. But the wines, especially the Pinots, retain their cult status, and Cabral has become a mentor to a new generation of talent. It might not be too much to say that Williams Selyem is the mother ship to the new acid freaks who practice the same kind of guerrilla wine making pioneered by Burt and Ed.

George Levkoff is one of these sons of Selyem. When I first tasted his wine at Cut in Los Angeles at the recommendation of the sommelier Dana Farner, I knew I wanted to meet him. Born on the Upper East Side of Manhattan, George was a hard-driving bond trader in Los Angeles when a friend who worked at a wine store changed his life. They were dining at Joe's in Venice, and the friend brought along two bottles of Williams Selyem, the 1991 and 1992 Rochioli Vineyard, which he felt would complement the grilled ahi tuna that was the restaurant's signature dish. "It was an epiphany," says George, when I visit him in his rented winery space just down the road from Selyem and Rochioli. (Westside Road, known as the Rodeo Drive of Pinot Noir.) "It was the first time wine had stood out as an equal partner in the dining experience, and I resolved pretty much right there that I'd move to Sonoma and make Pinot Noir." Levkoff, who reminds me of Buddy Hackett and is still enough of a New Yorker to wear a P. J. Clarke's T-shirt, actually made the move, eventually finding work with Cabral at Williams Selyem. A one-man operation, George owns no vineyards or winery, but he purchases fruit from five Russian River vineyards, makes bottles, and sells it all by hand. The wines, featured in some of the country's best restaurants, are superbly balanced, ripe but enlivened with zingy acidity.

Some of the new Sonoma Pinot makers cut their teeth in Burgundy, the holy land of Pinot Noir. The winemaker Alex Davis, of Porter Creek, studied wine making at Georges Roumier, one of the most revered domaines in Burgundy, before returning to his family estate just down the road from Rochioli to make very soulful Pinot Noirs and other varietals. If he ever gives up wine making, he could probably make a good living as a Leonardo DiCaprio impersonator, though he seems fiercely devoted to his biodynamically farmed vineyards, and it would take a good many manicures to get the dirt out from under his fingernails. Eric Sussman, of Radio-Coteau, apprenticed at Comte Armand in Pommard and Jacques Prieur in Meursault after studying agriculture at Cornell. Radio-Coteau is his joint venture with Bill and Joan Smith, who make some very fine Pinot under their own name. Radio-Coteau is a colloquialism he picked up in France, meaning broadcasting from the hillside, or word of mouth, which nicely captures the spirit of Sussman's venture and that of many of his Pinotphile neighbors. A Pinot Noir specialist, he buys grapes from cool-site vineyards, mostly in Sonoma County, and sells his beautifully balanced wines largely via his mailing list.

Ehren Jordan of Failla vineyards, the tallest man in Napa, also cut his teeth in France. He worked in the Rhône Valley with the peripatetic winemaker Jean-Luc Colombo before serving a brief apprenticeship with Helen Turley, who was around that time anointed the Wine Goddess by Robert Parker. When Helen had a falling-out with her brother Larry, Jordan took over as winemaker of Turley Wine Cellars, Larry's Napa Valley estate, and helped to seal its reputation as the ultimate source of rich, powerful old-vine Zinfandels. In 1999, Jordan took his first crack at Pinot Noir and quickly became enamored. He started Failla with his wife, Anne-Marie Failla, a recovering investment banker, in 2002 and bought land on a cool Pinot-friendly stretch of the Sonoma Coast near Flowers and Marcassin. While his Turley wines are known for their decadent opulence, the Failla Pinots have a much more restrained aesthetic, and he is not afraid to use the adjective "Burgundian" to describe them.

Basically, the new Pinot paradigm is pretty much the bizarro-world antithesis of planet Napa Cabernet, where power and volume are cardinal virtues. The new generation of Pinotphiles favor adjectives like "restraint" and "delicacy." Pinotphiles speak reverently about acid and brag about how early they pick their grapes. "I think the pendulum is swinging away from overblown wines," says Anthill's Web Marquez. "I feel like now wine making, especially with Pinot, is like learning how to use a recently acquired superpower. We have the ability to do whatever we want (from better vineyarding, technology, cellar practices, and general know-how), and we can make huge wines or very dainty ones. But now we all need to learn how to use and control that power . . .

and just because we have this ability doesn't mean we need to use it to the nth degree every time. I think the new generation is very attuned to that."

One way to achieve restraint is to seek out cool sites, which is why Jordan and many of the second-generation Sonoma Pinot pioneers have sought out the Sonoma Coast. Some of the chilliest real estate is within smelling distance of the Pacific, which is why Andy and Nick Peay, along with Nick's wife, Vanessa Wong, bought a fifty-three-acre ranch in the chilly inversion layer along the coast at Sea Ranch with plenty of fog and wind to moderate the California sunshine. (Vanessa is another French-trained winemaker, having worked at Lafite and Domaine Jean Gros in Burgundy.) In the past decade, they've produced increasingly sophisticated and celebrated Pinots while selling fruit to Failla and, yes, Williams Selyem.

Some of the best California Pinot Noirs (and Chardonnays) bear the Sonoma Coast designation. The problem is that this particular AVA, or American Viticultural Area, is so large and climatically heterogeneous as to be almost meaningless. If you look at the AVA on a map, it resembles a gerrymandered electoral district drawn by politicians to preserve a congressional seat. Should the word "coast" really be applicable to vineyards an hour's drive from the water? "That the appellation is so huge and covers areas with a twenty-degree temperature variation and very different soils makes a farce out of the idea behind appellations," says Andy Peay.

Many informed observers have started speaking of the true Sonoma Coast, or a west Sonoma Coast. Early pioneers such as Flowers, Marcassin, and Hirsch sought out the cooler westernmost areas of the coast in the early nineties, recognizing the potential for great Pinots and Chards. Matt Licklider, who is making some excellent Pinots and Chards under the LIOCO label, says, "I think the AVA is ripe for multiple secessions." He's one of many who would like to see a West Sonoma Coast AVA with the boundary defined by Highway 116. "Any vineyards west of there, we consider to be the Western Sonoma Coast. Wines grown on the true coast possess an undeniable link to their maritime origins—a link wines growing further inland lack."

Recently, Peay and some of his neighbors (Failla, Freeman, Littorai, Freestone, and Red Car) formed the West Sonoma Coast Vintners, which now has thirty-five members. The lesson here, as in Burgundy, is that the all-important name is the maker's.

Thomas Brown is a new superstar winemaker who crafts some of the most celebrated Cabernets and Zinfandels in the Napa Valley for clients like Schrader, Maybach, and Outpost. But his own pet project, Rivers-Marie, is devoted to the Burgundian varietals of Chardonnay and Pinot Noir. He routinely receives scores in the high 90s for his small-production Cabs, but for some wine geeks his most amazing laurel is a 94-point score for his 2004 Rivers-Marie Summa Vineyard Sonoma Coast Pinot Noir from Burghound's Allen Meadows, who worships at the shrine of Burgundy and generally has a low regard for California Pinot Noir. If you were lucky enough to be on the mailing list, you could have gotten this wine for just $50, far less than the average Napa Cabernet. Unfortunately, Brown only made sixty cases. He and his wife, Genevieve, have just bought the vineyard, though, so we can look forward to many more great vintages of Summa.

Generally speaking, these new-wave Sonoma Pinot Noirs are made in very small quantities, but they are far less expensive than Napa cult Cabernets or top Burgundies—most of them are in the $30 to $60 range—and they are extremely versatile at the table. While Burgundy serves as an inspiration for many of these winemakers, they are blessed with more consistent and clement weather, and you are less likely to get your heart broken by a bottle of Sonoma Pinot than one from the notoriously fickle Côte d'Or.

My Kind of Cellar:
Ted Conklin and the American Hotel

It's not that I don't love to pay two or even three times retail for a bottle of wine that's nowhere near maturity, which is the situation I often find myself in when I open a wine list, even in Manhattan. I'm a New Yorker; I'm used to being hustled. Yes, I know—my restaurant-owning friends have explained the economics to me, the expense of storage, the difficulty of finding mature Bordeaux or Barolo, blah blah blah. But I can't help dreaming about those old-school restaurant lists like '21' in New York, Bern's Steak House in Tampa, or Tour d'Argent in Paris, which list hundreds of bottles of mature-vintage wines, some of them with old-fashioned prices reflecting the fact that they were purchased on release. The American Hotel, in Sag Harbor, New York, has one of these drool-inducing lists. Its owner, Ted Conklin, sixty-two, bought and restored the derelict hotel in the former whaling village in 1972, opening a restaurant and gradually accumulating one of the best cellars in the country.

Historical records have nothing to say about the selection of beverages at the tavern owned by James Howell, which stood on the site of the present hotel when British forces occupied Sag Harbor in 1777, although Madeira and rum were at that time the favorite tipples of the colonists. The commanding officer of the redcoats was captured there in a daring midnight raid by Lieutenant Colonel Return Jonathan Meigs, a veteran of Bunker Hill, who crossed over from New Haven with 234 men in thirteen whaleboats. Meigs and his men killed or captured most of the British garrison, seized tons of supplies—including ten hogsheads of rum—and made it back to New Haven without the loss of a single American soldier. Despite the success of Meigs's raid, it took many years for Sag Harbor to recover from the devastation of the occupation. Ultimately, prosperity arrived as Sag Harbor became a major whaling port in the early part of the nineteenth century, when the American Hotel was built on the site of Howell's tavern. Its watering holes then were notorious enough to earn a censorious mention in *Moby-Dick*: "Arrived at last in old Sag Harbor; and seeing what the sailors did there . . . poor Queequeg gave it up for lost."

Sag Harbor's prosperity ended almost simultaneously with the discovery of gold in California. Whales were becoming scarce, and coal oil was replacing whale oil; most of the whaling ships sailed for San Francisco carrying many of the town's able-bodied young men. When Ted Conklin bought the American Hotel in 1972, it was a derelict shell with a coal stove and four outhouses. The cellar, now the repository of thousands of great bottles, was knee-deep in coal ash, which Conklin carried up the narrow stairs one bucket at a time. Sag Harbor was a blue-collar town, a dowdy stepchild of the fashionable summer resort towns of Southampton and East Hampton, albeit one with a strong literary tradition stretching back to James Fenimore Cooper's sojourn. John Steinbeck, Nelson Algren, and Spalding Gray lived here for many years; E. L. Doctorow, Wilfrid Sheed, and Thomas Harris all have homes in Sag Harbor. Conklin envisioned a place where plumbers and writers could mix, although there are probably more of the latter than the former these days, particularly in the summer, when Sag Harbor is invaded by well-heeled New Yorkers.

Only twenty-three at the time, Conklin had already opened and operated a successful restaurant in nearby Westhampton, rehabilitated a farm in upstate New York, gotten married and divorced. Although he'd been born in the city and spent his early years in suburban Manhasset, Conklin had deep roots in Sag Harbor. One of his forebears, Ananias Conklin, was among the first settlers, taking possession of land that would later be incorporated as Sag Harbor after having been, according to Ted, "kicked out of Salem, Massachusetts, by the same folks who sponsored the witch trials." Ted Conklin—who recently married his college sweetheart after a chance reunion in Palm Beach—now lives in the house built by Ananias in 1700, and while the purchase of the American Hotel must have seemed like a rash act at the time, he's clearly a man with a deep sense of history and tradition. He dresses as if he were still at Lawrenceville—blue blazers, chinos, and Top-siders. He's an avid sailor and has a deep affection for all things nautical, most especially the fifty-year-old seventy-five-foot Trumpy yacht that is docked at the marina just down the street from the hotel. His other great passion is for wine.

His palate seems to have kicked in early. "When I was in school, my parents drank Almaden Mountain Chablis, and I just knew it wasn't very good. When my mother discovered white Zinfandel, I had to move out of the house." For those who know Conklin, this story is fairly believable; he has firm opinions in matters of taste and decorum and doesn't suffer fools, or sweet pink wines, gladly. He has impeccable manners, but it's not hard to tell when he's annoyed or bored, even, sometimes, when the subject in question is wine. One gets the sense that his stolid WASP sensibility is slightly at odds with his epic epicureanism.

During his brief stint as a farmer he worked his way through Julia Child's *Mastering the Art of French Cooking* and learned about wine with the help of such authors as Frank Schoonmaker and Frederick Wildman. "In those days," he says, "wine meant Bordeaux, and you could afford it. You could actually buy Château d'Yquem." When he opened the hotel, Conklin was fortunate to have the guidance of a wine aficionado and distributor named Gus Gantz, who helped him stock the cellar of the hotel, after Conklin had excavated it, with Bordeaux, some of which is still resting comfortably there. He hired a French chef and has gone through many in the intervening years; the menu has always been fairly French, with a focus on local seafood.

Although he may have forgotten one or two of his chefs, he seems to remember every wine purchase, including the price. "One of my first purchases was the '66 Calon-Ségur," he tells me as he leads me into the labyrinth of the cellar. "It was $36 a case." The cellar, though very clean, looks utterly chaotic, with stacks of wooden cases and cardboard boxes creating narrow alleys and a wide variety of shelves and racks, but it's all accounted for on an Excel program that tells him and his staff the location of each bottle.

In the early days the list, currently 114 pages, focused mainly on Bordeaux, and it still has an amazing selection of treasures from that region, from the 1961 Gruaud Larose ($795) to the 2006 Lafite Rothschild ($1,400)—including many wines that are priced well below what they'd fetch at auction—although he believes that the great growths of Bordeaux are becoming too expensive. As much as he loves these wines, he seems offended by the idea of anyone spending four figures for a bottle. "The first-growth Bordeaux are becoming commodities. Once they become commodities, they don't have a place at the table." But he can't quite seem to break the Bordeaux habit—I notice many cases of expensive 2005s and 2006s—including Petrus and Lafite—among the stacked cases.

The cellar would be extraordinary if only for its collection of older vintages, including an extensive list of Burgundies, but it also reflects the new reality of the global wine village. Conklin keeps up, and he is currently very enthusiastic about New Zealand whites, Sonoma Pinot Noirs, and Argentinean Malbecs. He's also been a longtime booster of the top Long Island wines. Sitting on the front porch of the hotel, in between greeting the passersby on the sidewalk, he tells me, "There's never been more good wine in the world than there is today." And Ted Conklin is still discovering it and buying it, somehow finding more space in the cellar.

A Tuscan in the House:
Julian Niccolini and the Four Seasons

"This is New York," Julian Niccolini says, looking out over the famous Philip Johnson–designed Grill Room where Barbara Walters, Charlie Rose, and Governor George Pataki are eating lunch. "They know what they want. They know wine. They like to show off." He is explaining why a restaurant that has probably done more than any other to shape how Americans drink and perceive wine has no sommelier. "Since the beginning we had the idea that the customer knows what he wants."

The lack of a gatekeeper to the cellar is just one of the ways in which the Four Seasons remains the quintessential American restaurant. The restaurant's approach to wine, like its approach to food and the seating policy, reflects a smooth amalgam of the democratic and the plutocratic, of American informality and New York attitude: the customer is always right—not least because he's likely to be rich, powerful, and opinionated, or all three. Still, no customer is ever above and beyond Niccolini's coruscating European wit. Sitting in the serene oasis of the Pool Room with me one night—Grill Room for lunch, Pool Room at night is a formula to go alongside white wine with fish, red wine with meat—he stands briefly to bid farewell to a silver-haired banker with a gorgeous young thing on his arm, then sits again to refill my glass. "He has to get her home right away," Niccolini tells me. "His little blue pill is kicking in."

Ever since 1959, when it opened on the ground floor of Mies van der Rohe's Seagram Building on Park Avenue, the Four Seasons has had an enormous influence on American cooking, as well as restaurant service and design. If at this point it's no longer at the cutting edge of the food and wine revolutions it helped to foment, to this day it is exemplary in its approach to wine service and pricing, thanks in no small part to Niccolini, co-owner—with Swiss-born Alex von Bidder—and the guy in charge of the cellar.

From the very start, the Four Seasons was dedicated to showcasing California and even New York wine. In 1976—the same year as the Judgment of Paris in which California wines beat out the French in blind tasting—the then owner Paul Kovi organized the first of its barrel tastings of these wines and brought the word of Napa's emergence to the most important market in America. Twenty years later, Warren Winiarski of Stag's Leap vineyard said, "When Paul first invited us back in 1975, it was the first time we were taken seriously outside of California. It was a gesture that gave us all enormous confidence." The barrel tasting was replaced after a decade by an annual dinner featuring the latest vintage of the top growths of Bordeaux, an event that understandably remains hugely popular. In the meantime, shortly after the first barrel tasting, Kovi and his partner, Tom Margittai, hired Niccolini away from the Palace, then the most expensive restaurant in the country, to run their ailing Grill Room, and he turned it into New York's premier lunch spot for titans of media, advertising, finance, and fashion.

Niccolini more or less grew up in the food and hospitality business. A former resistance fighter, his father owned a small all-purpose general store in a hilltop town in Tuscany that sold food, wine, and dry goods and served homemade meals. From an early age, Julian was gathering wild porcini, transferring bulk wine from demijohns to small bottles, and helping his mother in the kitchen. At the age of sixteen he went to hotel school in Rome and from there to the Hôtel de Paris in Monte Carlo. Along the way his passion for wine, since he spent most of his vacations exploring the world's best vineyards, blossomed into expertise. He first visited Napa in 1977, and in 1979 he got to Montalcino, long before Brunello di Montalcino became famous in this country.

Although Kovi and Margittai had originally hired him for his smooth front-of-the-house skills, they soon handed him responsibility for the cellar and the dinners. Niccolini put together dinners featuring the wines of Montalcino and the Piedmont (home of Barolo and Barbaresco), anticipating and contributing to the explosion of interest in Italian wines in this country.

Today, years after Niccolini and von Bidder took ownership of the restaurant, the urbane Tuscan still runs the wine program single-handedly with a combination of great zeal and insouciance. ("Don't drink it, it's crap," he tells me, without tasting, when a customer sends a carafe of red over to the table.) In an era of wine directors and multiple sommeliers, Niccolini remains something of a passionate amateur, and while his by-the-glass selection is limited and his list conservative, his markups are also blessedly conservative, especially for a restaurant this expensive. The Mont-Redon Châteauneuf-du-Pape from the great 2007 vintage, for instance, was listed for just $77 in October 2011. The 1998 Krug might sound expensive at $390, unless you know that it goes for about $250 at retail. The cult Cabs—Colgin, Araujo, Bond—are represented. The plutocrats can order the 2007 Screaming Eagle for $2,500, while the more frugal may notice the 2007 Newton Unfiltered Cab for $95.

Much as he loves wine, you get the idea that Julian Niccolini wants us to keep it in perspective as an accompaniment to good food, conversation, and flirtation. "Is she attractive?" Niccolini asks, when a captain informs him that a patron wishes to say good-bye. Without waiting for an answer, he gets up and leaves his glass of Condrieu on the table in order to bid farewell to the lady in question.

Not Just Mario's Partner:
Joe "Vino" Bastianich Breaks Out

Although he's shrunk considerably since I first met him thanks to a long-distance-running habit, Joe Bastianich is cutting a very large figure these days. Once best known as the partner of the chef Mario Batali and the son of the chef Lidia Bastianich, both stars of the small screen, the newly svelte restaurateur has stepped into the spotlight recently. Since 2010 he's made a name for himself as a judge on Fox's *Master Chef.* He's a partner in the hugely successful Eataly, Manhattan's Disneyland for foodies. And he's published *Grandi Vini: An Opinionated Tour of Italy's 89 Finest Wines.* Bastianich has, in fact, created one of the most influential restaurant empires in America, but wine is his great passion, the subject that really gets his juices flowing.

He was born, as it were, into the business. His parents, refugees from Istria, an Italian province annexed by Yugoslavia, had worked in several restaurants in Queens before opening Buonavia in Forest Hills in 1970. "It was a blue-collar thing," Joe says of those days. Chefs weren't stars, and young Bastianich fils saw little glamour in the family biz. In 1979, though, they crossed the river to Manhattan, opening Felidia on East Fifty-Eighth Street. Drawing inspiration from Istria and Trieste, Lidia Bastianich's food was a hit almost from the beginning, highlighting a regional cuisine that was miles, literally and figuratively, from chicken parmigiana and spaghetti and meatballs. God knows I'd never tasted anything like it when my publisher took me there for lunch in 1984, nor had I ever drunk anything like the Barolo he ordered.

Lidia's son tried to trade restaurant row for Wall Street, spending three years at Merrill Lynch and Lehman before embarking on a pilgrimage to his ancestral home in 1990, drawn specifically by his passion for wine. "Ninety was a real turning point for Italy, not only a great vintage, but a transition, and I tasted all these great wines in barrel. I worked as a cellar rat from Friuli to Sicily." In Piedmont he apprenticed with two of the best producers of Barolo (known in Italy as "the king of wines and the wine of kings"), Bruno Ceretto and Luciano Sandrone; in Montalcino he apprenticed with Andrea Costanti.

Friuli, in the northeast, the region from which his parents hailed, is arguably the source of the greatest Italian whites. As Joe puts it in *Grandi Vini*, "In Friuli . . . the gently rolling foothills of the Julian Alps meet the warm, brackish lagoon of the Northern Adriatic . . . and the magical mixture of the respective cool and warm breezes—along with the *terroir*—create the climatic magic necessary to make long-lived, structured yet aromatic white wines." While there he worked with Livio Felluga, one of the best local producers. Before the end of the decade Bastianich would buy one of the area's historic wine estates, but in the meantime he returned to New York.

"I got into restaurants as a way to get back to wine," he says, sipping a glass of Barolo at his newest restaurant, Manzo, an Italian steakhouse set in the middle of bustling Eataly. He opened his first restaurant in partnership with his mother. Becco, in the theater district, featured an extensive Italian wine list with all selections priced at $15 (now $25). "But I realized at some point I couldn't work with my mom." It was Lidia who introduced him to his future business partner Mario Batali at the James Beard Foundation Awards in 1993. "We used to go out after work, hang out, eat, and drink," he recalls. They would become the Larry Page and Sergey Brin of the postmillennial Manhattan restaurant scene. Or maybe the Simpson and Bruckheimer, with Bastianich playing the Bruckheimer role—the focused, steady partner. "Joe has a cool head," Batali says. "I sometimes get too passionate." (That, his friends and colleagues would agree, is an understatement.)

In 1997, Joe purchased land in Collio, Friuli, including sixty-year-old Tocai vines planted in a beautiful south-facing bowl that looks like a natural amphitheater, along with an imposing, turreted thirteenth-century structure in the town of Butrio to serve as his winery. The following year he and the winemaker Emilio Del Medico produced his first vintage of Tocai (now called Friulano due to European Union regs), along with a white called Vespa, a blend of Chardonnay, Sauvignon Blanc, and Picolit that would become widely acclaimed. That same year he teamed up with Batali to open Babbo, a groundbreaking restaurant featuring Mario's inspired interpretations of the Italian classics. Its use of then-unknown ingredients like beef cheeks, wild fennel pollen, and lamb's tongue titillated the hell out of New York's foodies. It also featured a staggeringly comprehensive, all-Italian wine list, thanks to Joe, as well as a new serving portion, called a *quartino;* this was based on the *quarto*—quarter liter—common in Italian trattorias, except that instead of house plonk Babbo served serious juice, often from magnums. "Some people got mad and insisted on a glass of wine," Bastianich recalls. "I had to go to every table and explain that it was a by-the-bottle experience in a by-the-glass format, that it allowed you to control the amount of wine in your glass." When a bottle was ordered, every single glass was rinsed with a small amount of the wine to be served in order to avoid any chance of soap residue or cooking odors. New Yorkers were intrigued. With only eighty seats, Babbo had four sommeliers on the floor, and it had a huge impact on the wine culture of this country and spawned a new generation of sommeliers and enthusiasts.

As Joe's Friulian winery started getting serious reviews, he created another, this time in the emerging Maremma region of Tuscany, with Batali and his mother as partners. They produce a nice Morellino di Scansano (the local name for Sangiovese, of Chianti fame) along with a blend of international varietals on the Super Tuscan model. In 2008, Bastianich attained the ultimate fantasy of Italian oenophilia when he became a partner in Brandini, a winery in the holy region of Barolo—kind of the equivalent of marrying Carla Bruni or finding a perfect 1970 Ferrari Daytona.

Joe produced his first wine book, with Babbo's sommelier David Lynch, in 2002. *Vino Italiano* is a valuable and comprehensive survey of the country's numerous wine regions. The new book is a more personal take, his annotated greatest-hits list, and I only wish he'd taken the list all the way to a hundred. Even those who think they know the terrain will make some discoveries. He strikes a fine balance between traditional and new-wave producers, but he's not afraid to stand up for an unfashionable wine or to criticize conventional wisdom.

Grandi Vini should start more than a few well-lubricated arguments. Sassicaia and not Ornellaia? Fontanafredda and not Vietti? (Now, them's fighting words.) And why the hell are there only three wines from Joe's beloved Friuli? Is Brunello still Brunello? And does Merlot belong in your Chianti? These are questions that deserve to be argued, Italian-style, with lots of shouting and hand waving—or possibly contemplated with a glass of one of Joe's own wines, or one of his favorite eighty-nine, in hand.

The Wild Wizard of the Loire

Meeting the scholarly and genial Nicolas Joly in the picturesquely cluttered library of the eighteenth-century manor that houses his winery, you would be hard-pressed to imagine him dancing naked and burning rabbit skins in his vineyard at midnight, the image recently purveyed by a major French magazine. Joly is perhaps the world's leading practitioner of biodynamic viticulture, and as such he engages in some practices that might seem unconventional, although none of them involve naked dancing.

Joly is the proprietor of Coulée de Serrant, a domaine in the Loire Valley that borders the river and encompasses the ruins of an ancient castle destroyed in the wars between the Huguenots and the Catholics. ("Now we just have the war between good farming and bad farming," he says.) The vineyard was first planted in 1113 by Cistercian monks, and the excellence of its wines has been acknowledged for centuries. Louis XI spoke of "la goutte d'or" (the golden drop) in the wines, and Joly has a picture of Louis XIV touring the vineyards in a chariot. So prized was the spot that it became its own appellation, though it's contained within the Loire's Savennières appellation.

His parents bought Coulée de Serrant in 1961, when Nicolas was sixteen. He eventually attended Columbia Business School and worked for Morgan Guaranty in New York and London until something called him back to the land in 1977. "I loved learning about banking," he says over lunch in the medieval cloister on the property, where he lives with his wife, Coralie. "And it was a great life. But then one day I was finished with it."

Now, thirty years later, he seems like an unlikely cross between a professor and a farmer as he drives through the vineyards, repeatedly stalling his Pathfinder because he's in the wrong gear. He stops to taste the grapes, which are almost ready to harvest, as he expounds on the history of the place and the principles of medieval science. He has decided to start picking the day after my visit and will send his pickers through the vines at least five times, selecting only the ripest clusters. He likes to wait until some of the grapes on the clusters are shriveled and is more than happy if a little botrytis, or noble rot, has set in.

When he returned to Coulée de Serrant, he threw himself into the wine business. "I tried modern farming for two years," he says. On the advice of a consultant, he used weed killers and fertilizers. "Big mistake," he concludes. He was distressed to observe the effects on the vineyard, which he says had become a biological desert, devoid of microbial and insect life. In 1979, Joly stumbled on a book in English about biodynamics, a holistic approach to agriculture based on a series of lectures given by the Austrian philosopher Rudolf Steiner in 1924. The following year, Joly began applying biodynamic principles in his vineyard. He's been studying them, writing about them, and teaching them to an expanding band of disciples ever since.

I first encountered his wine more than twenty years ago when I ordered a bottle of the 1982 Coulée de Serrant at the Union Square Cafe in New York. I can still remember the stony intensity of that wine, and I have sought it out ever since, but it's not easy to find. In a good year Joly produces fewer than two thousand cases, about a quarter of which comes to the States.

As special as it is, Coulée de Serrant exemplifies many of the qualities of Savennières, a tiny appellation (with about a three-thousand-case annual production) in the Anjou region of the Loire, which seems to be superbly suited to the Chenin Blanc grape. Coulée, like all Savennières, is made entirely from Chenin

Blanc, and some connoisseurs think Savennières is the ultimate expression of Chenin Blanc (granted, it's a narrow field of competition). Quince is a flavor that recurs in tasting notes. The wines are often almost fierce in their youth, but they can age gracefully and improve for years, even decades. Whether Coulée is the finest Savennières or a unique expression of the seven-hectare vineyard—the correct answer is both—Joly is adamant that its quality has almost nothing to do with his wine making. "I really do almost nothing to the wine," he says. "It pretty much makes itself. Press it, put it in barrels, that's about it. All the work has been done before, in the vineyard." He doesn't add yeast—it's already there on the grapes—and he doesn't control temperature.

It's a cliché of winespeak 4.0, 2012 version, to say that wine is made in the vineyard rather than in the cellar. After years of increasing reliance on technology in the cellar, even New World wizards have started talking more about the importance of good raw material, (that is, grapes) and focusing more on the vineyards. But the cellars of many top wineries from Napa to Bordeaux have some very high-tech equipment designed to whip those naughty grapes into shape. Joly's cellar, by contrast, is eerily minimalist: a shiny pneumatic press, twenty-five or thirty old oak barrels, a small room stacked with unlabeled bottles of the 2009 vintage. Old school.

The French *appellation contrôlée* system, which came into being in the nineteen thirties to codify hundreds of years of regional practice, is based on the idea that wines should uniquely reflect their place of origin, and Joly fiercely defends it. But he believes that a wine is unlikely to convey the unique aspects of soil and climate—what the French call *terroir*—if you bombard the soil with pesticides and fertilizers and then manipulate the results in the cellar. "There are lots of good wines today," he says, "but there aren't that many unique wines."

The specific practices of biodynamic viticulture can sound a little wacky—like burying a cow horn packed with manure in the vineyard—although many of them have an intuitive logic. The rabbit skins, for instance. In biodynamics, pesticides are verboten; instead, the pest in question (when large enough) is discouraged by the ashes of its deceased brethren. When Joly developed a rabbit problem, he burned a skin or two and spread the ashes in the vineyard. He says it worked. While Joly emphasizes that these principles need to be adapted to a vineyard's specific conditions, there are common practices. Teas made of nettle and other plants are sprayed on the vines, and manure is used in lieu of fertilizers.

Critics of biodynamics point out that Coulée de Serrant has always been a highly regarded wine, and some suggest it was an even greater wine before the adoption of the biodynamic regimen. I have tasted only a few of the older wines and would hazard that they were excellent, if leaner and less rich. The two latest vintages I tasted were both wonderful and utterly unique wines: the 2008 was very plush and full-bodied, almost sweet but vibrant, a youthful and powerful beauty like Milla Jovovich in *Resident Evil*. The 2007 was more voluptuous and decadent, with a honeyed quality that put me in mind of Ava Gardner in *The Barefoot Contessa*.

In 2000, Nicolas founded Return to Terroir, a group for like-minded organic and biodynamic producers that includes such heavy hitters as Zind Humbrecht, Domaine Leflaive, Movia, and Araujo vineyards. If this philosophy borders on the mystical, tasting these great wines seems to present fairly compelling empirical evidence of its success. Coulée de Serrant would be on many connoisseurs' lists of the world's greatest wines, a white that can combine great richness with piercing intensity, a wine that is a compelling expression of a particular place and the personality of the man who denies he made it.

Is Biodynamics a Hoax?

Burly, heavily bearded Stuart Smith has been tending his vineyard atop Spring Mountain with his brother Charlie for more than forty years. The Smith brothers have gained a quietly loyal following for their Smith-Madrone wines, despite eschewing such Napa conventions as new French oak, irrigation, and Robert Parker raves. Stu, the more loquacious of the brothers, has been known to complain about the alcohol content and prices of many Napa wines—both too high in his estimation. Recently, he has directed his contrarian streak at a fashionable new target: biodynamic viticulture.

Biodynamics is a system of organic agriculture based on the teachings of Rudolf Steiner, the Austrian theosophist, and specifically on a series of lectures he delivered to a group of farmers in 1924. Biodynamics uses many of the basic principles of organic farming—no pesticides or chemical fertilizers—but goes further, relying on practices like planting and harvesting according to solar and lunar cycles. Some of the most revered domaines in France, including Domaine de la Romanée-Conti, Domaine Leroy, Coulée de Serrant, and Zind Humbrecht, adhere to it, and in recent years it has been gaining converts in Napa and Sonoma—Araujo, Benziger, Grgich Hills, Sinskey, and Quintessa among them. In 2009 Stu Smith created a local stir when he published a letter in Santa Rosa's *Press Democrat* charging that "biodynamics is a hoax and deserves the same level of respect we give witchcraft." He has continued his assault on a Web site called Biodynamics Is a Hoax.

"Rudolf Steiner was a complete nutcase," he writes, "a flim-flam man with a tremendous imagination, a combination, if you will, of an LSD-dropping Timothy Leary with the showmanship of a P. T. Barnum."

In order to demonstrate his point, he quotes Steiner at some length—something he claims proponents are reluctant to do—and there's some wild stuff to quote, about ghosts, Lemurians, and the jellyish beings who inhabited Atlantis. The most emblematic and controversial practice of biodynamics involves burying a cow horn stuffed with manure at the time of the autumnal equinox; on or around the spring equinox, the horn is disinterred and the manure diluted in water (a mixture known as BD 500) and sprayed over the vineyard.

"You see, by burying the cow horn with the manure in it," Steiner wrote, "we preserve in the horn the etheric and astral force that the horn was accustomed to reflect when it was on the cow. Because the cow horn is now outwardly surrounded by the Earth, all the Earth's etherizing and astralizing rays stream into its inner cavity. The manure inside the horn attracts these forces and is inwardly enlivened by them. If the horn is buried for the entire winter—the season when the Earth is most inwardly alive—all this life will be preserved in the manure, turning the contents of the horn into an extremely concentrated, enlivening and fertilizing force." To which many oenophiles might well respond, "What the fuck?"

In my experience, Smith is correct that most biodynamic proponents would rather talk about results than quote Steiner (with the notable exception of the voluble and erudite Nicolas Joly of Coulée de Serrant). Robert Sinskey of Sinskey Vineyards in Carneros is a case in point. In 1990, he told me recently, he and his winemaker, Jeff Virnig, went to look at one of their Carneros vineyards that was in decline. "One look at the soil told us that life was out of balance," he said. They couldn't penetrate the surface with a shovel, so they broke it up with a pick. They couldn't find any earthworms in the ground, and there was little humus (organic soil matter such as decomposed leaves and other plant material). Until then, they'd tried to kill off anything in the soil that might compete with their vines and to add back anything the vines needed by applying fertilizers. "We had, in essence, sterilized the soil," he said.

· They applied BD 500 prep to that vineyard the following year. "The microbe-rich concoction jump-started life," Sinskey concluded. "Within a few years, the soil rebounded with microbial activity, earthworms, and mycorrhizal fungi. The original vineyard that motivated this journey turned around to become one of our favorite sites and produced one of our most distinctive wines."

The obvious question for biodynamic producers is whether organic farming, which eschews herbicides and pesticides without reference to Steiner or to cosmic forces, would yield similar results. A research paper titled "Soil and Winegrape Quality in Biodynamically and Organically Managed Vineyards," published in the *American Journal of Enology and Viticulture* in 2005, compared the two approaches and found few differences. But most of the certified biodynamicists I've spoken to over the years, none of whom were obviously certifiable, started with organic farming before moving on to Steiner's methods, which all of them claim to have given them superior results and healthier vineyards.

Jeff Dawson, who works as a biodynamic consultant with Araujo and Quintessa vineyards in Napa, considers the fact that Araujo's Cabernet has ripened well ahead of its neighbors in recent years "a tribute to biodynamics." (A skeptical neighbor insists this is because the site is warmer than most.) Dawson became interested after working at a biodynamic garden at Fetzer Vineyards in Mendocino and marveling at the quality of the produce. After studying Steiner's teachings, he created a biodynamic garden for Steve Jobs. "He was a raw-food vegan, and he loves sweet fruits and vegetables," he says of Apple's founder, and quotes his former boss, whom I presume to have had a scientific cast of mind, as saying, "Steiner knew what he was talking about." Stu Smith would be rolling his eyes by this point and declaring there's no scientific basis for the claims of biodynamics. And he's right. There isn't.

Dawson paraphrases Steiner when addressing such skepticism. "Science has cast its net on the world of nature," he tells me. "That net is not fine enough to catch all the aspects of creation." Many proponents seem to believe that science will eventually catch up with the tenets of biodynamics, particularly with regard to the influence of the solar and the stellar systems on plant and animal behavior.

The minimal claim to be made for biodynamics, it seems to me, is that it fosters a more intimate approach to the land and that its products are less likely to contain the toxins that have for many decades been commonly employed in conventional agriculture. Then there's the question of the quality of the congregation. Domaine de la Romanée-Conti and Domaine Leroy, to name just two examples, are widely acknowledged to be among the greatest wineries on the planet. Many people want to belong to the same church, even though critics like Stuart Smith would argue that these properties were already great *before* they made the switch. Biodynamics certainly dovetails with the now inescapable green consciousness. Whether it is a manifestation of an original holistic approach to nature or a crock of BD 500, wine lovers will be hearing about it more often in the years to come.

The Modigliani of Healdsburg

David Ramey was driving on a dusty road through the land of tequila and mescal when he had what he describes as his *coup de foudre*—otherwise known as his road-to-Mexicali moment—and realized, improbably, that he wanted to make wine. "I suddenly thought, wine makes people happy," he says. "And it's the intersection of art and commerce." For a California guy who'd recently graduated from Santa Cruz with a degree in American literature, there wouldn't seem to be anything preordained about this choice, which entailed returning to school to catch up on chemistry and other courses he'd disdained as an undergraduate before enrolling in the Department of Viticulture and Enology at UC Davis, the West Point of the California wine industry. But in retrospect it was a brilliant decision.

Ramey turned out to be a natural. After a stint at Château Petrus in Bordeaux in 1979, he returned to northern California with a more nuanced vision of wine making than the technocentric version he'd been steeped in at Davis and eventually became a leader of the post-Mondavi generation who helped make the nineties a golden age for Napa and Sonoma. Unlike some of his contemporaries', Ramey's style always favored balance over power. His wines were never the fattest, or the ripest, or the most alcoholic— his aesthetic more Modigliani than Botero. Tasting a Ramey Chardonnay alongside a Kistler—as I did when I first visited him in the late nineties—was a fascinating study in contrast, the Ramey vibrant, chiseled, and fresh, the Kistler tropical, buttery, fleshy, and sweet. It was the difference, I thought then, between

Kate Moss and Pamela Anderson. In the nineties the super-rich style was ascendant; now balance and freshness are the new buzzwords, and even Steve Kistler is preaching the gospel of restraint and finesse. Ramey never lacked recognition, but he's now beginning to look like a prophet. Not that he didn't sometimes question the wisdom of his principles.

"Could I get higher scores by making riper, less acidic wines?" he says, as he sips a glass of his 2008 Russian River Chardonnay at Spoonbar in Healdsburg, the ridiculously picturesque town in Sonoma where he lives and works. "Absolutely." Gruff tends to be his natural tone of voice. He pauses to check out the fashionable, exuberant crowd at the bar. After years as a sleepy backwater frequented by farmers and ex-hippies, Healdsburg is suddenly the kind of place where you see people in Prada eating tapas. "You can't drink these heavy, fat wines," he says. "On the other hand, you don't have to go to the other extreme just because there are wines of excess." Which is to say that his wines, for all their precision and restraint, tend to be more come-hither than their Old World counterparts, his Chardonnays just a little more voluptuous than the average Puligny-Montrachet, his Cabs less tannic than the typical Médoc. Ramey is proud to be a California winemaker, happy to be the beneficiary of the climate, and while he loves French wines, he's not trying to imitate them.

He seems equally adept with both whites and reds. After his stage at Petrus, the mother ship of Merlot, he went to Matanzas Creek and made some of the first serious Napa Valley Merlots. Moving on to Chalk Hill, he garnered attention for his Chardonnays. He then went on to make acclaimed Cabernet-based wines at Dominus and Rudd, while founding his eponymous winery in 1996. Ramey Wine Cellars initially specialized in Chardonnay, made from grapes purchased from some of the cooler vineyards in Sonoma. I still remember the first one I tasted at the French Laundry in Yountville, a racy, mouthwatering Hyde Vineyards Chard, having been steered to it by the sommelier.

Ramey continued to work for Rudd, receiving some stellar scores from the critics, before finally devoting himself full-time to his own wines, at a winery he built in Healdsburg. And he's justifiably proud that he and his wife, whom he married at Petrus, own the whole operation and that they didn't start with a large fortune derived from another industry. "You've got mega-millionaires buying their way in," he says, "and you've got scrappy young winemakers making tiny amounts of wine that's hard to find on the market. Then there are your big corporate conglomerates. By contrast, we're like a chef-owned restaurant." Fortunately, it's a chef-owned restaurant that, though not huge, has enough seats to accommodate demand.

Ramey Wine Cellars is too big to qualify as a cult winery and too small to make the owners rich. But the conservative business model, which might have seemed a bit frumpy five or six years ago, might be the perfect one for the post-crash economy. Like his wine making, his pricing has always been restrained compared with that of his competitors, given the relative critical acclaim. Now, when wineries that once turned away customers for $200 bottles of Cab are secretly cutting deals and accumulating inventory, Ramey is more than holding his own. His delicious 2007 Napa Valley claret, a Cabernet Sauvignon–dominated Bordeaux blend, sells for around $40, and it's ready to drink at this moment, unlike many of the big Cabs from that excellent vintage. (He makes more complex and expensive Cabs, too, the single-vineyard Pedregal from Oakville being the rarest and dearest.)

"I've lived through three cycles of the California wine industry," he says. "We had recessions in '91 and '92 and again in '02 and '03." While he admits that the recent economic meltdown briefly depressed sales, he had his best year ever in 2010. It doesn't hurt that the man whose name is on the bottle is on the road much of the year, meeting restaurateurs and retailers. "A lot of my colleagues," he says, "haven't worked hard enough to establish themselves in the market."

For a winemaker, Ramey seems to be an uncommonly good businessman, but his decision to make Syrah might have been a case of listening to his heart more than his head. In 2002 he planted two vineyards' worth on the cool western side of the Sonoma Coast appellation, inspired by his love for the Syrahs of the northern Rhône. The resulting wines have been lavishly praised but aren't, as many of his colleagues have discovered, easy to sell, and he's scaled back production since the 2007 vintage. A local joke goes: "What's the difference between a case of Syrah and a case of the clap? You can get rid of the clap." I love Ramey's Syrahs, which are much more reminiscent of Côte Rôtie than they are of jammy Barossa Shirazes, and they make the case for this grape as convincingly as any in California. My advice is to try them and buy them while they're still unfashionable. They are great values.

I also have a special fondness for his Chardonnays, which seem to me to strike a perfect balance between the elusive virtues of white Burgundy and the hedonistic pleasures of other California Chardonnays. Imagine if Christie Brinkley spoke French. Oh, wait, she does. Maybe David Ramey should consider hiring her as a spokesmodel.

The Odd Couple

Is there such a thing as the perfect match? Having been married four times, I've done my share of research on the subject of compatibility in the realm of eros. But the pairing of food and wine is perhaps even more bedeviling. Is there a perfect wine for oysters? For Camembert? For baked lobster with sunchoke braised in red wine and a fava sprout bergamot emulsion? Does fish always call for white wine? In your search for answers to these questions you could do worse than to go to New York's Le Bernardin, the Michelin three-star temple of piscine cuisine. Aldo Sohm, who was named Best Sommelier in America in 2007 and Best Sommelier in the World in 2008, is masterful at matching food and wine. He has converted more than one skeptic, including my wife, to the concept of pairing. "I can make the food look good," he says. On the other hand, the chef Eric Ripert, his boss, likes to drink red Bordeaux with pretty much everything, including oysters. This must make for some interesting discussions in the kitchen.

Among the mentors that Ripert studied under on his way to becoming America's best seafood chef was the great Joël Robuchon, who shares his taste in wine. "When Robuchon came to Le Bernardin," Ripert tells me over a lunch at Ben Benson's Steak House in midtown Manhattan, "he was offered the wine-pairing menu. He just said, 'Bring me Bordeaux.' I agree. I love Bordeaux. I'll even have it with salad." Indeed, he is sipping a 1995 La Conseillante, a Bordeaux from the Pomerol district, with his Caesar salad. This kind of thinking exasperates Sohm, an earnest and intense Austrian who came to the States in 2003 and has spent hundreds of hours working out the concepts of wine and food pairing. Watching them work together, I couldn't help thinking that the puckish Ripert enjoys winding Sohm up and throwing him nearly impossible challenges. The French-born Ripert loves to feign indignation whenever Sohm recommends a wine from his native Austria, despite the fact that Austrian Rieslings and Grüner Veltliners are an insider's secret, beloved among chefs and sommeliers for their food friendliness. Even when he's not playfully tormenting Sohm, Ripert poses some pretty serious difficulties with his exotically spiced and sauced seafood, like the aforementioned baked lobster (so far, so good) with red-wine-braised sunchoke (uh-oh) and a fava sprout bergamot reduction (what the fuck?). Sohm is currently recommending a sake for this particular dish, though he could probably come up with any number of other interesting and enhancing accompaniments. Fortunately, most of us are seldom faced with this sort of thing at home, but Sohm's insights are transferable.

"I like to compare food and wine pairing to relationships," Sohm says. "The food and the wine should be equal, and they should enhance each other. Some pairings are just okay, they go along without really hurting each other, but they don't really interact. Some just suck. And then there's the best possible matches, where the food and the wine transform and elevate each other."

Red wine with meat, white with fish, remains one of the most venerable rules of wine pairing, and Sohm acknowledges that it's a good starting point. "Life is simple," he says, "but it's not that simple. Otherwise I'd be unemployed." He likes to break or at least stretch the rules, though only up to a point. "I remember once when I was in school, someone asked just before a test if cheating was allowed. And the teacher said yes, but getting caught isn't. And wine pairing is like that. If you break the rules, you have to make sure it works."

Although Le Bernardin's menu is devoted almost exclusively

to seafood, the wine list is about equally divided between reds and whites. The chef wouldn't have it any other way, of course, and Sohm often matches white fish with red wine. First of all, he points out, the sauce is at least as important as the base, and if a fish is served with a red wine sauce like a red wine béarnaise, then the white wine rule is suspended. Cooking methods can also influence the match. Poached fish, he says, with its delicate taste, usually calls for white. "I had a customer recently who wanted to drink Shafer Hillside Select with a poached halibut." This is one of Napa's finest Cabernets, a powerful red loaded with fruit and tannin—a great wine, but not for all purposes. "In this case, the wine isn't as good as it should be, and neither is the food." (Chef Eric, of course, might beg to differ, but I've got to go with Aldo on this one.) Generally speaking, tannic, hard-rock reds don't dance well with light fish dishes.

"If fish is pan roasted or grilled, you get those roasted, richer flavors, and then you can move more in the direction of red wine." Sohm often recommends Pinot Noirs or red Burgundies (made from Pinot) for such dishes. One pairing featured halibut casserole with morel mushrooms and a 2007 Flowers Pinot Noir from the Sonoma Coast. The earthiness of the morels and the chicken stock in the casserole helped to make this a stellar combination, even though conventional wisdom would have called for a white. Sohm has even been known to match white wines with red meat; he points out that Tafelspitz, the boiled beef specialty of his native Austria, is traditionally served with Riesling or Grüner Veltliner, a match that is mediated by the bouillon in which it's served. (Cue chef Ripert rolling his eyes and reaching for a Pauillac.)

When in doubt, Sohm says, Champagne is probably the most versatile food wine in the world and particularly well suited to Le Bernardin's complicated cuisine, a point that he emphasized recently when he matched an eight-course tasting menu with eight different Champagnes for the benefit of my wife, who drinks only bubbly. As the meal progressed from lighter, uncooked dishes to heavier fare, the wines likewise progressed from light and citrusy Blanc de Blancs to heavier vintage Champagnes based on Pinot Noir. He explained the rationale throughout, and by the end of the meal Anne was a convert. "I used to think you guys were full of it when you talked about these perfect wine and food combinations," she said, "but I can see there's something to it."

There is, indeed. Oysters and Chablis, like Troilus and Cressida, or Taylor and Burton, have an undeniable chemistry, as do grilled steak and Cabernet Sauvignon. Certain flavors tend to enhance each other, as Eric is the first to concede. On the other hand, even Aldo would be willing to admit that love is mysterious, and taste is a matter of taste. If you love California Chardonnay and you want to drink it with a grilled rib eye, go for it. If red Bordeaux's your thing and you want to drink it with Dover sole, don't let a sommelier or a wine snob make you feel self-conscious. Tell him that's how Eric Ripert rolls, as does his pal Joël Robuchon. My own footnote: if someone else is paying for a bottle of Petrus, or Yquem or La Tâche, don't worry about the food. If it clashes, give it to the dog.

Mondavi on Mondavi

1998

Not so long ago the phrase "California wine" belonged in the same book of oxymorons as, say, "living poet" and "Dutch cuisine." You knew, on some level, that such things existed, but you didn't necessarily want any of them at your dinner table. Today, thirty-two years after Robert Mondavi founded his eponymous winery in the Napa Valley, wine has become California's second-most-glamorous export, and Napa has become one of the world's celebrated wine regions. (Just ask Mondavi's neighbor the winemaker Francis Ford Coppola.) Wine buffs and collectors from around the world put their names on waiting lists in the hope of acquiring a few bottles of the latest boutique Cabernet from Colgin or Screaming Eagle. A personalized Napa Valley winery has become a popular trophy for American plutocrats, and the formerly rustic town of St. Helena brims with the kinds of polo-shirted tourists who also seek out Aspen and Santa Fe. Meanwhile, nearly all their fellow citizens have learned how to pronounce "Cabernet Sauvignon." In his boosterish memoir, *Harvests of Joy,* Robert Mondavi doesn't take any less credit for these developments than he deserves.

Like his dowdier peers Ernest and Julio Gallo, Mondavi is the son of Italian immigrants. His father, Cesare, arrived in Minnesota in 1906 and, after a stint in the iron mines, opened a grocery store in a mining town called Virginia, where Robert and his younger brother, Peter, were born. Robert's description of their childhood might best be characterized as polenta pone: "Family; hard work; high spirits; healthy, hearty meals—my childhood was a daily infusion of all four." With the passage of the Volstead Act, in 1919, Mondavi senior became involved in the grape business. Under the terms of Prohibition, any family was permitted to make two hundred gallons of wine for home consumption, and the Italian residents of Virginia, Minnesota, elected to do just that, appointing Cesare Mondavi as their representative to travel to California and buy grapes to be shipped north. When Robert was ten, Cesare moved the family to Lodi, California ("the grape capital of the United States"). There he became a wholesaler of grapes and, shortly after repeal, the co-owner of a Napa Valley winery called Sunnyhill, now Sunny St. Helena. Upon graduating from Stanford in 1937, Robert decided to join the family business. Sunny St. Helena didn't grow its own grapes—using only purchased fruit—but it did everything else: pressing, fermenting, and shipping the stuff out in railroad tank cars.

When Robert joined the family business, viticulture in the Napa Valley was a marginal enterprise. Fifty years earlier, however, Napa had seemed well on its way to oenological prominence. The vineyards of France had been devastated by phylloxera, a tiny root louse, and the resulting wine drought presented an opportunity to California viticulture. In the late eighteen seventies, state-of-the-art wineries were established by two German immigrants, Jacob and Frederick Beringer, and a Finnish fur trader named Gustave Niebaum. Beringer Brothers and Niebaum's Inglenook were among the pioneers of a frenzied Napa grape rush; by 1887, more than sixteen thousand acres of Napa were under the vine, at which point the dread phylloxera struck the valley. Then, thirty years later, just when the root louse was being brought under control, along came the tambourines of the temperance movement. The dark ages of Prohibition and the Depression crippled the fledgling industry. Some of the wineries that had survived by selling grapes and altar wine damaged the reputation of California after repeal by shipping spoiled wine that they had been holding during the dry years. In those days, most winemakers barely understood the chemistry of fermentation, according to the historian James T. Lapsley, "and they lacked the technology to control it even if they did." Most wineries were undercapitalized; there was no national network for wine sales and distribution. And there were few consumers. Immigrants who considered wine a staple of daily life often made their own. Most of the wine that came out of California—the product of high-yielding, inferior grape varietals—was a sweet beverage of the type that is now most commonly associated with brown paper sacks. And the shortcomings of these wines were only highlighted by the propensity of their manufacturers to adorn them with French names like Chablis and Burgundy.

Only a few visionaries recognized the great potential of the Napa Valley. One of them was the agronomist André Tchelistcheff, a former Russian aristocrat who, fleeing the revolution, ended up in France, where he studied wine microbiology at the Pasteur Institute while holding down a series of jobs in the French wine industry. In 1937, he was hired as a winemaker by Georges de Latour, a native of Bordeaux who had become wealthy selling French rootstock to California grape growers and at the turn of the century had bought a Napa estate, Beaulieu Vineyard. Tchelistcheff brought French wine-making expertise and a sense of high purpose to the Napa Valley. Centuries of grape growing had allowed the French to parse the viticultural landscape into hundreds of regions and subregions based on nuances of soil type and microclimate. Tchelistcheff attempted to do something similar in Napa, identifying at least three climatic regions in the valley and replanting the Beaulieu Vineyard with grapes he deemed most suitable. From the end of the thirties until the seventies, his Georges de Latour Private Reserve Cabernet Sauvignon was a benchmark, and Robert Mondavi was among a number of winemakers whom he inspired.

In 1943, when the Mondavi family moved upmarket by acquiring the Charles Krug Winery, Robert hired Tchelistcheff as a consultant. (He would turn to him again, a couple of decades later, when he went off on his own.) Despite plenty of wine-making experience, Mondavi has never really been the man in the cellar, though he has been very smart, and fortunate, in hiring wine-making talent. At Krug, it was his brother, Peter, who assumed the wine-making responsibilities. Robert was the public face of the Krug Winery and a tireless promoter of his own product and of the Napa Valley in general. In 1952, Krug was among the first wineries to establish a tasting room for visitors, and when Mondavi wasn't entertaining visitors at the estate, he was traveling the country glad-handing restaurant owners and distributors.

A power struggle developed between the two Mondavi brothers and led to Robert's departure from the Charles Krug Winery: the valley's version of the Cain and Abel legend. As Robert tells the story, it all began when he first visited the great wine regions of Europe, in 1962, and experienced an oenological epiphany. After he toured the Old World châteaus and tasted the great wines of Bordeaux and Burgundy, "a great business and creative venture took shape before my eyes," he recalls. "I wanted to take American technology, management techniques, and marketing savvy and fuse them together with Old World tradition and elegance in the art of making fine wine." He returned to Napa all fired up: "I wanted my family and our company to commit ourselves to a true quest for excellence in our vineyards, in our wine making, and in our marketing and sales." But, he says, his vision did not interest the rest of the family—which is really to say his brother, for their father had died in 1959.

According to Robert, it was a mink coat that started the war. In 1963, Robert and his wife, Marge, received an invitation from President John F. Kennedy to attend a state dinner at the White House.

"Flattered though we were, Marge and I were very nervous," he recounts. "We were just small-town people running a small family business. . . . How in the world would we fare at the Kennedy White House, with the charismatic president and his famous wife, surrounded by all the glamour of Camelot? Marge also had a more specific worry: What in the dickens should she wear to a White House dinner? What dress? What shoes? What bag? What jewelry? What coat?" Mondavi's admirers and his detractors alike will probably be astonished at this self-portrait of the king of the Napa Valley as a shy, charisma-challenged bumpkin. About the shoes and the dress we learn nothing, but the couple eventually settled on a mink coat from I. Magnin, in San Francisco. "When he heard about that mink, my brother, Peter, couldn't understand it," Robert says. A snit became a sulk that simmered until it became, two years later, a fistfight. At one of those big family gatherings that are so conducive to the airing of grievances, Peter accused Robert of spending too much money on travel and promotion. Then he accused his older brother of taking money from the winery. How else, he demanded, could Robert have afforded to buy the mink coat? "Say that again and I'll hit you," Robert warned Peter. He said it again. "Then I gave him a third chance: 'Take it back.' 'No.' So I smacked him, hard. Twice."

The rift never healed. Many years later, the older brother triumphed in an acrimonious lawsuit. In the meantime, since their mother had sided with Peter, Robert, at the age of fifty-two, was on the street. He decided to start from scratch in pursuing his vision of producing world-class Napa Valley wines. It was a daunting mission, quite aside from the question of capital; in 1965, there was still no significant American market for the kind of wine Mondavi hoped to produce. Julia Child was still trying to wean Americans away from tuna casseroles and chipped beef. On the other hand, as everyone had long observed, the climate in Napa was practically perfect for ripening grapes, whereas the temperamental Gallic weather in Bordeaux and Burgundy resulted in vintages of wildly uneven quality.

After buying a piece of a well-situated old vineyard called To Kalon, Mondavi turned his attention to designing a winery that would make a statement. His architect, Cliff May, wanted to place the mission-style winery with its faux campanile far back against the hills, but Mondavi chose a spot within sight of Highway 29, where its yawning archway could attract visitors and serve as a kind of billboard for the enterprise. Its silhouette, which appears on the labels of Robert Mondavi estate wines, has since become iconic—at least as recognizable among wine lovers as that of the tower at Château Latour. Inside the winery, Mondavi presided over a series of technological innovations. He had been among the first winemakers in this country to use new French oak casks, in order to impart complexity and structure to Cabernet Sauvignon—a practice he had observed at the great châteaus of Bordeaux. But Mondavi also embraced American-style technology wherever he could, cheerfully calling his "the test-tube winery." Not surprisingly, America's first great wine region tended to rely heavily on science in the form of fertilizers, filters, and additives. The results weren't always happy, however. In the past, the California wine industry had been plagued by spoilage; in the attempt to make a clean, stable product, Mondavi and those who followed him went too far down the road of sanitation, filtering and sterilizing the living beverage almost to death. "Only later did we discover that this rigorous cleaning—part of what we call the suppression of fault—stripped the wine of vital essences, flavor, and character," he writes. Still, unlike many who adhered to the high-tech gospel of the Department of Viticulture and Enology at the University of California at Davis—which became a combination think tank and training ground for the industry during the seventies and eighties—Mondavi was always willing to reconsider and subsequently curbed his technological excesses.

The event that certified the arrival of the Napa Valley as a major wine region didn't come until 1976, when the British wine connoisseur Steven Spurrier organized a blind tasting in France—the famed Judgment of Paris. The tasting was to pit some of the most venerable French wines from Burgundy and Bordeaux against some of the Napa Valley upstarts, and Spurrier made a trip to Napa to handpick the American entrants. California Chardonnays were matched against white Burgundies—which are also made from Chardonnay grapes and are generally regarded as the highest expression of that grape. California Cabernets went up against some of the greatest red wines of Bordeaux, including a 1970 Château Mouton Rothschild and a 1970 Haut-Brion. The judges, nine in all, were French, and their oenological credentials were impeccable, which made the results all the more surprising. The top-scoring white wine was Mike Grgich's 1973 Chateau Montelena Chardonnay. Two of the other top four white wines chosen were also American. In the red category, the winner was Warren Winiarski's 1973 Stag's Leap Wine Cellars Cab. Naturally, the hosts were indignant. The French press at first ignored the results and later tried to explain them away. One or two of these dozens of explanations were remotely plausible. French *grand vin* tends to be made for the long haul and to show more awkwardly in youth than the ripe, flirty wines of California. Then again, the patriotic French tasters presumably would have been on the lookout for hints of California glitz. At any rate, the Spurrier tasting made an enormous impression on both sides of the Atlantic. Mondavi professes himself to have been "tickled to death by the outcome," but none of the representative American wines that Spurrier chose were his, and that had to rankle. Still, whatever frustration he felt at sitting out the big event must have been ameliorated by the fact that the two winners, Grgich and Winiarski, were alumni of his cellars. His vision for the industry had been resoundingly endorsed.

Mondavi continued to expand and proselytize, seeming less

like a voice in the wilderness and more like an elder statesman. His 1974 Cabernet Sauvignon Reserve, released around the time of the great tasting, has become something of a legend. And in 1978 the French came calling. Baron Philippe de Rothschild, the proprietor of Château Mouton Rothschild, invited Mondavi to participate in a joint venture in the Napa Valley. If Mondavi still needed vindication, this was it. Indeed, he can scarcely conceal his pride. "My parents came to America without a penny in their pockets," he writes. "Now, thanks to hard work and the ability to turn humble grapes into fine wine, the names Rothschild and Mondavi were going to stand side by side." Together, the two men built a limestone-clad, postmodern winery. Yet the venture nearly capsized: it was plagued by huge cost overruns, and consumers were initially skeptical about the wine, Opus One, when it was released at $50 a bottle. And then, just a year after the first vineyards were planted, phylloxera struck again. The dread root louse swept through the valley during the next decade, wiping out millions of dollars' worth of vines. This, however, was a mixed curse: the epidemic forced the vineyards to replant, but the new plantings tended to be genetically superior and to reflect advances in the understanding of climate, soil, and grape types.

The cost of replanting was one of the reasons that Mondavi decided, in 1993, to take the winery public. Shortly afterward, he appointed his older son, Michael, president in an effort to end a long power struggle between Michael and his brother, Tim, which threatened to become a replay of the earlier family feud at Charles Krug. *Harvests of Joy* only hints at the family dramas behind the corporate success story. Mondavi confesses that his fierce and single-minded ambition damaged his family, but he doesn't really show us how. His portrait of his saintly, silent wife, Marge, is typical: after buying the mink, she more or less disappears from the narrative. The reader is occasionally puzzled by flattering references to a Mondavi employee named Margrit Biever until, near the end of the book, Mondavi mentions that she became his second wife. And we learn little about his sons, who will lead this hugely successful company into the new century. One senses, if not a *King Lear*, then certainly a *Rich Man, Poor Man* of viticulture awaiting its bard. If *Harvests of Joy* were a wine, we would have to say that it was a little disjointed, lacked complexity, and had too much residual sugar. But then it's entirely fitting that Mondavi's most eloquent message still comes in a bottle.

Postscript: In 2004, Robert Mondavi and his family lost control of the company they'd spent decades building in the wake of the Robert Mondavi Corporation's $1.3 billion sale to Constellation Brands. Robert Mondavi died in May 2008 at the age of ninety-four. Julia Flynn Siler's *House of Mondavi* fleshes out the story.

The Red and the Black

Does Bordeaux Still Matter?

This might seem like a foolish question given that the 2009 and the 2010 futures campaign set record prices, and given that Asian buyers in general and the Chinese in particular have embraced the region's wines, especially the first growths, as if they were aphrodisiacs. Many younger sommeliers and enthusiasts think of Bordeaux as the General Motors of the wine world—kind of a dinosaur. For wine buffs with an indie sensibility, it's the equivalent of the Hollywood blockbuster, more about money than art. At a 2009 Acker Merrall & Condit auction, there was booing when the auctioneer announced an offering of Bordeaux. "Let the Asians overpay for it," one bidder remarked. If I were the owner of a château in Bordeaux, I would be worried that the world's hottest restaurant, Copenhagen's Noma (voted Best Restaurant in the World for 2010 and 2011 in *Restaurant* magazine), hasn't got a single bottle of Bordeaux on its very extensive wine list.

In spite of, or, more likely, because of, the fact that Bordeaux has produced the world's most famous wines for hundreds of years, slagging it has become a new form of snobbery. As someone whose first love was Bordeaux, I can't quite join the beat down, and several recent close encounters have reignited my passion.

The most improbable of these took place at Terroir, a wine bar in Manhattan's East Village run by Paul Grieco, a very influential sommelier known to advocate the obscure and the artisanal. Of the fifty wines he serves by the glass, not one is a Bordeaux. So I was surprised to discover him pouring several late one night for a raucous and seemingly appreciative audience that included some of the city's top sommeliers. Overall it was a younger crowd—lots of tats and piercings and facial hair. Grieco himself sports a pencil-thin mustache, soul patch, and RIESLING tattoo.

The wines in question were part of a portfolio of small-grower Bordeaux imported by Daniel Johnnes, wine director at the four-star restaurant Daniel, who is famously passionate about Burgundy. Had these guys gone over to the dark side, or was it possible that a backlash to the backlash was fermenting? "I was tired of listening to the wine cognoscenti bash Bordeaux," Johnnes told me. He went there to seek out small, family-owned properties in the lesser-known appellations and came back with a handful of artisanal wines with traditional Bordeaux character in the $20 to $30 range. It was a tough crowd that night, but most of us were very impressed with them.

Among those struggling for elbow room in the tiny space was burly, bearded Pascal Collotte, the proprietor of Château Jean Faux, who looked as if he might have just come across the bridge from Williamsburg. He poured me a glass of his 2007, a delicious, hearty Merlot-based red that was every bit as ingratiating as its maker. Collotte worked as a cooper—a barrel maker—before buying a hilly estate just outside Castillon, and he was the first Bordeaux proprietor I've ever met who wasn't dressed like a tweedy English aristocrat. He explained that wines with the Bordeaux Supérieur label have stricter yields and higher alcohols than those labeled generic Bordeaux, although they are less illustrious—and expensive—than the classed growths of Pauillac, St. Julien, and Margaux.

It's a long way from the East Village to the manor houses of the Médoc, and no address is more emblematic of classic Bordeaux than Château Lafite Rothschild, which is one of four first growths listed in the famous 1855 classification. (Château Mouton

Rothschild, owned by another branch of the Rothschild banking family, was added in 1973.) The château itself is a relatively modest, eighteenth-century dwelling, but Lafite's preeminence in the market is perhaps better reflected in the circular cellar designed by Ricardo Bofill, its central vault supported by sixteen massive pillars under which oak casks of Lafite age fragrantly. After a lackluster period, since 1982 Lafite has regained its place at the top of the Bordeaux hierarchy with a succession of great vintages. More recently, it has become the object of a kind of cult in the Far East, particularly in China. A Sotheby's auction in Hong Kong in November 2010 ratcheted up the market even further. Three bottles of the 1869 vintage sold for $232,692 each. This wine is obviously a great rarity, but cases of the 1982 vintage, still widely available at auction, sold for $131,859, or more than $10,000 per bottle. This kind of madness may gladden the hearts of auctioneers and château owners, but it tends to depress the average wine drinker and to harden the perception of Bordeaux as a commodity rather than a beverage.

Perhaps it's best to think of the first growths of Bordeaux as the haute couture of the wine world. Not many of us will consume them, but they serve as a kind of reference point, and it's remarkable that those named in the 1855 classification have maintained their reputation and position 150 years later. The 1855 classification didn't include wines from the right bank of the Gironde River, in the appellations of Pomerol and St. Émilion, but critical consensus has made Cheval Blanc, Ausone, and Petrus unofficial first growths. The right-bank wines, based on Merlot rather than Cabernet Sauvignon, tend to be more immediately seductive. Petrus, virtually unknown until the English wine writer Harry Waugh championed it in the nineteen forties, became—at least until the Chinese discovered Lafite—the most expensive of them all.

On my fifty-fifth birthday, with the help of some generous friends, I tasted many of the top 1955 Bordeaux, including several first growths, and was astonished by the beauty and depth of these wines that were fermented the year I was born, the best of which have a great many years ahead of them—possibly a good omen. This is one of the signal glories of Bordeaux, its ability to age and improve for decades. The 1955 La Mission Haut-Brion, a second growth, is one of the finest wines I have ever tasted. A few months later, I was invited to taste the first growths of 1982, described by James Suckling, the former *Wine Spectator* editor who helped organize the tasting, as "the first modern vintage of Bordeaux." Some have suggested that the vintage was too warm, too low in acid to be classic and long lasting, but the tasters agreed the wines were brilliant, though several were just beginning to show their full potential. (Just for the record, we all ranked Lafite well behind Latour, Cheval Blanc, and Mouton.) A couple weeks later my Bordeaux infatuation was further stoked at a pre-auction dinner at Sotheby's in New York that was devoted to the top wines of the 2000 vintage. (Latour and Cheval Blanc were once again the standouts.) If too young to show all of their colors, they were awe inspiring and already a hedonist's delight.

I will probably be long gone before these wines reach their peak and I doubt my children will be able to afford them. The Chinese might have consumed them all by then. (One hopes at least that they don't mix their Lafite with Sprite, a persistent rumor.) But the ineffable experience of Bordeaux, which Cardinal Richelieu once described as having "an indescribable sinister, somber bite that is not at all disagreeable," has for centuries set the standard for great wine and is available at almost all price points. The lesser-classified growths, second through fifth, sometimes outperform the first, and the wines from less prestigious appellations like the Haut-Médoc, Fronsac, and Côtes de Castillon can be terrific values, especially in great vintages like 2005, 2009, and 2010. And yes, it's possible to find a good one for less than ten bucks. Although I'm not ready to surrender my "Bad to the Beaune" T-shirt, which flaunts my passion for Burgundy, I'm rediscovering the joys of Bordeaux. Dare to be unfashionable and try some this season.

The Exquisite Sisters of Margaux

The name Margaux was famous long before Ernest Hemingway's son Jack named his daughter after the wine he was drinking on the night she was conceived. Besides Papa Hemingway, Thomas Jefferson and Sir Robert Walpole were among the fans of this Bordeaux, one of four first growths named in the famous 1855 classification (along with Lafite, Latour, and Haut-Brion). This particular château gave its name to an entire appellation in the southern Médoc region of Bordeaux, which has caused some confusion and a fair amount of disappointment, since many of the wines sold under this name aren't all that good. In the whole appellation, only Château Palmer has ever challenged the founder, so to speak, and although ranked as a third growth, it has in some vintages surpassed Margaux and, in all the others, provided a fascinating comparison to its eminent rival.

Nothing could provide a more stark contrast than the architecture of the châteaus themselves, among the most dramatic in all of Bordeaux. Designed in 1810 by Louis Combes in the neo-Palladian style, Margaux is a stately pile with clean lines and a three-story pediment supported by Ionic columns. Palmer was built in flamboyant Second Empire style with two fanciful pointed turrets, lending a touch of Bavarian whimsy of which Walt Disney would have approved. Both buildings are so iconic that it's sometimes difficult to remember that it's what is under the ground, rather than above it, that truly shapes the character of the wines. The two properties share a border, close to the Gironde River, and are blessed with superb soils and drainage.

Margaux has the longer history as a wine-producing property. Legend holds that Edward III had a castle on the premises in the fourteenth century, when the British occupied Bordeaux and developed their taste for the wine they called claret. The property itself was owned by a series of noble families, and in 1771 its wine was the first Bordeaux to be listed for sale at Christie's, when claret was changing from a pale pink beverage to the bolder red wine we know and love today. It was classified as first growth in 1855 and lived up to its rank for most of the next century. But the wine seriously underperformed in the nineteen sixties and seventies, until it was bought by André Mentzelopoulos, a Greek tycoon whose French residency came in handy after the government quashed the proposed sale of the estate to National Distillers, an American company.

The Mentzelopoulos family turned the estate around almost immediately, and their first vintage, the 1978, was the first great wine from the estate in decades. Today, Margaux is owned and managed by the unconscionably glamorous, strawberry-blonde Corinne Mentzelopoulos, with the very able help of Paul Pontallier, one of the most highly regarded winemakers in Bordeaux.

The first time I met Pontallier he was hosing down the winery floor dressed in a Harris-tweed sport jacket over a vest, a knit tie, and knee-high Wellingtons. He arrived here in 1983, which happened to be a very good year in Margaux—better than in the more northern Médoc appellations—and produced a wine that has become legendary (Palmer also made a terrific 1983). Under his stewardship, there have been many great wines since then, including the 1990 and the 2000, although probably none has raised such a buzz of anticipation as the 2009, which is widely touted by early tasters as *the* wine of an extraordinary vintage. Typically, the elegantly modest Pontallier gives credit to the untranslatable French concept that embraces the soil, topography, drainage, weather, and everything else unique about a particular vineyard by saying that "the 2009 seems to have enhanced the intrinsic qualities of Château Margaux's *terroir*." The genius of the place, he believes, "consists in producing wines of inimitable aromatic finesse and complexity, of great density on the palate, and yet of a surprising softness."

"Margaux wines are recognized to be the most feminine wines of the Bordeaux region," according to Thomas Duroux, the wine-maker at neighboring Château Palmer. "They show less power than the wines of Pauillac or St. Estèphe, but more delicacy, more precision." While such generalizations don't always apply across the board, this is usually true of his wines, which sometimes seem almost Burgundian, and at other times like a Pomerol. It's unique among the wines of Bordeaux's left bank in its high proportion of Merlot (about half), which might account for its singular, supple character. Margaux, by contrast, is mostly Cabernet Sauvignon, giving it a little more heft but making it less approachable in its youth.

The property is named for Charles Palmer, a wellborn English general who fought under Wellington and was almost as well-known for his success with ladies of the court as for his military victories and his decision to purchase Château de Gascq, which seems to have been sealed during a "turbulent" stagecoach ride with the beautiful Marie de Gascq. He expanded her estate, replanted the vineyards, and was, by all accounts, his own best salesman and worst enemy. His personal charm and his friend-ship with the prince regent, the future George IV, helped to seal his wine's reputation among the British aristocracy, even as his extravagance eventually led him to bankruptcy. Palmer was forced to sell in 1843, and the estate was still in turmoil when the 1855 classification was made, which might explain why it was ranked a third growth; its quality since then has long exceeded its ranking, a fact reflected in its price. Palmer made many great wines while Margaux languished in the mid-twentieth century, and the 1961 remains one of the greatest legends of Bordeaux—certainly one of the best wines I've ever tasted. Curiously, it often excels in off vintages—like 1999 and 2002—and sometimes fails to dazzle in purportedly stellar years.

In 2004, the Bordeaux native Thomas Duroux took over the wine making at Palmer after serving as the winemaker at Tuscany's renowned Ornellaia (essentially an imitation of the domaines where he'd grown up). Describing Palmer's singularity, he credits its *terroir* and its high percentage of Merlot, but also a historical element that he needs to honor. "Our wines are known for their elegance and their Burgundian style, and each team of Palmer winemakers has tried to respect that." Unlike most of the big boys of Bordeaux, for instance, they seldom use more than 50 percent of new oak barrels for the *grand vin,* aging the remaining wine in casks a year or two old.

Like Pontallier, Duroux is ecstatic about the 2009 vintage, which will start appearing on these shores in the fall of 2012. It's possible to find the spectacular 2005s here and there, and both Palmer and Margaux are brilliant, though neither is cheap or ready to drink. Less expensive is the 2006, which, according to Pontallier, "is an excellent vintage that may have been considered as a great one should it not be born after 2005."

Fortunately, after years of underperforming, some of their neighbors in the Margaux appellation have started to produce wines worthy of the illustrious name. Château d'Issan—perhaps best known for its picturesque moated castle, allegedly where Eleanor of Aquitaine was married to Henry Plantagenet—has finally begun to live up to its third-growth ranking. Brane-Cantenac and Boyd-Cantenac have improved steadily in recent vintages, as have stablemates Giscours and du Tertre. They're worth looking for, particularly since the great 2005 vintage, though it should be noted that these wines often take at least a decade to show their stuff. Château Margaux doesn't reveal its full glories for twenty years in a great vintage. In the best of all possible worlds, each of us would be drinking the 1990 Margaux or the 1989 Palmer tonight. But you can experience the signature genius of both properties earlier, for much less money, via their secondary wines, Alter Ego de Palmer and Pavillon Rouge de Margaux.

Big Aussie Monsters

When they shoved a metal dinner tray through a slot in the door of his room, Benjamin Hammerschlag was beginning to think that he'd probably made a big mistake and that he'd be going back to his day job in a Seattle grocery store. He was staying in what passed for a hotel in the Frankland River region of Western Australia—"a pub full of misshapen humanity, pretty much at the end of the earth," as he describes it—while seeking out premium wines to import to the States. A week later, with only two prospects in his sights, he woke near dawn in yet another crummy hotel room, this one in the Barossa Valley, to find the walls literally seething with millipedes: "By this time I was pretty depressed." Fortunately, wine making in both regions was more advanced than the hospitality industry, and Hammerschlag is a persistent and highly competitive son of a bitch with a very good palate. Over the past ten years he has assembled a portfolio, Epicurean Wines, that represents something of a new wave in the Australian invasion.

At the time of his unpromising first visit, Hammerschlag was working as a wine buyer for a supermarket called QFC in Bellevue, a wealthy suburb of Seattle. (Wine would seem to run in his veins; his forebears ran a chain in Manhattan called Flegenheimer's, the first stores to bring California wines to New York, and they eventually had thirteen branches before Prohibition.) In a few years he almost doubled QFC's wine turnover, deciding in the process that he had a "popular palate." Among the crowd-pleasers he discovered for his clients were old-vine Shirazes from Australia's Barossa

Valley, which had just begun to trickle into this country, thanks to a few boutique importers like John Larchet's Australian Premium Wine Collection and Dan Philips's Grateful Palate. "It was a style of wine that Americans loved," Hammerschlag says, "rich and powerful and generous and all about instant gratification." Some Aussies, according to Hammerschlag, refer to these big Barossa Shirazes as "leg spreaders." However, given the sheer size and power of these behemoths, stereotypically masculine metaphors seem more appropriate to me; high-octane potions like Kaesler's Old Bastard Shiraz remind me more of a muscle car like a Dodge Charger or a Viper than of a starlet, more of Russell Crowe than Naomi Watts.

The only problem with these South Australian reds, it seemed to Hammerschlag, was that they were pretty hard to find. Elderton's Command Shiraz or Clarendon Hills' Astralis, for example, were made in small quantities from vines, including Shiraz and Grenache, planted in the early twentieth century. (Old vines, it's generally conceded, make more intense and powerful wines than younger ones.) Although Grange, Penfolds's prototype for premium Australian Shiraz, dates back to 1951, when its chief winemaker, Max Schubert, came home from a visit to Bordeaux determined to make a world-class wine, it remained something of a one-off until the eighties, when others began making big, rich Barossa Shirazes. In just a couple of decades, Australia became a wine-making superpower, and Australian winemakers started circumnavigating the globe spreading their fruity high-tech gospel.

Much as Hammerschlag loved the big badasses, he was presumptuous enough to believe there was room for some finesse and a more specific sense of place (Grange uses grapes from all over South Australia) and that he could coax even better wines from the country if he could find the right talent. "I consider myself a talent agent," he says. Upon arriving in Adelaide in 1999, he made the rounds of the wine stores and accumulated thirty-six bottles of local reds he then tasted in his bug-infested hotel room and finally started working the phone. He was lucky enough, and early enough, to find a core of extremely talented young winemakers, including Dan Standish, the winemaker at Torbreck; Ben Glaetzer, who was involved with his family's estate; Ben Riggs, a six-foot-five winemaker who worked in Napa, Bordeaux, and Italy before focusing on making Shiraz on his home turf of McLaren Vale. In the years since he signed them, Hammerschlag has become more and more intimately involved in the wine-making process, a commitment that has nearly ruined his teeth—the result of tasting through thousands of barrels of tannic young reds.

"I go for that tightrope quality," he said, through his dingy choppers one spring evening in 2006 at the Soho Grand Hotel, as we slurped the 2002 Kaesler Avignon Proprietary Red, which would make a really good Châteauneuf-du-Pape. "Pushing the limits, but still maintaining balance and harmony." To put it another way, Hammerschlag's Fruit Loops have fiber, and his muscle cars have precise handling and even, sometimes, luxurious interiors. (A car buff, Ben in fact drives a 1968 Dodge Charger around the high-altitude vineyard he purchased in the McLaren Vale.) They have the big ripe flavors and good-day-mate charm that have made Aussie wines so popular. Dan Standish's 2001 The Standish, for instance, was at that point the most satisfying young Aussie red I'd ever tasted—an old-vine Shiraz that has complex leather and coffee aromatics, an unbelievably voluptuous and viscous texture, and a long, lingering finish that left me alternately giddy and awestruck. Ben Glaetzer's two old-vine Shirazes, Amon-Ra and Mitolo's GAM, were already legends in their second vintage, having racked up exceptional ratings in *The Wine Advocate* and elsewhere, although like many of Epicurean's wines they are made in tiny quantities. All in all, it was an exhilarating tasting, and when we finally parted late that night and I staggered home to my apartment in the Village, I was as wildly enthusiastic about South Australian reds as everybody else (drunk or not) seemed to be.

I didn't imagine it would take five years, but when we finally met again at Manhattan's Gotham Bar and Grill in 2011, the balance of power in the wine world had shifted significantly.

Somehow this boom had gone bust in the last few years, at least in terms of imports to the States. Despite the success of Yellow Tail, or perhaps because of it, Oz lost its mojo. Overall imports dropped by 15 percent in 2010, and the cognoscenti seemed to snub the category, partly out of a shift in fashion toward (buzzword alert!) finesse and elegance, away from sheer power and alcoholic punch. Whatever the reality, Australian wines were perceived as being fruit bombs, unsubtle and overripe. Pinot was suddenly king, and sommeliers—a powerful new force in the wine world over the past decade—were railing against high alcohol. It certainly didn't help when Robert Parker, previously a big champion of premium South Australian Shiraz, stopped visiting and handed responsibility for the country to a subordinate.

When I met Hammerschlag at the Gotham Bar and Grill, he admitted that his chosen turf was "a category that's out of fashion right now." He attributed this fact partly to the strength of the Australian dollar and partly to the shifting tastes of "the gatekeepers," namely the critics and sommeliers. "Customers still like this stuff," he claimed, while acknowledging it's harder to sell Australian wines now than it was five years before. When I asked if his winemakers had modified their practices at all in response to changes in the market, he shrugged. "They're trying to make wines reflective of their regions, just like they always have." And the fact is that South Australia is conducive to "rich, dark voluptuous wines." They ain't dainty, and they're not meant to be.

Hammerschlag and others are pinning their hopes on the 2010 vintage, which will soon be heading to these shores, to raise awareness and help turn the tide. "It was spectacular across the board," he told me, sipping an amaro at the bar at Gotham. "The best in twenty years." It will be interesting to see if the vintage can help revive the country's image. Other areas have recovered their mojo after losing credibility. Red Burgundy was rightfully slumping in the marketplace in the late seventies and early eighties thanks to high yields, lazy wine making, and an overreliance on chemical fertilizers. In 1985 some Austrian vintners decided to beef up their wines with antifreeze, and the resulting scandal nearly destroyed that market. But both regions have come back stronger than ever internationally. And it's not as if the Australians have done anything wrong, unless it's a sin to make ripe, rich, high-test reds—the vinous equivalent of a 1966 Pontiac GTO. Presumably, there are still millions of consumers who don't have any beef against power and opulence. If Hammerschlag has anything to say about it, Aussie reds will soon regain their place at the American table.

Is Cornas Finally Having Its Moment?

When I'm at a restaurant with a sommelier I trust, I often ask him to pick something for me. After all, sommeliers are on the front lines, tasting every day, seeking out treasures, and they certainly know their own lists better than I do. Unlike my collector friends, who tend to search out the classics—the known commodities—the somms have their palates primed for what's new. They are looking for the next great region, the next great maker. Recently, two of my favorites have picked a Cornas—both of which I liked very much. Moreover, I've heard several young winemakers express their admiration for Thierry Allemand, the rising star of Cornas. Is this appellation finally having its moment?

Some ten years ago I found myself clinging to the base of a vine in the Les Ruchets vineyard, high above the town of Cornas, with the serpentine Rhône River just beyond, trying not to slide downhill. My luggage had been lost somewhere between New York and Marseilles; for the third day in a row I was wearing Gucci loafers, which didn't provide much purchase on the steep, rocky hillside as I attempted to assist Jean-Luc Colombo and his crew harvesting Syrah grapes. I could well understand why many of these granitic vineyards, too steep for a tractor, had been abandoned in the early part of the twentieth century.

As far as I can tell, Cornas hasn't really been fashionable since the era of Charlemagne. Ten years ago, Jancis Robinson wrote a piece describing her failure to fall in love, or even in like, with this wine. "'Virile' is a favourite description of Cornas with Frenchmen," Robinson wrote. "'Obdurate,' I would suggest is nearer the mark." She described one wine as having "all the charm of the Reverend Ian Paisley." I know what she means. Cornas has always been a rustic wine, with formidable tannins and, sometimes, a barnyard funk that suggested a lack of hygiene in the cellar. The first few examples I tasted made me wonder if the grapes had been stomped by someone with very stinky socks.

If it was ever beloved, its reputation was long ago eclipsed by Hermitage and Côte Rôtie to the north. All three appellations make powerful red wines exclusively from the Syrah grape, which has grown here at least since Roman times. The steep granitic vineyards were hard to farm, and many were abandoned, even as Côte Rôtie and Hermitage were gaining international renown and Syrah was being planted everywhere from Stellenbosch in South Africa to the Santa Rita Hills in California. A few hardy growers like Auguste Clape and Noël Verset carried the torch of the appellation, making traditional, earthy Cornas for the faithful. A good Cornas is like the Delta blues, soulful and earthy, though not for everyone.

As is often the case, it took an outsider to cut through the cobwebs in this ancient village. Jean-Luc Colombo, an oenologist from Marseilles, moved here with his wife, Anne, in the nineteen eighties, first establishing a consulting business and later buying vineyards. Like the Chicago players who electrified the rural sound of Charley Patton and Robert Johnson, Colombo introduced modern viticultural methods, including new oak barrel aging and destemming, and created cleaner, more modern versions of Cornas that seduced some critics while outraging some traditionalists. Colombo is the epitome of the modern flying winemaker, a compact dynamo who consults with some hundred-plus clients in the Rhône Valley and beyond. On my most recent visit he started the day with clients in Châteauneuf-du-Pape, met me some seventy miles south for lunch in Marseilles, drove half an hour up the Côte Bleue to tour some vineyards he's leased near St. Julien les Martigues, raced two hours north to the Alpilles in Provence to taste through twenty barrels in the cellar of his client Mas de la Dame, stopped off in St. Rémy for dinner, then drove another two hours north to Cornas, where we arrived about one in the morning. "Zis day, she is fairly typical," he tells me, as we sip Calvados in his living room.

Like his friend Michel Rolland, the famous Bordeaux winemaker and consultant, he has sometimes been criticized for allegedly making internationally styled wines that don't speak of their place of origin. In recent years Colombo has dialed back on the use of new oak and developed a lighter touch. In the meantime, a new generation of younger winemakers has stepped in, reviving abandoned vineyards and adopting those of retiring winemakers like Noël Verset and Robert Michel. The most influential of these is Thierry Allemand, the son of a factory worker who grew up in the town of Cornas and embraced its wine-making traditions, apprenticing with Robert Michel at the age of eighteen. Allemand bought an overgrown vineyard with ruined stone terraces and gradually rehabilitated it, producing his first wines in 1982.

Duncan Arnot Meyers of Arnot-Roberts, which has gained cult status for its Sonoma Syrahs, cites Allemand as a huge influence. "I think his wines are some of the most expressive bottlings of Syrah on the planet," he says. It's a sentiment I've heard frequently in the last couple of years. Bearded and bare of pate, Allemand lives with his wife and four children in an old stone house in the town of Cornas and works his vineyards almost entirely by hand. Like many young winemakers around the world, he has looked to the past for inspiration, using whole grape clusters, including stems, and aging in neutral (that is, used) barrels, which don't impart toasty flavor to the grapes. A leader of the natural-wine movement, he uses very little sulfur to preserve the wines, a risky strategy that seems to work for him—I have yet to taste an off bottle. His wines are very earthy and even rustic—you'd never mistake a bottle of Allemand Cornas for Australian Shiraz—but they have a freshness and lift that were lacking in most old-school examples.

In the past few years many vineyards have passed from the old guard to a new wave of young winemakers. Among the new kids on the block is Franck Balthazar, who inherited five acres of ninety-year-old vines in 2003, and Guillaume Gilles, a disciple and heir of Allemand's mentor Robert Michel, who retired in 2006. Vincent Paris, Matthieu Barret, and Gilbert Serrette are rising stars.

Although the young generation seems to be respectful of the traditions, one is less likely to encounter a really stinky bottle of Cornas these days. But a good one will always be more earthy and even gamy than a New World Syrah. Black licorice is part of its flavor profile, and the wines usually show an earthy bass note. Even in lighter vintages like 2006 and 2007 it's a pretty big wine, requiring red meat or braises to balance its power. It's not a summer red. The old-school wines often took years to shed their tannin, if indeed they ever did, and even now most Cornas needs at least five years to round out and open up. If you find an older bottle, you might be in for a treat; it will cost you far less than a similar vintage from Hermitage or Côte Rôtie. I had a 1990 Robert Michel La Geynale the other night that was really singing. The blues, of course.

Barbera: Piedmont's Everyday Red

Just outside the walls of the turreted medieval castle that crowns this hilltop village is the gate to the Vietti winery, which clings to the steep hillside. Spreading out below the compound on all sides are vineyards that produce some of the most coveted of Barolos. Made from the difficult Nebbiolo grape in just five villages in the Piedmont region of northwest Italy, Barolo has been known since the nineteenth century as "the king of wines and the wine of kings," thanks in part to its association with the house of Savoy. Luca Currado, whose family has grown grapes here for centuries, directs my attention to an anomaly on the hillside, an area with slightly darker, redder leaves. "That's Barbera," he says. "My secret Barbera vineyard."

Barbera is a grape usually planted on less expensive real estate, and it's generally considered a lesser cousin to the Nebbiolo and used for the region's table wine. "Barbera was the wine of the people," Currado explains, but thanks to Vietti and a few other determined producers it has in recent years become a star.

It was traditionally grown in cooler, less desirable plots in Alba, the province that encompasses both Barolo and Barbaresco, and in the neighboring province of Asti, best known for bubbly Asti Spumante. Barbera has a very deep ruby color and a full body. For years it played a secret, supporting role in the production of Barolo, where it was often used to supplement the color and body of Nebbiolo, which can be low on both. When Luca joined the family winery, his father wouldn't let him near the Nebbiolo. The young winemaker worked instead with Barbera from their holdings outside the Barolo appellation. The more he worked with Barbera, the more he became convinced of its potential, given the right sites and restricted yields. When a patch of Vietti vines in the Grand Cru region of Castiglione required replanting, he took charge of the project, secretly replacing the Nebbiolo vines with Barbera. Eventually, some of the neighbors noticed. "They were laughing," he says. "They went to my father and asked why we'd planted Barbera in prime Barolo land. My father was pissed off." But eventually he seemed to forgive his son, due to the quality of the wine from those rogue vines. In fact there was a precedent for Luca's experiment. His great-grandfather went to America, becoming an engineer, after his older brother inherited the winery. (He worked on the Sumner Tunnel in Boston, among other public-works projects.) When the elder brother died, he returned to Italy to run the family business. He planted a small patch of Barbera on the hill beneath the house for his personal consumption, out of nostalgia for the table wine of his youth. These vines have survived to the present, although many of the Vietti vineyards were confiscated by the Fascists when it was discovered that the family was supporting and sheltering partisans.

The wines produced by these very old vines, planted in 1932, are a testament to the potential of Barbera in ideal sites. A 1990 Vietti Scarrone Vigna Vecchia (old vines), which Luca opened for me at the winery alongside a flight of Barolos, pretty much stole the show, even as it demonstrated a family resemblance with its tar, leather, and mushroom notes. Like Currado himself, who wore a very well-tailored bespoke shirt over dirty jeans and work boots, it seemed to oscillate between sophistication and rusticity.

Vietti wasn't the only producer who saw in Barbera a potential Cinderella; another champion was the late Giacomo Bologna, a motorcycle-riding, jazz-loving bon vivant who inherited a property called Braida some ten miles east of the town of Asti. Like an old Hollywood studio head ordering cosmetic procedures for a starlet, Bologna set about to reshape Barbera, which is typically very high in acid and low in natural tannins. (The latter, which most of us are familiar with from over-steeped tea, act as a preservative, allowing a wine to develop complexity over time.) He planted Barbera on prime, sun-drenched slopes and picked the grapes later than his neighbors, with the idea of softening the sharp acidity. He aged the juice in new French oak barrels, which further softened the sharp edges while lending some wood tannins. The idea of barrel aging Barbera was first proposed by the famous French oenologist Émile Peynaud, who consulted at a winery in Asti in the nineteen seventies. In 1982, Bologna created Bricco dell' Uccellone, a barrel-aged vineyard-designated Barbera that changed the perception of the grape in the Piedmont region and moreover achieved international recognition. Unlike the rustic table wine beloved of Piedmontese farmers, poured out of pitchers at kitchen tables, this was a Barbera that had been to college, maybe even graduate school. It was suitable for high-end wine lists.

Other makers have followed the examples of Bologna and Vietti, planting the grape in better real estate and giving it the spa treatment in the cellar, creating premium barrel-aged examples in both Asti and Alba. According to Currado, Barbera d'Alba is typically more feminine and sophisticated, while Barbera d'Asti is more powerful and bold; he likens it to Angelina Jolie and Alba to Grace Kelly. Undoubtedly he knows whereof he speaks, although winemaker styles can sometimes trump terrain.

Some thirty years after Bologna started experimenting with French oak barrels, there are many styles of Barbera, including simple table wines meant to be consumed early. In this category, price is a reliable indicator of quality and ageability. Wines in the $15–$20 range should be easy to appreciate on release, tossed back with a pizza or a simple pasta. Barbera specialists like Bologna and Hilberg-Pasquero inevitably make great juice. But some of the best come from makers of Barolo and Barbaresco, like Vietti, Giuseppe Mascarello, Sandrone, Giacomo Conterno, and La Spinetta. It's a great wine to keep in mind when you pick up the list at an Italian restaurant. Even when softened by barrel aging, Barbera is relatively acidic for a red, which makes it the ideal companion for any dish that features tomatoes. The chef Thomas Keller, who honed his pasta-making skills in Luca Currado's grandmother's kitchen before opening the French Laundry, became a fan during his stay there. "They're simple and easy to appreciate," he says. Currado sees it as a bridge between New World and Old World reds. "It's sexy but earthy," he posits, "and Barolo's more reserved and severe." And while Barolo can take years and even decades to mellow out and become palatable, even the most sophisticated Barbera is approachable—and downright convivial—in its youth.

Reasons to Be Cheerful: Barolo and Barbaresco

Now that the war is over, the Piedmont is thriving. Since 1996, the region has enjoyed an amazing string of successful vintages, and somewhere along the way modernists and traditionalists seem to have signed a truce. Happily for consumers, its great Nebbiolo wines, Barolo and Barbaresco, are still less renowned than Bordeaux and Burgundy, but no less worthy of respect.

Like Burgundy, the historically independent Piedmont is full of proud farmers and small estates. Like Pinot Noir, the signature red grape of Burgundy, Nebbiolo is thin-skinned and temperamental and yields wines of tremendous aromatic complexity. Unlike Burgundy, which seems to get a great vintage every three years or so, the Piedmont has been on a roll since 1996 with only a single washout vintage, the soggy 2002. The 2003 vintage was somewhat mixed, complicated by the hot weather that affected all of Europe. Most of the top wines of Piedmont's Barolo and Barbaresco districts still sell for well below $100, and many retail for less than $50, even in this era of a pathetically weak dollar. And just in case you're a pedant, the region is more than complicated enough to absorb a lifetime of study.

In Italy, Barolo has long been known as the king of wines, in part because of its association with the house of Savoy and the family of Vittorio Emanuele II, the first king of a unified Italy, in part because of its unquestioned preeminence. Most commentators agree that the wine as we know it, a dry 100 percent Nebbiolo, was probably conjured into being in the early nineteenth century by the French oenologist Louis Oudart, who was working for the

Marchioness of Barolo. Generally speaking, the Barolo denomination, situated south and west of Alba, produces bigger, longer-lived wines than Barbaresco, to the north and east of the town, though the similarities outweigh the differences.

Angelo Gaja, who is to the Nebbiolo grape what Yo-Yo Ma is to the cello, has a favorite analogy to describe its discreet charms. "Cabernet is like John Wayne," he told me over dinner at Guido da Castiglione, a hillside restaurant not far from his home in the little town of Barbaresco. "When he walks into a room, no one else exists. All the men want to be him, and the women want to sleep with him. Nebbiolo is like Marcello Mastroianni. He walks into the room with a woman on his arm, and he makes the woman look more beautiful." His point is that Nebbiolo will never be as powerful or as self-sufficient as Cab; it requires food in order to present itself at its best.

"Cab is like a guy who's a show-off; Nebbiolo is shy and seductive," says Angelo's twenty-eight-year-old daughter, Gaia Gaja, who joined him in the business in 2001. With a name like hers, how could she stay away? Gaia grew up in the village of Barbaresco, where wine is pretty much the only game in town. At the local grade school, she and her friends made wine and grappa with grapes they brought in from their family vineyards. Like her father, Gaia has an excess of nervous energy; she drums her fingers on the table at New York's Insieme as she waits for my verdict on her 2003 Barolo Sperss.

"Barbaresco is a little sweeter, with notes of balsamic, violets, cumin, and spice," Gaia says. "Barolo is deeper and has more tobacco, mushrooms, and licorice." The timeworn descriptor for the smell of Barolo is "tar and roses." Many devotees find the funky scent of white truffles, which are native to Piedmont, in aged examples of both, and it's hard to think of a better accompaniment to a risotto with white truffles.

Along with Renato Ratti and Domenico Clerico, Angelo Gaja

was among the pioneers who experimented with new production methods, including the use of new French oak barrels, to make Nebbiolo more accessible. In the past, a typical Barolo, which might spend five years or more in huge casks called *botti,* would take twenty years or so to shed its formidable tannins and show the full range of its charms. Since the mid-eighties a debate—verging on a battle—has raged between the traditionalists and the so-called modernists. Producers like Aldo and Giacomo Conterno, Giuseppe Rinaldi, and Bartolo Mascarello in Barolo and Bruno Giacosa in Barbaresco upheld the traditions, including long fermentation and aging in giant chestnut *botti.* Until his death in 2005, Bartolo Mascarello led the battle against *barriques*—the smaller barrels that began showing up in the seventies—the traditionalists believing that new French oak, with its vanilla flavor, masks the true character of the Nebbiolo grape and the Piedmont *terroir.*

Aldo Conterno, looking very much the epitome of tradition in English tweeds when we met at his estate in 2005, proudly informed me that his Barolos weren't drinkable in their first decade of life. By law, Barolo must be aged at the winery for three years before release, and some makers like Conterno hold their wine back even longer, but these traditional wines are made for the patient and for those with wine cellars.

Not long ago these fierce, old-school Barolos seemed in danger of extinction. In 1973, Robert Mondavi visited the area and met the young Angelo Gaja, among others. Mondavi was at that moment helping to usher in a new golden age of wine making in Napa, and Gaja was inspired to do something similar. "It's *fantastic* what Mondavi did for California," he says. "He saw the potential before anyone else. Also here he saw the potential. He says that everyone in Piedmont is sleeping. And he's right. We were all sleeping." In other words, tradition needed a jolt of innovation if the wines of the Piedmont were to become a force in the emerging international marketplace, which was increasingly shaped by New World palates and the demand for bolder, fruitier, more precocious wines. Gaja and fellow modernists like Altare, Sandrone, Scavino, and Valentino believed the old, recycled *botti* were frequently tainted with bacteria and adopted new equipment and production methods such as rotary fermentors and *barriques* to soften the acid and tannin that make Nebbiolo so formidable in its youth. The small French oak barrels increase oxygen contact with the young wine, speeding its evolution, and sometimes impart those toasty vanilla flavors (which the traditionalists deplore). In 1985, according to Luca Currado, the fourth-generation winemaker at Vietti in Castiglione Falletto, the revolutionaries staged a festive "Bonfire of the Botti" in Barolo, burning a pile of the old casks to symbolize their rejection of tradition.

Bartolo Mascarello, fiercely traditionalist about wine making but a progressive in his politics, emblazoned "No Barrique, No Berlusconi" on the label of his 1999 Barolo; the slogan quickly became a rallying cry for the old school. When I first visited the Piedmont around this time, tensions were running high. When I met Giuseppe Rinaldi, a close friend of Mascarello's, he was lying in the driveway in front of his Beaux Arts villa in Barolo, poking a wrench into the innards of his Yamaha dirt bike. Clearly, dinner was going to be late. A wry, modest former veterinarian who inherited his father's estate, Rinaldi doesn't speak English—his wife translated—but when we finally sat down at a nearby restaurant, he made his point emphatically as he dumped some 1997 Barolo into his risotto. He railed against new oak and what he saw as the pandering to the global market. "If you have a particular wine with a particular smell and taste, it's silly to waste it, to make a standard wine for international taste." Later, we were joined by his neighbor Chiara Boschis, a chic, petite young woman in a Prada sport ensemble, who holds a doctorate in economics and speaks fluent English. Boschis comes from an old wine-making family, but since she purchased an estate called Pira, she's been turning out an "international" sexy beast of a Barolo that had recently copped 96 points from Robert Parker. With her arrival the talk veered from wine to the less contentious area of politics. They were united, at least, in their disdain for Berlusconi.

By the mid-nineties it seemed the modernists had won the battle, promoting a richer, darker, and yet softer style of Nebbiolo that could be enjoyed much sooner than the old-school juice. I like to call them wines of cleavage, hey-there-big-boy reds that seem designed to grab the attention of critics looking for the wow factor. These wines were making stars of their makers even as they revitalized the moribund local agricultural economy. But a few loyalists, myself included, couldn't help noticing that some of the new-school wines from the eighties weren't aging all that well, that they were either cracking up or failing to evolve over time into something more interesting, which is the mark of truly great wine and one of the particular glories of Barolo. Far from achieving greatness after thirty or forty years, like, say, the 1964 Giacomo Conterno Monfortino or the 1982 Bruno Giacosa Santo Stefano, they were washing out before they hit their teens.

"The only way we can survive," says Luca Currado, the cosmopolitan proprietor of Vietti, "is to make a wine that reflects the region." Currado stands somewhere in the middle of the debate, which seems like a good place to be.

Over the past twenty years many of the brash upstarts have quietly revised and refined their techniques, sometimes reducing the amount of new wood they use, while some of the traditionalists have quietly adopted newfangled tools; the battle lines are not so sharply drawn as before. But even the most modern styles are slow bloomers by New World standards. Powerful structured vintages like 2004 and 2006 will benefit from a decade of aging, in most instances, and will continue to develop long afterward. The very good 2007 vintage is more approachable and seductive; many of the wines were drinking brilliantly on release in 2011, although they will certainly benefit from age.

One way to become enamored of Nebbiolo is to start with Barbaresco, the precocious sister of Barolo. Barbaresco regulations require only two years of aging, which means that the wines are released into the marketplace earlier. The local cooperative, the Produttori del Barbaresco, might just be the world's best wine-producing co-op and is a great source of high-quality, accessible, but age-worthy Barbarescos in the $30 to $50 dollar range. They usually shine within a few years and also age extremely well: I was blown away by a bottle of 1982 Barbaresco from the Produttori that a friend opened for me in 2011.

Caveat emptor: as with Burgundian Pinot Noir, inconsistency and mystery are part of what draws some of us to this region and this grape. If you are looking for something utterly unique, a wine that in the same breath can smell like flowers and the dirt and compost they spring from, a wine that could hardly be mistaken for a wine from any other part of the globe, you need to visit the Piedmont, if only in the glass.

Blood, Sweat, and Leaps of Faith

The sun has yet to clear the peaks of the Palisades above the vineyard, and the grapes are still cool to the touch as the pickers, along with a groggy journalist visiting from New York, move up the manicured rows of Sauvignon Blanc, slicing the clusters and dropping them into small plastic bins that are emptied into larger collection bins at the end of each row, where Bart and Daphne Araujo go through the grapes, picking out leaves and discarding sunburned grapes. "I love the first day of harvest," says the elegant, silver-haired Daphne as she plucks out a shriveled grape.

This is the twentieth harvest since the couple bought the Eisele Vineyard, which was first planted in 1886 and has since become renowned for its Cabernet Sauvignon. Today they are harvesting a small lot of Sauvignon Blanc planted in a cooler area of the vineyard. This small patch of white grapes is less than an acre, and it's picked in just over an hour. The journalist is tired and bleeding copiously after slicing his hand with the scimitar-shaped harvesting knife, but the Araujos seem positively exhilarated as they stride back to their house for breakfast, past meticulously pruned vines laden with knee-high clusters of purple grapes. Almost as many clusters are scattered on the ground, victims of a recent purge, sacrificed in order to concentrate the flavors of the surviving grapes, which Bart predicts will need another two to three weeks of hang time. The thirty-two acres of Bordeaux varietal vines yield an average of just sixteen hundred cases of their top Cabernet Sauvignon, one of the Napa Valley's iconic wines.

Certain privileged sites yield great wine as a result of some serendipitous combination of geology, topography, and micro-climate. Located on an alluvial fan in the northeastern corner of Napa near the hot-springs town of Calistoga, this one was cel-ebrated long before the Araujos bought it in 1990. Beginning in 1975, Joseph Phelps purchased grapes from the Eisele family and made a Cabernet that would become one of Napa's defining wines, though for some reason Phelps passed when the Eiseles decided to sell the vineyard, at which point Bart Araujo pounced.

A San Francisco native, Araujo went to USC with ambitions of becoming a major-league baseball player until injuries forced him to reconsider. After Harvard Business School, he returned to California and founded a successful construction business. He met Daphne, a landscape architect, when she applied for a job. Bart then sold his firm and began prowling Napa in search of a great vineyard. "How do you make a small fortune in the wine business?" goes a joke that has a predictable punch line: "You start with a large one." The Araujo narrative is in many ways the archetypal Napa story of a successful entrepreneur who brings his fortune and his business acumen to bear on a second career pro-ducing wine with his name on it. The birth of Araujo vineyards coincided with the creation of the so-called cult Cabernets like Harlan, Colgin, and Bryant Family, wines made in small quanti-ties (two thousand cases or fewer) in a richer, riper style than the old-guard Napa Cabs. But Bart and Daphne's story is unique, due to the history of the vineyard they purchased and their hands-on, fanatical devotion to every detail of grape growing and wine mak-ing; whenever I call Bart, he seems to be in the vineyard. "After we purchased the property, I sat down and tasted the wines made from these grapes over the years," Bart told me, "including the 1971 Ridge Eisele Vineyard made by Paul Draper, the '74 Conn Creek bottling, and the '75 Joseph Phelps. Whoever made the wine, there was this signature earthy mineral element that seemed to come through."

If the vineyard deserves most of the credit, the Araujos go to extraordinary lengths to help it along. In the nineties they began farming organically; later, they began to make the switch to biodynamics. After reading an article one day, Bart says, he realized that many of his favorite French estates, including Domaine Leroy, Domaine Leflaive, and Chapoutier, employed the holistic approach to agriculture based on the teachings of Rudolf Steiner. He began to explore the subject and eventually employed Jeff Dawson, who had previously worked as Steve Jobs's gardener, to make the conversion. In 2002, Araujo was certified by Demeter, the nonprofit biodynamic organization, named after the Greek goddess of the harvest. Bart cheerfully admits that he doesn't understand all of the intricacies of this arcane field. "But, hey," he adds, "I'm a Catholic. I'm used to making leaps of faith." He then notes that the vineyard is far healthier than it was before the switch, and ripens earlier.

Ripeness is all, as Edgar reminds us in *King Lear,* and this subject is one of the most controversial in the wine world. In the Napa Valley, with its clement, un-European weather, growers have the luxury of ripe fruit year in and year out. But the question remains, how ripe is ripe? In recent years the tendency has been to pick later and later, which results in much higher levels of both sugar and alcohol; the former converts to the latter. Some claim these big voluptuous fruit bombs appeal to the palates of certain influential critics and tend to win blind tastings. But in the twenty years of the Araujos' stewardship, the Eisele Cabernets have stayed fairly consistently in the 14 percent alcohol range—on the low side by 2010 Napa standards—which might explain why the vineyard's signature flavors come through from vintage to vintage. There is almost always an earthy component, more common in Bordeaux than in Napa, and an herbal note, which Bart speculates may have something to do with the numerous olive trees that surround the vineyard. Tasting through twenty years of Eiseles with the winemaker Françoise Peschon, who worked at Haut-Brion before coming to Araujo, I was more than once reminded of the earthy, stony character of that great Bordeaux first growth, possibly my favorite. The 1991, the Araujos' first vintage, was especially complex, with many years of life ahead of it. The 1995 was a Baby Huey of a wine, young and huge. When I commented that the 2005 was a real princess of a wine, Bart said, "Yes, but one with a career." In other words, it has everything: deeply voluptuous texture with rich mocha flavors as well as the structure to improve for decades. The 2007 and the 2008 are worthy successors.

Coincidentally, less than an hour after tasting the 2007 Araujo, I had lunch with a winemaker who brought along a Cab of the same vintage that had just been given 99 points by *Wine Spectator*, and it was fascinating to compare them. Absolutely nothing on the menu, except possibly dessert, could have stood up to this jammy, super-ripe, super-rich, high-octane Cabernet. Actually, it was dessert unto itself and tasted a lot like blueberry pie. No doubt there's an audience for this kind of wine—indeed, the winemaker told me it was already sold out. And it probably doesn't matter that it might not develop and age gracefully over the next twenty years. I'm all for diversity, and I've got nothing against floozy bimbos—I've been known to watch the odd episode of *Rock of Love*—but tasting this wine made me instantly nostalgic for the sophisticated and nuanced Araujo.

I still have a small scar from that harvesting knife. But I'm happy to report that the 2010 Sauvignon Blanc turned out very nicely.

The Woman with All the Toys

I honestly can't think of many people I envy, but if I had to come back as someone else, I think it would be Ann Colgin. No, wait . . . on second thought, I think I'd come back as Ann's husband, Joe Wender. It's not just that she's a babe, or that she has houses in Napa and Bel Air, or that she knows practically everybody you've ever heard of, or that she's a serious philanthropist. That's the least of it.

When Joe met her at an Henri Jayer dinner at Spago, all the Goldman Sachs executive knew about her was that she worked for Sotheby's as a wine expert. Waiting for the restaurant's notoriously slow valet parkers, he chatted her up enough to pave the way for a phone call. "Joe's a Francophile," Ann says. "He wasn't much interested in California. He told a friend we'd met, and his friend said, 'Oh my God, she makes that wine that's impossible to get.' Joe had no idea." The next time he saw her, over dinner at New York's Le Bernardin, Wender ordered a bottle of Colgin Herb Lamb Cabernet from the wine list. The *carte du vin* was decidedly French when he proposed to her the following year at Paris's three-star L'Ambroisie.

As I recall, she was wearing white shoes, gingham, and a big floppy straw hat when I first met Ann more than a decade ago at the Iroquois Steeplechase in Nashville, Tennessee. A Texan who'd attended Vanderbilt, she seemed right at home with the horsey set on that hot afternoon, when I encountered for the first time her signature brand of earthy, down-home glamour and learned that she was an art and antiques expert who'd fallen in love with the Napa Valley in the late eighties. Coincidentally, I'd recently returned from Napa, where I had tasted the first vintage of her eponymous Cabernet Sauvignon with the winemaker Helen Turley—the first time I'd ever tasted a wine out of barrel and still one of my most vivid vinous memories. I didn't realize then that I was witnessing the birth of a legend.

That first vintage, the 1992, and several subsequent vintages were made from purchased grapes in a leased cubbyhole of the Napa Wine Company, which was about the size of a sauna—not exactly a grand provenance. It was made by Helen Turley, who was on the verge of being dubbed the Wine Goddess by Robert Parker. I remember being amazed that I could detect olive notes among other flavors in this Cab, which was richer and more concentrated than any I'd ever tasted. I've since lost my notes but can still conjure that taste. (That vintage was called Colgin-Schrader, the winery having started as a joint venture with her first husband, Frederick Schrader, who has, since their divorce, launched the highly acclaimed Schrader Cellars.) Since then, Colgin has become famous—along with Bryant Family, Harlan, and Screaming Eagle—as one of the cult wines that redefined the concept of Cabernet in Napa.

Ten years later I find myself racing through a series of steep switchbacks up Pritchard Hill in Ann's little two-seat Mercedes, with my wife, also an Anne, sitting in my lap, and finally arriving some thousand feet up the side of the mountain at the gate of the new property, its dramatically situated Mediterranean house and adjacent circular winery overlooking Lake Hennessey and the Napa Valley. The winery's a little bit like a boutique version of Lafite's round *chai* in Pauillac. And here's the other reason I really envy Joe Wender—because beneath the house, with its dramatic views and art treasures, the wine cellar is stocked with not only verticals of Colgin but also drool-inducing, large-format rarities from Burgundy, Bordeaux, and the Rhône.

Ann finally has a facility that seems adequate to her ambitions. (Although I might opt for a more dramatic name than IX Estate; she and Joe were married up here on 9/9/2000.) The 124-acre property has 20 acres of vines, planted in 2000, which will significantly boost the Colgin label's production without nearly taking care of all the supplicants waiting for a slot on her mailing list.

Ann started out buying Cabernet grapes from the Herb Lamb Vineyards on the eastern hillside above the town of St. Helena. In 1996 she purchased the Tychson Hill, a sloping, five-acre parcel north of St. Helena that was planted in the nineteenth century by the pioneering winemaker Josephine Tychson. She restored the modest nineteenth-century farmhouse, which she now calls home, and replanted the vineyards under the supervision of her superstar vineyard manager, David Abreu. (Honest, there really are superstars of viticulture.) The two-and-a-half-acre plot now produces a brooding, complex Cabernet that always tastes utterly distinct from Herb Lamb, thanks to a unique dark-soil type it shares with the nearby Grace Family Vineyards. A third Colgin bottling, a Bordeaux blend called Cariad, comes mainly from Abreu's Madrona Ranch vineyard on the steep slopes west of St. Helena. Cariad is usually the most Bordeaux-like and restrained of these, though it often shows an exotic spiciness early. Finally, there are the incredibly promising Cabs and Syrahs from the new IX Estate property.

In recent years the wines have been made by Allison Tauziet, who spent ten years in Bordeaux before returning to the States to work at Napa's Far Niente. Since 2005 she's worked at Colgin alongside the oenologist Alain Raynaud, of St. Émilion's Quinault L'Enclos, who flies over regularly from Bordeaux. Since Helen Turley's tenure the style seems to have remained relatively consistent. Like all of the Napa Valley cult wines, Colgins are rich and concentrated and voluptuous in texture; compared with traditional Bordeaux or old-style Napa Cabs, the tannins are much softer in their youth. But I usually find Colgin less flashy and flirty in its youth than some of the other cult Cabs, a little more mysterious and reserved on first acquaintance. For pure, decadent pleasure I recommend the new Syrah, which debuted with the 2002 vintage and is so sexy and voluptuous that it should probably be banned.

As enviable as Ann Colgin's life appears, it might not be quite as perfect as some of her wines. For all of their travel, her frequent-flier husband insists that all luggage be carry-on. "I haven't checked a bag in nine years," she says. "I used to have a bag just for my shoes." Confidential to AC: I'd let you check as many pieces as you liked.

The Whole Spice Rack: Old-School Rioja

Don't get me wrong, I have nothing against fruit. But I sometimes get tired of all this super-extracted, alcoholic grape juice that seems as if it ought to be served on toast rather than in a glass and that tastes as if it doesn't come from anywhere in particular. These are wines that somehow remind me of a blind date I had in 2005 with a woman exactly half my age. Our conversation had lots of italics and exclamation marks and very few parentheticals or semicolons. Much as I like some of the bold, new postmodern Riojas from producers like Artadi, Allende, and Roda, I sometimes crave the sepia tones of traditional Rioja, which tastes the way old Burgundy should but seldom does—and for a lot less money.

What we now think of as the old-school Rioja was created in the eighteen fifties, when French wine brokers arrived in Spain after odium and later phylloxera had devastated their own vineyards. They introduced oak barrel aging to the region, which had previously specialized in light, fruity, short-lived plonk. Two nobles, the Marqués de Murrieta and the Marqués de Riscal, helped to develop and market this Bordeaux-style Rioja, and both bodegas are still flourishing. The Riojans took to barrel aging the way the Italians took to noodles, substituting American for French oak and developing an official hierarchy that culminates with *reserva* (at least twelve months in oak, two years in bottle) and *gran reserva* (at least two years in oak and three in bottle). *Crianzas,* released after just two years, are apt to have a strawberry-vanilla freshness, whereas the *reservas* and *grandes reservas* will exhibit the mellow, secondary flavors associated with age—flavors evocative of autumn rather than summer. And those with bottle age can suggest practically the entire spice rack, not to mention the cigar box and the tack room. Somehow you get the idea that this is how red wine used to taste.

If the old school had a central campus, it would be a series of buildings clustered around the railroad tracks at the edge of the medieval town of Haro, including the bodegas Muga and López de Heredia. Both houses are run by the direct descendants of their founders, and both keep several coopers employed year-round, making and repairing barrels and maintaining the huge *tinas*—the swimming-pool-sized oak vats in which the wine is fermented and stored. Old oak doesn't impart a woody flavor to the wine, and both wineries believe it's superior to stainless steel. In addition to its old-school wines, notably the *gran reserva*, which spends three years in old American oak barrels, Muga makes a more modern expression of Rioja with French oak under the Torre Muga label, including a new postmodern luxury cuvée called Aro. Not so López de Heredia, the hardest-core reactionaries of Rioja, makers of Viña Tondonia.

Tondonia is one of those secret passwords whereby serious wine wonks recognize their own kind. The winery was founded in 1877, and apparently its practices have changed very little since. The Tondonia vineyard is beautifully situated on a high south-facing plateau outside Haro. For reasons not entirely clear to me, the complex itself resembles a Swiss or Bavarian village. Inside, it looks like the set of a low-budget horror movie, with ancient and vaguely sinister-looking machinery, huge blackened *tinas,* and a fluffy black mold blanketing almost everything. Some of the vats are as old as the winery, and pixieish María José López de Heredia, great-granddaughter of the founder, is convinced that the petrified sediments and natural yeasts in the *tinas* are an important part of the wine's distinct flavor.

Far below the fermentation and storage vats, in a series of tunnels carved out of the limestone, tens of thousands of bottles dating from the nineteen twenties slumber beneath the pillowy mold. "The spiders eat the cork flies," López de Heredia explains cheerfully as I swipe a vast cobweb off my face. Any minute now, I feel certain, Vincent Price is going to jump out at me. The sense of eeriness is gradually dispelled, replaced by a mounting sense of exhilaration and wonder as she uncorks bottles in the subterranean tasting room. I start with, of all things, a 1995 rosé—this being her idea of a young wine—and move on to the 1981 Gran Reserva Blanco, made mostly from the indigenous white grape called Viura, which tastes fresh and lively for its age. The tasting of reds begins with the ethereal 1985 Tondonia, which has an amazing nose of cinnamon, clove, leather, tobacco—the whole spice box, plus the stable and the library. You could sniff this forever. And while this might seem like one of those annoying instances where you have to listen to a writer tease you with descriptions of stuff you will never see or taste, in fact most of these wines were released at fifteen or twenty years of age, and are still possible to find with the help of Wine-Searcher.com. In this regard, López de Heredia reminds me of Orson Welles's embarrassing commercials for Paul Masson—"We will sell no wine before its time." (Check it out on YouTube, along with the outtakes featuring a thoroughly sozzled Orson.)

Across the street, Muga is releasing its *grandes reservas* on a slightly more accelerated schedule. Prado Enea Gran Reserva is a special bottling of the best grapes from the Muga vineyards in the best vintages. You can probably find 2001 and 2004 at retail through 2012; both have the kind of spicy complexity that develops only with age. And if you're lucky, you might even find older vintages. A 1976 *gran reserva* that I shared with the bearish, gregarious Juan Muga at a restaurant in Haro lingers in memory as one of the best old Burgundies I never drank. Marqués de Riscal,

Marqués de Murrieta, and Bodegas Montecillo are also good sources of traditional Rioja. Next time you're feeling palate fatigue from trying to chew the latest super-extracted New World Merlot, you might consider checking out the subtle and delicate charms of an old *gran reserva*.

Zowie!

The very name of the organization, so at home in a comic book speech bubble, is highly evocative of the wine that it promotes, ZAP being the official abbreviation for the Zinfandel Advocates & Producers, which in 2010 celebrated its twentieth anniversary in San Francisco. Judging from my experience of previous festivals, I can assure you it wasn't pretty. Teeth were stained, voices were booming, wine was guzzled and spilled. Whereas most wine tastings involve spitting discreetly into silver buckets in order to maintain a modicum of sobriety and critical judgment among the tasters, a great deal of wine seems to get swallowed at ZAP's Grand Tasting at San Francisco's Fort Mason Center, although one participant claimed it was slightly more subdued than usual in 2009. Similarly, some observers have detected a new wave of more sophisticated Zins, but Zinfandel, like rock and roll, is never going to be subtle.

Generally a big, high-alcohol red, with explosive fruit flavors ranging from raspberry to blackberry, Zin calls out for such all-American fare as barbecue and chili. "No wimpy wines" is the long-standing motto of Ravenswood, a winery that helped put red Zinfandel on the map, and it could also be ZAP's rallying cry.

Ravenswood's founder, Joel Peterson, was a cancer immunologist at San Francisco's Mount Zion Hospital before he lost funding for his research. His interest in wine had been passed along by his father, Walter, a physical chemist and charter member of the San Francisco Wine Sampling Club. In 1972, Joel started working with Joseph Swan, one of the pioneers in the rediscovery of Zinfandel, which had been widely planted around California in the nineteenth century by Italian immigrants. (It was finally genetically identified as being identical to Primitivo, a southern Italian varietal.) Many of these vineyards survived, partly out of neglect and partly because of the popularity of white Zinfandel, a cloyingly sweet blush wine created at Sutter Home vineyard in 1975. To increase the concentration of its red Zinfandel, its winemaker Bob Trinchero had bled off some of the just-pressed juice before fermentation. A thousand gallons of this pinkish wine was fermented separately, but the fermentation stopped before the sugar was converted to alcohol, resulting in a sweet beverage that soon became the most popular wine in America.

A lot of old-vine Zin also went into Gallo's so-called Hearty Burgundy, the first dry red wine that many of us future enthusiasts ever tasted—I well remember my first jug, consumed along with some Thai stick on the shore of Onota Lake in Pittsfield, Massachusetts. But winemakers like Peterson and Paul Draper of Ridge Vineyards believed that Zinfandel had a higher calling and that great red wines could be crafted from the old vines, which, as they age, yield fewer grapes but deliver more intense flavor. In 1976, Peterson launched Ravenswood using Swan's winery and four tons of old-vine Zinfandel bought from local growers. Pictures of him at this time show him with elbow-length blond hair, looking like a lost member of the Eagles. Peterson didn't have the money to buy his own vineyard and cultivated relationships with growers, particularly those with old vines, some of which dated back to the nineteenth century.

The Ravenswood slogan came about when his business partner of the time insisted at one point that they needed to make a white Zinfandel in order to get profitable. Peterson refused. "I told him I'd never make a wimpy wine," he says. Instead, he came up with Vintners Blend, an inexpensive red Zinfandel crafted from dozens of vineyard sources, which has become an international best seller with an annual production of around 500,000 cases. At about eight bucks retail, it's a great value and a great introduction to the easy pleasure of Zinfandel.

When I was getting married in 2006, I chose to pour a crowd-pleasing red complex enough to intrigue the oenophiles in the group: a Zin, the 2003 Ridge Geyserville. Until fairly recently, if you wanted a good Zinfandel, you simply had to look for one that started with the letter *R*. Kent Rosenblum, a veterinarian from Minnesota who'd fallen in love with Zinfandel after moving to Alameda, launched Rosenblum Cellars in 1978. Ridge, Ravenswood, and Rosenblum are still the big three of Zin, though they have helped to inspire several new waves of Zinophilia.

Larry Turley was an emergency-room physician when he launched Turley Wine Cellars in the early nineties. (I have no useful hypothesis as to why so many Zinfanatics have medical backgrounds.) A courtly, gentle giant who originally hails from Kentucky, Turley and his wine-making sister, Helen, rocked the wine world with their first vintages, which seemed to crank up the volume and power (and alcohol) in a category that was already known for being over the top. Turley later turned over the wine-making duties to Ehren Jordan, one of the few men in Napa tall enough to look him in the eye. Although the Turley style was once synonymous with excess—and helped spawn an arms race in which everyone seemed to be going for riper, fruitier, fatter wines—most Zinophiles agree that Jordan has in recent years refined the style, which isn't so surprising given the fact that he crafts some extremely elegant Pinot Noirs for his own Failla label. But make no mistake, these are still big, bad reds that almost require a spoon.

More recently, the mailing list that Zin freaks have been over-subscribing is that of Carlisle, which launched its first commercial vintage in 1998, although its founder, Mike Officer, had been making wine in his garage for many years before he launched a winery under his wife's maiden name. (Officer sounded a bit forbidding.)

He was a software designer who first caught the wine bug at eighteen when his older sister, a restaurateur in San Francisco, poured him some choice California classics from Trefethen, Chateau St. Jean, and Freemark Abbey. Throughout his twenties, his hobby became all consuming, his garage more and more crowded with barrels, until, he says, "it was time to fish or cut bait."

Like Peterson before him, Officer relied on the friendships he'd developed as an amateur winemaker to secure access to fruit from old Zinfandel vineyards, most of them in Sonoma's Russian River Valley. Along the way he became president of the Historic Vineyard Society, a nonprofit organization founded to preserve the heritage of old, mostly pre-Prohibition vineyards that constitute an amazing resource for California winemakers. "Every time someone buys an old-vine vineyard and rips it out," he says, "we lose a piece of our history."

Eventually, he was able to purchase a vineyard planted in 1927, which he renamed Carlisle. Although the majority of vines are Zinfandel, recent research has uncovered other varietals as well. So far, thirty-one black varietals have been identified in the Carlisle Vineyard, including of course Petite Syrah and also Syrah, Peloursin, Alicante Bouschet, Grand Noir, Petit Bouschet, Carignan, Tempranillo, and Merlot. Officer thinks there's another ten or twelve in there. Many of these old "Zinfandel" vineyards have a similar diversity. "I do a lot of walking, and all of a sudden I look at a vine and go, 'Whoa, what's that?' We take tissue samples and send them to UC Davis, where they have a database of fifteen thousand cultivars. Once they run DNA on our samples, they can tell us what we've got." This genetic resource might someday be the basis for reviving certain varietals, and in the meantime it makes wines like Ridge's Geyserville or Lytton Springs and Carlisle's Carlisle Vineyard more complex and nuanced.

Officer's friend Morgan Twain-Peterson is one of the newest stars on the Zinfandel scene. As Joel Peterson's son, he would seem to have wine in his veins—he made a bit of a name for himself with a Pinot Noir called Vino Bambino, which he first produced when he was five years old and continued to make until he went to college at Vassar. After graduate studies at Columbia he went back to Ravenswood, then refined his wine making with stints at Australia's McLaren Vale and at Lynch Bages in Bordeaux. Returning to California, he founded Bedrock Wine Co. and, in partnership with his father, bought a vineyard planted in 1886 (which he informed me was owned at that time by my wife's great-grandfather George Hearst). The ancient Zin was interplanted with more than twenty other varietals; because only about 60 percent of the grapes are Zinfandel, he doesn't designate the wine as such.

"I didn't make a straight Zin my first two years at Bedrock," he says. "I have a more classically trained palate and thought it lacked the requisite balance." Zinfandel fans will be grateful that he overcame his scruples—and possibly Oedipal issues—and now makes two vineyard-designated Zinfandels as well as the sublime Heirloom, a blend of Zin (about half) and more than twenty other varietals, that is, in my opinion, an instant California classic. "The Rock in a velvet smoking jacket," reads my tasting note on the 2009. Those who prefer their wrestlers turned actors shirtless—and this would include many hard-core Zinophiles—will find plenty of Zins out there that fit the bill.

Heartbreak Hill

or, The Golden Slope

Becky Wasserman:
The American Godmother of Burgundy

In March 2010 a group of American investors assembled by the former sommelier Robert Bohr purchased some twenty acres of prime Meursault vineyards for some 13 million euros, sealing a trend whereby wealthy American oenophiles buy into the fabled vineyards of Burgundy. In 2002, long before the Goldman Sachs Conspiracy Theory became a major interdisciplinary body of knowledge, a band of rich Americans led by Joe Wender and his wife, Ann Colgin, bought Camille Giroud, a small but venerable Burgundian negotiant. In wine circles, the headliner in this transaction was Colgin, the founder of Colgin Cellars, renowned for its small-production, big-ticket Cabernet Sauvignons from the Napa Valley. However, most of the ten original investors were, like Wender, partners in Goldman Sachs. Was this just a friendly confederation of well-heeled Burghounds looking for bragging rights and first crack at some old bottles for their personal cellars? Was it part of an incredibly intricate scheme for wine-world domination, possibly some sort of prescient countermove against the nascent Chinese interest in the rival region of Bordeaux? Or was it yet another example of the influence of Becky Wasserman, the American-born Earth Mother of Burgundy, who acted as the matchmaker in this particular Franco-American union? I say the last.

Wasserman grew up on East Seventy-Seventh Street, the daughter of a Wall Street broker she describes as "an elegant alcoholic" and a Hungarian ex–prima ballerina. She attended the Rudolf Steiner School on East Seventy-Ninth: conspiracy theorists should note that Steiner is the father of biodynamic agriculture, an approach embraced by many of the domaines she imports to the United States. Coincidence? At Hunter College High School her teacher Madame Brody introduced her to the French existentialists, and she associated "with terrible girls with pretensions peering at Dylan Thomas drinking at the White Horse Tavern." After a year at Bryn Mawr, she married "a Harvard fellow" and moved to Cambridge. Her memories of Harvard at that time: "Leary and Alpert, Gregory Corso and Allen Ginsberg auditing an Auden course. A friend had spent a year in France at Les Baux and introduced us all to good wines, wonderful cookbooks (Charles Baker), and soufflé au Grand Marnier. If it was French, it was good—the whole shebang, the art, literature, food, wine, the Revolution, the clothes." It would take a divorce and several years before she finally sailed for France with her second husband, "who had left Merrill Lynch to go to art school."

They found a crumbling barn in the town of Bouilland and restored it, in part with cast-off materials from neighbors who were replacing their ancient flagstone floors with linoleum. The couple had two children, Peter and Paul. Peter, who now works with his mother in sales, reports that his childhood was idyllic in many ways, growing up on a more or less self-sustaining farm, complete with ponies, "although there were some drawbacks to growing up in the family of an artist in the sixties," he says. "My parents didn't cut my hair, and in rural Burgundy they didn't get that. I was subject to some serious bullying, but my parents were oblivious."

Her husband, Becky says, "collected Burgundies and au pair girls." Foreseeing the end of her marriage, Becky took a job as a broker for a barrel maker, selling French oak barrels to California winemakers, including Robert Mondavi. By the time her marriage was over, she'd fallen in love with the wines of Burgundy and was desperate to make a living and keep the house in Bouilland. "I had to become rapidly self-supporting as I had no trust fund, no alimony, no amour propre." After working for Kermit Lynch and the Troisgros brothers, she started her own company, which specialized in the export of small-domaine wines from the Côte d'Or and a few other regions of France. Her third husband, Russell Hone, a veteran of the English wine trade, joined the company in 1985; he holds the titles "company father" and "chef." He's a formidable cook, having collaborated on a series of Time-Life cookbooks with the late Richard Olney.

When I arrived unannounced one March afternoon at their office in the former chancellery of the Dukes of Burgundy, on a cobbled street in the town of Beaune, the couple were just sitting down with their staff for lunch, a lamb and kidney stew cooked by Russell. Becky promptly invited me and my companion, Beaver Truax, a veteran New York wine merchant who's known the couple for years, to join them. "Beaver," she said, "do I look like Aubrey Beardsley?" She cupped her halo of curly gray hair between her hands. "Russell says I look like Aubrey Beardsley."

"I thought I said you looked like Oscar Wilde," Hone said, as he poured me a glass of 2009 Michaud Morgon, a Cru Beaujolais from their portfolio.

Truax assured her she looked like neither, and as a polite guest I concurred, though I did think she looked as if she'd been drawn by Edward Koren for *The New Yorker,* one of his hirsute sophisticate-eccentrics. I was as impressed by the level of marital banter as I was with the meal. The staff lunch is a daily ritual that serves as a tasting forum and often draws guests who just happen to show up around twelve thirty. "We see these heads in the window," says Becky, "which is terrific, because Russell is incapable of cooking for less than twelve." Clearly a man of large appetites and enthusiasms, he can take no credit for his towering height, but his Falstaffian girth is presumably his own accomplishment. He is also widely reputed to have both an excellent palate and an extraordinary memory for older vintages.

The couple began hosting Burgundy symposia for passionate amateurs in 1997, welcoming a dozen guests to Bouilland for an intensive week of tasting and touring, enlisting the help of such experts as Clive Coates and Allen Meadows. An early guest was Joe Wender, who returned the following year with his wife, Ann Colgin. Wender asked Wasserman to let him know if she ever spotted an investment opportunity, and not long afterward she enlisted him to help rescue the foundering negotiant firm of Camille Giroud, with whom she'd worked for years. In addition to its venerable name, the firm had significant stores of older Burgundy vintages. Through her contacts, Wasserman then found David Croix, a twenty-three-year-old fresh out of oenology school, who has since become one of the most respected winemakers in the region, though his hiring had to have been something of an act of faith. At Camille Giroud's winery in an unpretentious nineteenth-century warehouse in the center of Beaune, Croix is now turning out thirty cuvées from Burgundy's humblest appellations to its grandest.

When Wasserman heard whispers that the Domaine Duchet was for sale, she contacted another symposium alum, the real estate investor Richard Forbes, and again hired Croix to make the wine. The estate, Domaine des Croix, is named for a stone cross in the courtyard of the domaine, with a nod to the winemaker. And while she had no part in the recent sale of Domaine René Manuel, her former employee Dominique Lafon, who now runs his family domaine in Meursault, was one of the principals in the deal, one of many top Burgundian producers whose wines she exports to the States.

A few days after I meet her in Beaune, Becky is eager to talk about the humble side of Burgundy over lunch at the old stone farmhouse in Bouilland. "There's so much emphasis on the famous domaines and the Grands Crus," she says, "that I'm afraid people are overlooking appellations like Monthélie and Savigny and Marsannay. Burgundy can be so expensive, but there are wonderful bottles for $30 or $40." Russell, who has prepared another lamb stew, this one with lots of garlic over a white bean puree, pours me a glass of 2002 Sylvain Pataille Marsannay, an inexpensive red that's one of the best things I've tasted during a week in Burgundy. "It's always the small things that have intrigued us the most," Becky says. "The handmade, the artisanal. That's really what Burgundy is about."

A Grace Kelly of a Wine:
Puligny-Montrachet

The first time I remember drinking white Burgundy was in 1985, shortly after I returned to Manhattan after a sojourn at graduate school. The bottle in question was a birthday present from my wife, a 1982 Carillon Puligny-Montrachet. I'm not entirely sure whether it was a Premier Cru, from the middle slope of the gently rising hillside adjacent to the famous Grand Cru Montrachet vineyard, or a simple Village wine from lower down, but I was so blown away that Puligny-Montrachet immediately became my favorite special-occasion white.

Over the years I've learned to love Meursault, Chassagne-Montrachet, and even select New World Chardonnays, but I've always maintained a soft spot for the wines of Puligny, a tiny village on the lower slope of the famous hillside known as the Côte d'Or. Puligny-Montrachet is located in the southernmost part of the Côte de Beaune, home of the best white Burgundies, made exclusively from the Chardonnay grape. In 1879, in an effort to boost its own profile and the price of its wine, Puligny attached to its own name that of its most famous vineyard. Le Montrachet had long been hailed as the world's greatest dry white wine. Claude Arnoux, writing in 1728, could find no words in either French or Latin to describe its splendors (an example that wine critics should sometimes ponder). Thomas Jefferson was such a big fan that after tasting the 1782 vintage, he ordered an entire 130-gallon cask, according to John Hailman's *Thomas Jefferson on Wine*. Must have made for quite a party. More recently, it was the wine that Grace Kelly brought over to wheelchair-bound Jimmy

Stewart's apartment in *Rear Window*, along with a meal from the '21' Club, a delivery that I'd willingly break my own leg for. The problem, from the point of view of a thirsty world, is that there are only twenty acres of this hallowed ground. However, the adjacent hillsides, with their similar aspects and limestone-rich geology, produce wines with a distinct family resemblance that often approach the level of the Big M. (Why Montrachet itself is always considered superior to, and worth more than, wines from vines just a few feet away is a question that wouldn't necessarily be elucidated by a book-length analysis.)

So it was a natural, even brilliant move on the part of the former mayor of Puligny to co-opt this famous name. Unfortunately for him, though, the Montrachet vineyard straddled the border between Puligny and Chassagne, and the residents of that village, hearing of Puligny's application, quickly followed his lead. "And thus the bigamous marriage was proclaimed, on 27 November 1879," Simon Loftus writes in his book *Puligny-Montrachet*. "Puligny became Puligny-Montrachet . . . at the same time as Chassagne took the same partner, from that day forth." The two villages had a long history of rivalry, which was exacerbated by the shared name. While I love some of the wines of Chassagne, those of Puligny seem to me to have greater precision and refinement. When I ask Jacques Lardière, the winemaker at Louis Jadot, which makes some five different Pulignys, what distinguishes the wine of that commune from its neighbors, he says, "Aristocracy." This is a very short answer for the garrulous poet of Beaune, who describes wine making as the process of "seeking the unconscious of the earth," but I think I know what he means. Even without that takeout scene in *Rear Window*, Grace Kelly might easily come to mind.

Lardière took me on a tour of the Côte de Beaune vineyards, some marked off by tangible boundaries like a streambed or a road, others distinguished only by invisible shifts in the bedrock or soil type. The untrained eye might not register the borders, but a thousand years of observation and tasting have drawn the lines.

As we drove north from Santenay, we passed Chassagne and shortly arrived at the inner sanctum, the walled vineyard of Montrachet, located in the middle of the hill—the sweet spot. For such a famous piece of real estate the landscape isn't very dramatic—a ten-degree slope ribboned with vines. I have to admit I was a little disappointed. Below, on a gentler slope, is Bâtard-Montrachet, also a Grand Cru, and above, on the steepest part of the hill, is Chevalier-Montrachet. Thanks to erosion, the latter has very sparse soil, some of which ends up downhill at Bâtard; the wines of Chevalier are generally thought to be leaner and more elegant, those of Bâtard fatter and richer. Montrachet, in the middle, is said to strike a balance between the two. I can vouch for these generalizations thanks to the generosity of several movie studios that employed me in the late eighties. I spent a fair amount of Paramount's and Universal's money comparing these three Grands Crus at the Chateau Marmont in Los Angeles, which for some reason was well stocked with older vintages from Bouchard Père & Fils. There were only two or three solid items on the room service menu—apparently, the management of the then-raffish establishment where John Belushi met his end assumed its patrons weren't deeply interested in food. But just in case you ever find yourself wondering what to eat with a fine Montrachet, I can assure you that a tuna melt works very well.

To the north of the Grands Crus, on the same southeast-facing slope, are the Premiers Crus of Puligny-Montrachet, wines I learned to love after the demise of my screenwriting career. They can attain similar heights, occasionally even surpassing the Grands Crus in the hands of a great producer like Domaine Leflaive, the ne plus ultra maker of Puligny. The vineyards higher on the hill, like Les Caillerets and Champ-Gain, tend to yield somewhat more structured, flintier wines, while those lower down, contiguous with Bâtard, tend to be rounder, though still marked by a mineral note. From the flatlands below the hill come the so-called Village wines, the third declension of greatness, entitled to be called Puligny-Montrachet, though the vineyard itself is generally not specified. Village wines from the better domaines like Leflaive, Carillon, Sauzet, and the newcomer Pierre-Yves Colin-Morey can be very special wines despite their third-tier ranking.

Leflaive is the superstar of the appellation, the reference standard for Puligny-Montrachet. (Domaine de la Romanée-Conti makes a few barrels of Montrachet every year, but unless you own a private jet, you probably shouldn't worry about it.) Anne-Claude Leflaive, whose family has been in Puligny since 1717, converted the domaine to biodynamic viticulture in 1997, and such is the quality of the wines that many of her neighbors followed her example. Exponents of this cosmically conscious version of organic farming inevitably cite Leflaive to lend credence to this controversial set of practices. Its best Premier Cru is probably Les Pucelles, while its Grand Cru Chevalier-Montrachet is undoubtedly one of the world's greatest white wines—celestial juice—more than worthy of being delivered by Grace Kelly.

The American-owned Maison Louis Jadot is a very good source of Pulignys at all levels. Shortly after touring the great Chardonnay vineyards of Beaune with Lardière, I retraced our journey in the cellars of Jadot, tasting through the wines of Chassagne, Puligny, and Meursault. Remarkably, each vineyard had a distinct flavor profile, but the Pulignys seemed to me more high toned, steely, and vivid than their neighbors. More recently, I repeated this experiment in Manhattan—with the wines of most of the top producers of Puligny, and a few Chassagnes and Meursaults thrown in for good measure—with the help of Daniel Johnnes, the wine director of Daniel Boulud's restaurant group, who spends a good deal of time in Burgundy. Even with many different winemakers' signatures, a decisive Puligny character was evident. "There's an energy and a tension in Puligny," Johnnes said. "Chassagne and Meursault are softer, less high toned." Inevitably, we started comparing these great white Burgundies with women. Having agreed that Puligny was a beauty with distinctive bone structure, slightly more angular than curvaceous, I mentioned the model Carmen Dell'Orefice, and Daniel countered with Gwyneth Paltrow, though I still think it's hard to improve on the Grace Kelly analogy, one that seemed all the more apt as we moved on to older wines from the 1992, 1993, and 1995 vintages.

Puligny acquires great complexity with age, and the best Premiers and Grands Crus can improve for decades, although the Village wines can often be enjoyed on release. The 2007 vintage was much more successful for white Burgundy than for red; tasting through more than a dozen 2007s, we didn't encounter a single dud, with the exception of one bottle that was corked. The 2008s are classic Pulignys, while the 2009s are riper and more lush, which makes this a good transitional vintage for those who are accustomed to New World Chardonnays.

I haven't spoken to my second wife in many years, but if I ever do, I should probably thank her for that first bottle of Puligny-Montrachet.

Secrets of Meursault

When I visited Dominique Lafon at his château in Meursault, he was a little bleary-eyed but exuberant, having just returned from Paris, where he had celebrated the completion of a complicated transatlantic deal that significantly increased the acreage he would be tending. Thanks in part to some deep-pocketed American investors, the chain-smoking Lafon, who looks like a shorter, weathered version of Liam Neeson, was essentially splitting the old René Manuel estate, which includes some of Meursault's best vineyards, with his friend and neighbor Jean-Marc Roulot.

Lovers of great Meursault would soon be celebrating the news, too. Lafon and Roulot are basically the Han Solo and Luke Skywalker of this small village in Burgundy's Côte de Beaune, source of one of the world's most famous and coveted white wines. The other great maker, the legendary and reclusive Jean-François Coche, of Domaine Coche-Dury, would be Obi-Wan Kenobi. Coche inspires reverence in the wine world, and his whites trade for prices that induce vertigo in all but the wealthiest of collectors. Fortunately, Meursault has many other excellent winemakers, far more than neighboring Puligny-Montrachet. It's a picturesque and prosperous village, at the heart of which is a Gothic town hall with a multicolored enamel-tiled roof. Although some red wine is produced here, Meursault's renown is based on the quality of its whites, made from the Chardonnay grape.

Thomas Jefferson was a fan of Meursault, and for a great many others this is the quintessential white Burgundy, easy to pronounce and easy to love, generally fleshier and flirtier than the svelte, steely wines of Puligny. Whether or not the R&D people at General Mills were fans of Meursault, they seem to have mimicked its classic flavor profile when they came up with Honey Nut Cheerios. Hazelnut, in particular, seems to be a recurring tasting note. While there are no Grand Cru vineyards here, there are many fine Premiers Crus, and most aficionados agree that the Perrières vineyard is worthy of Grand Cru status. But Meursault, like its neighbors, has a dirty little secret on which its future might hinge.

But first, some history: Domaine Lafon came into existence when Dominique's great-grandfather Comte Jules Lafon married Marie Bloch, who owned land in Meursault. A man of great energy, a well-traveled bon vivant, art collector, and gourmand, he bought the best vineyards in the village in between two circumnavigations of the globe and founded La Paulée de Meursault, the bacchanalian post-harvest feast that survives to this day. The current *comte* seems to share many of the qualities of his ancestor, although when Dominique took over the estate in 1984 it was in fairly dismal shape. The young Lafon renovated the cellar, experimented with organic, and finally converted to biodynamics, the holistic agricultural system inspired by the teachings of Rudolf Steiner. In short order he created a rich, full-bodied Meursault that achieved international stardom. His Perrières is particularly admired; the 1996 is easily one of the best white wines I've ever tasted.

Meanwhile, Jean-Marc Roulot took over his family domaine in 1989 somewhat reluctantly, sidelining a successful career as a stage and film actor. Tall and slim, with a hawkish nose and a wry wit, he crafts wines that are a little leaner and racier than Lafon's, which has made him a favorite with sommeliers and other fans of high-acid wines. He really hit his stride with the 1992 vintage—I recently tasted his 1992 Perrières, a beautiful and complex wine that seemed to have another decade of life. Roulot buffs are thrilled that the Domaine Manuel deal will greatly expand the supply of Roulot Meursault, which has never been easy to find.

But there's a troubling mystery that Lafon and Roulot are beginning to confront. Although Meursault is approachable in its youth, experienced tasters tend to agree that a Premier Cru Meursault from a good year is at its best around the seven-to-ten-year mark—or at least they did until recently. There is now a general consensus that something changed for the worse starting with the 1995 vintage. Many of the wines of that vintage and subsequent ones evolved far more quickly than they were supposed to, suffering from premature oxidation, a.k.a. premox, that gave them an unwanted resemblance, in taste and color, to sherry. In 2011 I hosted a tasting of vintages going back to 1985 with some sommelier friends, and while there were some transporting moments, we also experienced some real disappointments; five out of sixteen bottles suffered from some degree of oxidation, including the two bottles that had us all drooling in anticipation—2002 Perrières from Roulot and Lafon.

Many white Burgundy makers have been in denial about this, but by now most acknowledge the problem, although no one has come up with a simple explanation. One theory links the premox phenomenon with the trend toward "natural" wine making and a decreasing use of sulfur, which acts as a preservative. Faulty corks have also been blamed, some claiming that around 1995 many cork manufacturers started bleaching corks with hydrogen peroxide, which interacts with—and oxidizes—the wine in the bottle. The practice of *bâtonnage*—the periodic stirring of the lees (the yeasty sediment) in the barrel—has also been cited as an oxidative factor, although it's unclear why it would have started causing problems in 1995.

Lafon, for one, is not afraid to talk about premox, and he's attacking the problem on several fronts, working with scientists at the University of Bordeaux, experimenting with corks and coatings as well as higher levels of sulfur, and he's sharing and comparing notes with his neighbors. He seems confident that younger vintages will behave like the Meursaults of yore. One can only hope. Many white Burgundy lovers have told me they've cut back on their purchases or stopped buying altogether.

Personally, I'm trying to keep the faith for the present, despite frequent disappointments. Reason would seem to dictate caution, but love and the lower appetites have nothing to do with rationality. Drinking a great, mature Meursault is one of life's more intricately nuanced pleasures, and even young ones have a unique and thoroughly beguiling flavor profile. Recent vintages, tasted now, have been good to excellent. The 2009s are very rich and ripe, the kinds of whites that provide an easy transition for California Chardonnay drinkers. The 2007s and 2008s are more classic and less opulent, with brighter acid. I particularly like the 2008s; recent bottles from Jobard, Ente, Roulot, and the rising star Pierre-Yves Colin-Morey have been superb. For a Meursault-like experience on a budget I would recommend the whites of neighboring Auxey-Duresses and Monthélie. Once you taste a really good bottle of Meursault, you may find that you're willing to risk the occasional stinker in order to relive that incomparable pleasure.

Jacques's Domaine

Back when Jacques Seysses arrived in the sixties, Burgundy was nearly as famous for its provinciality as for its sophisticated wines. If the archetypal château owner of Bordeaux was a polished man of the world in English tweeds and Lobb shoes, the stereotypical Burgundian vigneron was a taciturn peasant in a beret and gum boots who hadn't ranged any farther than his great-grandfather, who'd occupied the same house and land. Seysses, by contrast, was a handsome, well-traveled, multilingual gourmet with a sophisticated palate developed under the tutelage of his father, Louis, who owned a biscuit company and was the president of the Club des Cent, a fraternity of oenophiles and gastronomes. Young Jacques visited all of France's three-star restaurants and wineries like Domaine de la Romanée-Conti and Ramonet while he was still a kid. After sojourns at Morgan Guaranty and at the family biscuit company, Seysses followed his heart to Burgundy, where he apprenticed at the Domaine de la Pousse d'Or under Gérard Potel.

In 1967 he and his father bought a small domaine in Morey St. Denis, a sleepy village between the much more famous towns of Gevrey-Chambertin and Chambolle-Musigny. Morey is probably the least famous of the Côte de Nuits appellations, although it contains within its boundaries five Grand Cru vineyards—the highest category in the Burgundian hierarchy. "I was a newcomer in the most traditional wine-making region in the world," says the eternally youthful, silver-haired Seysses. The newly minted Domaine Dujac (a playful moniker signifying the domaine of

Jacques) had a piece of three of these, Clos de la Roche, Clos St. Denis, and Bonnes Mares.

Seysses's first vintage was the abysmal 1968, the grapes of which he sold off in bulk. He was luckier with the great 1969 vintage and luckier still when an American beauty, Rosalind Boswell, came to pick for the 1971 harvest. "The competition was not ferocious," Rosalind Seysses said modestly, some thirty-five years later, over lunch in the former abbey in which she and Jacques have raised their family and grown their winery. (In fact, I have it on good authority that she was a celebrated debutante whose marriage saddened many bachelors back in her native San Francisco.)

Thanks to Rosalind and the importer Frederick Wildman, a fair portion of the production has come to these shores almost from the beginning, while his father's connections helped Jacques place his wines in some of France's best restaurants. Seysses continues the grand tour of France's gastronomic shrines, although he now does so by bicycle, traveling thousands of kilometers a year, inevitably arriving at the end of the day at some two- or three-star restaurant. "We're bicycle people," Jacques exclaims, beaming at his svelte wife as he helps himself to another serving of lamb and pours out more 1985 Clos de la Roche.

In the summer of 2005, thirty-year-old Jeremy, who has a master's from Oxford as well as a degree in viticulture from the University of Dijon, followed in his father's footsteps when he also married an American, Diana Snowden, a twenty-seven-year-old UC Davis graduate who looks about a decade younger and has become an integral member of the Dujac wine-making team. The two met while they were both working as interns at Robert Mondavi in Napa. They had only a few dates before Jeremy returned to France, but he was taken enough to send her a plane ticket to France for Christmas.

Jeremy tried to escape the family business. He worked at the Monterey Bay Aquarium for six summers and studied biology at

Oxford, but he also joined the Oxford University Wine Society, becoming part of the blind-tasting team that crushed Cambridge three years in a row. "All of a sudden," he told me a decade later as we tasted through the 2009 vintage in the Dujac cellar, "wine was not something that only people of my parents' generation could be interested in but something that young people could be interested in too." After Oxford he studied viticulture in Dijon, worked as a wine sales rep in London for two years, and finally embraced his fate, returning to the tiny village of Morey St. Denis and assuming more and more responsibility. "I suppose 2004 was the first vintage for which I was really in charge," he says, "but my father continues to be present to this day."

The following year was memorable on several fronts, starting with weather that made for a nearly perfect vintage. Jeremy's wedding to Diana, held at the sixteenth-century abbey of Clos de Vougeot, was a convocation of Burgundian royalty and an international wine-world event. Diana, who was by then working alongside Jeremy as the domaine's oenologist, gave a speech in French, and Jeremy, who speaks the language of Shakespeare flawlessly, gave his speech in Peter Sellers–style heavily accented English, much to the amusement of the Yank and Limey contingents.

The other, less publicized occasion for celebration at Dujac that year was the purchase of prime vineyards of the former Domaine Moillard, which includes choice slices of Chambertin, Vosne-Romanée Malconsorts, and Romanée St. Vivant. This purchase was the cause for a lot of drooling in the wine world. None of these wines, which had their debut with the great 2005 vintage, are terribly easy to find, or inexpensive; fortunately, the Seysses family launched a negotiant label, called Dujac Fils & Père; these wines, made from purchased grapes, are less expensive than the domaine wines and sometimes very nearly as good.

The Dujac style strikes many as the epitome of Burgundy. "Dujac has an aromatic complexity which is utterly compelling," says Burgundy expert Robert Bohr. "It's not foursquare, and it's not powerful; it's pretty and perfumed and elegant." Like others, including Seysses, Bohr attributes this style in part to the old-fashioned practice of vinifying with the stems intact—a practice also followed at Domaine de la Romanée-Conti. Once universal, this practice is relatively rare in Burgundy today, and it seems as if Jeremy is using a slightly lower percentage than his father did, but these wines retain an unmistakable signature, even as it seems that the 2005s and the 2009s may surpass the high standards of earlier benchmarks. For whatever reason, I find the aromatic profile unmistakable and haunting in the best sense.

A few years back I found myself at a Burgundy dinner, sitting in the dining room of the British wine master Jancis Robinson, along with Stephen Browett of Farr Vintners and Heston Blumenthal, the chef of three-star Fat Duck. I was daunted in the presence of these experts and prepared for a thoroughly nerve-racking evening until I stuck my nose in the first glass and experienced a thrill of recognition. It was as if I'd pressed my nose to the skin of a former lover—I knew that this wine could only be from Domaine Dujac, that it was almost certainly its signature Grand Cru Clos de la Roche. And I got lucky with the vintage, which was 1995, having tasted it not long before at the domaine. (This took some of the sting out of a humiliating episode in Jancis's company the week before, when I'd utterly failed to identify one of my favorite Bordeaux, La Mission Haut-Brion, going so far as to idiotically insist that the wine in question wasn't a La Mission.) After nailing the Dujac, having established my chops, I was free to kick back for the rest of the night, though in fact I came out of retirement an hour later to identify a second Dujac. On the one hand, the style was Dujac, and, on the other, the vineyard and the vintage shone through. You can't ask any more of a wine than to be unique and unmistakably itself.

Starchild and the Marquis:
Earthiness Meets Refinement in Volnay

Guillaume d'Angerville and Frédéric Lafarge would seem to be unlikely friends; the former is a tall, sartorially elegant, multilingual aristocrat who spent years in New York and London as a banker; the latter seems very much a man of the soil, a modest, bespectacled farmer with deeply calloused hands who is most comfortable in Wellingtons. Such is Frédéric's affinity for the rhythms of the natural world that Jeremy Seysses, of Domaine Dujac, calls him "Starchild"; Guillaume, on the other hand, is very much at home on the streets of Paris. They grew up together in the medieval hillside village of Volnay and attended the same school in nearby Beaune, their fathers taking turns driving them back and forth. But whereas Michel Lafarge encouraged his son to join him in the family wine business, Jacques d'Angerville sent his only son away. "He basically pushed me out," Guillaume told me when we met at his eighteenth-century manor house, the finest house in the village of Volnay. "He told me there was no room for me at the domaine. In retrospect I see that he did me a great favor." Guillaume went on to a successful career with J. P. Morgan in New York and London; his classmate Frédéric stayed in Volnay, with brief stints in Champagne and Bordeaux, working alongside his father in the vineyards and eventually, after he married, moving in to the house next door to his childhood home.

When Jacques d'Angerville died suddenly in the summer of 2003, Guillaume, then living in Paris, suddenly inherited one of Burgundy's most venerated domaines in the midst of the most torrid summer in recent history. "It was a real baptism by fire," he says. (You may recall 2003 as the summer in which hundreds of un-air-conditioned French senior citizens died as a result of the unprecedented heat wave.) Fortunately, he was able to consult his old friends the Lafarges, whose house and thirteenth-century cellar, its walls padded with black mold, is just a two-minute walk down the hill. Since that first vintage he has continued to consult with the Lafarges, and he has followed their lead in converting to biodynamics, that cosmically conscious version of organic agriculture based on the teachings of Rudolf Steiner. "We taste at each other's cellars several times a year and share information about *biodynamie*," d'Angerville says.

Michel Lafarge, the snowy-haired former mayor, had closely observed with his piercing blue eyes more than sixty vintages in Volnay, including the similarly sizzling summer of 1959. "Michel is the wise man of the village," d'Angerville says, and he continues to work alongside Frédéric in a collaboration that a family friend describes as "seamless." The same word might well be used for their wines.

Volnay is located in the Côte de Beaune, the southern half of Burgundy's Côte d'Or, and many snobs insist on the superiority of the Côte de Nuits, to the north, but Jacques-Marie Duvault-Blochet, who owned the Domaine de la Romanée-Conti in the mid-nineteenth century, was equally proud of his holdings in Volnay. Although Volnay doesn't have any official Grands Crus, more than half of its vineyards are Premiers Crus, the second-highest category. If I had to limit my Burgundy buying to just one village, this would probably be it.

The wines of Volnay have been highly regarded since at least the Middle Ages, when the Dukes of Burgundy owned vineyards here and exported the wines to the court. Volnay as we know it is a red wine made from Pinot Noir, although for many centuries it was a light pink, and that perhaps partly explains its reputation as one of the most ethereal and delicate wines of Burgundy. The word "feminine" invariably comes up. (The neighboring commune of Pommard, which generally has heavier soils, is said to produce much more structured, masculine wines.) "Silky florality" is how the wine importer Peter Wasserman sums up the stereotype of Volnay, although he insists the reality is more complicated. There is real diversity in the 527 acres encompassed by this village of some three hundred people, but the level of quality and consistency is almost unmatched in Burgundy, a region whose wines have sometimes reminded me of British sports cars of the sixties in their fickleness and undependability, although both are happily more predictable today than in years past.

Today it's a given that the best wines here and everywhere else are estate bottled, produced, that is, by the people who grow the grapes, but through the nineteen twenties most of the grapes grown in Burgundy were sold to large negotiants who vinified and bottled the finished wine, frequently blending them with heartier wines from the sunny Rhône Valley and elsewhere. Guillaume's grandfather Sem, infuriated by this practice, sued some of the large Beaune negotiants, who thereafter boycotted his grapes. As a result he became a leader of the estate-bottling movement in Burgundy, selling his wines in Paris and then, with the help of Frank Schoonmaker, in the States. Thanks to that connection, the d'Angerville Volnays have long been available here.

Sem d'Angerville was a painter and an engraver who studied at the École des Beaux-Arts in Paris before inheriting the estate from an uncle. Along with the manor house, it included some of the best vineyards in Volnay, notably the Clos des Ducs, a dramatically sloping, southeast-facing plot enclosed within an ancient stone wall and blessed with a spring mid-slope, providing hydric relief in drought years such as 2003, when his grandson took over. (If you can find the 2003, buy it.) Clos des Ducs is one of the benchmark Burgundies, more powerful than the typical Volnay but more delicate than, say, a Chambertin, and is capable of aging and improving for decades. (A 1964 that Guillaume opened for me was sensational.) The other desert-island wine of the appellation would be Lafarge's Clos des Chênes, from a midslope vineyard on the south side of the village, although there are many other excellent vineyards, and producers, in Volnay.

Hubert de Montille will be familiar to viewers of the film *Mondovino* as the crusty defender of old-school traditions and the scourge of alleged American critical influence on French wine making. His Volnays were indeed classical to the point of being austere, requiring decades to reveal their shy charms. Montille still totters around the village but finally turned over the reins to his son Étienne in 2001, and the latter has made these wines much more accessible without, so far as I can tell, resorting to any technological harlotry. The Premier Cru Taillepieds is the domaine's signature wine.

The other big marquee in Volnay is Domaine de la Pousse d'Or, which made a name for itself in the last century under the leadership of Gérard Potel, who was the third driver in the car pool that transported young Guillaume and Frédéric, along with his own daughter, Agathe, to school in Beaune. Potel's first vintage from the vineyard called Bousse d'Or, the 1964, is one of Burgundy's modern legends. After his sudden death in 1997 the domaine went through a shaky period of experimentation, but it has recently recovered its form.

The 2009 vintage was a great one in Volnay, and throughout Burgundy, a real French kiss of a year, in which all but the top wines will be approachable and even wildly flirtatious on release, unlike the similarly heralded 2005, which at the moment is wearing a chastity belt. Even the basic Village wines—the ones labeled simply Volnay—are delicious, ripe, and complex. The 2008 isn't quite as come-hither, although many connoisseurs love this vintage, and many winemakers feel that these wines, while slightly less ripe, are more nuanced and more reflective of their specific sites of origin, which is what we pay for in Burgundy.

Off the Main Drag: Savigny-lès-Beaune

Carved in stone above the doorway at Château de Savigny, and elsewhere in the little town of Savigny-lès-Beaune, is the motto "Les vins de Savigny sont nourrissants, théologiques et morbifuges." I'm not certain what it means for a wine to be "theological"; "nourishing" seems like a comparatively safe and mundane claim. As for that last adjective, the Burgundy expert Jasper Morris suggests "it means either disease chasing or perhaps death defying." Whatever it means, it's a pretty grand claim for a wine that hasn't had much hype in the years since that inscription was first chiseled in the seventeenth century. Savigny-lès-Beaune is one of the less celebrated appellations of Burgundy, in part because the village is off the beaten path, located several kilometers from Route 74, the north-south artery of the Côte d'Or. This obscurity makes for some great values.

Directly across the street from the Château de Savigny, now an airplane and motorcycle museum, is the winery of Domaine Simon Bize, housed in a sprawling shed, presided over by fifty-something Patrick Bize, the diminutive, laconic fourth-generation proprietor. His great-grandfather founded the domaine in 1880, one of three consecutive Simon Bizes, and he inherited it, somewhat reluctantly, in 1972. "I didn't even like wine," he told me, "and I didn't want to work in the vineyards or the cellar." Fortunately, he grew to love his birthright, especially the vineyard work. He seems to know every vine on his patchwork, nearly fifty-acre domaine.

For many years, the Bize Savignys have been an insider's secret for budget-conscious connoisseurs. Patrick isn't prone to hype—he doesn't say much of anything as he hands me samples of his 2009s from tank and cask, or later when we drink some older wines in front of a roaring fire in his office. When pressed about the 2009 vintage, about which most critics and winemakers are rapturous, he ventures only that "it's a good vintage."

Bize doesn't do anything cutting-edge in the winery—vinification being pretty traditional and straightforward—but his yields are always well below those allowed by the authorities, which makes for wines with more concentration, and he's willing to pick later than his neighbors and risk losing his crop to ensure ripeness. That wasn't really a problem in the warm 2009 vintage, where even the basic Village wines from less-favored exposures got more than enough rays to ripen, and even Patrick's less conscientious neighbors managed to produce some pretty voluptuous juice. That said, even in a hot vintage Patrick's wines can be forbidding in their youth—especially the Premiers Crus—and generally need a few years of bottle age after release.

Traditionally, Savigny was known to produce a light and delicate red wine, and it cultivated this image to the point of blending white grapes in with the reds when the wines were too robust, according to the importer Peter Wasserman. In recent years, the reds have gained weight, in keeping with contemporary tastes, and white grapes, grown on the mostly limestone-rich sites, are vinified separately to create some tasty Burgundy and Savigny Blancs—not so surprising when you consider the proximity of the hill of Corton just north of the appellation, source of the majestic Corton-Charlemagne.

Another overachiever in the neighborhood is Domaine Pavelot, now run by Hugues Pavelot with plenty of help from his father, Jean-Marc, genial giants who tower above their neighbors and outperform most of them. Hugues, who did a stage in Australia before returning home, is the fourth generation of Pavelots to tend vines in Savigny. The Pavelots' Dominode is often considered the first among the many Premiers Crus, although Bize's Vergelesses, from a rocky, well-exposed vineyard at the north end of Savigny, vies with it for supremacy in the appellation.

The humble image of Savigny-lès-Beaune is slightly compromised by the presence of Domaine Chandon de Briailles, an eighteenth-century limestone manor house set within a small park laid out by the great landscape designer André Le Nôtre, who created the gardens of Versailles. Since 1834, the domaine has belonged to the noble de Nicolay family, but for much of the twentieth century it was neglected until Nadine de Nicolay moved down from Paris in 1984 to take charge. (She has since been joined by her children, Claude and François.) Knowing virtually nothing about viticulture or wine making, Nadine learned on the job, converting to organic and eventually biodynamic farming and transforming an undistinguished estate into a very good one. Although the domaine is probably best known for its Grand Cru Cortons, from the appellation just north of Savigny, it also makes several excellent Savigny-lès-Beaunes, including the Premier Cru Fourneaux and Lavières and a lighter Village red, all for less than the average Russian River Pinot Noir.

Savigny reds and whites represent very good value; while prices up and down the Côte d'Or took a big jump in 2009, you can find very good Village-level Savigny for $30, and the best Premiers Crus can be had for less than $60. There is, however, one notable exception to this rule. Those who feel uncomfortable drinking relatively inexpensive Burgundy will be happy to know that the renowned Domaine Leroy, based in Vosne-Romanée and owned by the dynamic, chic, and controversial Madame Bize-Leroy, makes a Savigny-lès-Beaune Les Narbantons that retails for several hundred dollars. It's a very good wine, made from extremely low-yielding old vines. I recently tasted the 2006 and was impressed with what Bize-Leroy had achieved in a very difficult vintage, although some critics argue that the powerful, concentrated house style overrides nuances of the *terroir*. At the very least, I'd say it isn't exactly a typical Savigny-lès-Beaune, but I certainly wouldn't turn my nose up if someone offered to pour me a glass.

Typically, Savigny is more Sunday-night-with-roast-chicken than let's-impress-the-client, which is not to say that it's simple. The better Savigny reds, particularly the Premiers Crus, can be extremely complex, and they can age and improve for years, even decades. The transplanted New Yorker Becky Wasserman, also known as the godmother of Burgundy, told me a story about entertaining a client at a restaurant in Bouilland, a few miles up the road from Savigny. The client had ordered a 1979 Jayer Vosne-Romanée Cros-Parantoux, a legendary wine from the most celebrated maker of the past century. Patrick Bize shambled over to their table and poured two glasses of something from a magnum for Wasserman and her client. "It just bloomed in the glass, and the bouquet became more and more heady," Wasserman said. "The Jayer retreated. I finally asked Patrick what it was—a magnum of 1929 Bize, never moved from the cellar."

Peasants and Plutocrats: La Paulée de New York

"What I love about Burgundy is the authenticity," says Daniel Johnnes, the hyperactive, diminutive dean of American Burgundy geeks, over an omelet at Balthazar in SoHo. "You meet a Burgundy grower, they're farmers, they spend half the day on their tractors. You shake their hands and they are calloused. When you meet a château owner in Bordeaux, his hands are smooth and he's wearing a foulard." As generalizations go, this one is pretty accurate and helps explain how special this region is for Johnnes, a self-professed "working guy" whose family were union organizers and whose father took him to protest marches in the sixties.

Two days after our lunch, he welcomed more than thirty Burgundian winemakers to New York for the tenth La Paulée de New York, and more than a few of them looked as if they'd just climbed off a tractor. Not the least interesting aspect of the event was the reverence with which these French farmers were received by several hundred of America's wealthiest and most powerful citizens, more than a few of whom travel in private jets and chauffeured Maybachs, and all of whom had paid twelve hundred bucks for dinner.

Johnnes modeled his New York celebration on La Paulée de Meursault, which was founded in 1923 when the vigneron Jules Lafon gathered his neighbors for a fall feast to celebrate the harvest. (Jules's grandson Dominique was on hand for the 2010 New York Paulée—one of the most cosmopolitan vignerons in the group.) Johnnes first fell in love with French food and wine when he lived in France as a student in the seventies. Originally, he studied cooking but eventually turned his attention to wine, becoming sommelier at Drew Nieporent's Montrachet, in what was then the wasteland of Tribeca. With its mix of casual downtown ambience and sophisticated cuisine, the restaurant helped reshape the concept of fine dining in Manhattan, and Johnnes had a significant impact on the emerging American wine scene. The list was devoted to Burgundy, and Johnnes began traveling to the source, the fabled Côte d'Or. In 1989 he invited a few of his favorite Burgundy makers to New York. "It was kind of wild. Most of them had never been to the States," he says. "I think two of them had never been on a plane." He continued to invite Burgundian vignerons to meet American oenophiles at Montrachet, and in 2000 he launched his New York tribute to La Paulée de Meursault, an event that has become an institution in the wine world, the annual American gathering of Burgundy nuts.

Actually, "nuts" might be overly kind. You have to be more than a little mad, and more than a bit of a masochist, to love Burgundy. Johnnes, with his infallible good cheer and his deep reserves of common sense, is probably the exception, although even he compares the search for great Burgundy to the quest for the holy grail. It's a fickle and unreliable lover, its mood and complexion seeming to change from one bottle to the next. Burgundy is like the girl with the curl in the nursery rhyme. When she's good, she's very, very good, and when she's bad, she's horrid. Case in point, the La Paulée collectors' dinner, an intimate $3,750-a-head feast that preceded the main event and featured wines dating back to 1966, none of which cost less than four figures per bottle and many of which were no fun to drink. The evening, which I attended thanks to the generosity of a friend—and her husband's illness—reminded me of the old Richard Pryor joke that cocaine is God's way of telling you you have too much money. The same might be said of old Grand Cru Burgundy. What's even crazier is that most of the participants weren't even shocked—Burgnuts being used to having their hearts trampled on, a price they're happy to pay for the moments of rapture and ecstasy.

The tenth annual La Paulée de New York had many satellite events, seminars, tastings, and even an auction, but the main event was the Saturday night dinner, a bacchanal the likes of which my liver hoped not to experience again for at least another week or two. The meal itself, presided over by the great Daniel Boulud, who has been La Paulée's head chef from the start and since 2005 has employed Johnnes as his wine director, would have brought an appreciative tear to the eye of Diamond Jim Brady. It's a thoroughly hedonistic experience and a thoroughly communal one. Collectors bring their best and oldest bottles of Burgundy to share with their tablemates. I brought a 1990 Rouget Echézeaux and a 1993 Anne Gros Richebourg—which in most company would've been superstars—but I frankly felt like a piker, given some of the other offerings. Early on a jeroboam of 1992 Leflaive Bâtard-Montrachet, a 1992 Coche-Dury Meursault-Perrières, and a magnum of 1985 Ramonet Montrachet appeared at our table. I knew I must be intoxicated to the point of hallucination when I found myself looking at three jeroboams (each the equivalent of four regular bottles) of Domaine de la Romanée-Conti La Tâche from the sixties in front of me—1964, 1966, and 1969, collectively worth more than a brand-new Range Rover. No, they were indisputably real, unlike the magnum of 1989 La Tâche, which was almost certainly a fake, one of more than a few. Like celebrities, great Burgundies breed impostors.

I wish I could tell those of you who weren't in attendance that these three holy of holies were crappy, or merely okay, but I can't. Just when I was about to swear off the stuff forever, which I was considering after the collectors' dinner, I was suddenly wondering how much money I could get for my eight-year-old Audi, or if I could just trade it for a single 750-milliliter bottle of the 1964 DRC La Tâche. Anybody out there in the market for a used Audi TT?

Sitting across from me was the violinist Itzhak Perlman, but the big star at our table was Aubert de Villaine, a.k.a. God, the seventy-one-year-old proprietor of Domaine de la Romanée-Conti, one of the few Burgundian vignerons who probably sports a foulard from time to time, although on this occasion he was wearing a very elegant tweed jacket and a green silk tie. But even the aristocratic de Villaine seems to be attuned to the true peasant spirit of Burgundy, clapping his hands to "Je Suis Fier d'Être Bourguignon," and singing along with les Cadets de Bourgogne, a twelve-man choir of gray-haired bons vivants Johnnes had flown in for the occasion.

When I asked about the lyrics of another song that I couldn't make out, he winked and said, "Let's just say in Burgundy there is an affinity between the appreciation of wine and of women." There was a virtual receiving line to kiss his ring—half of his time, he admitted to me, was spent dodging requests from the rich and famous to visit the Domaine de la Romanée-Conti—so I decided to skip the subject of wine and talk about opera, one of his great passions, and though I know very little about it, I thought I got more and more brilliant as the evening progressed.

If de Villaine was the Angelina Jolie of the night, he was almost upstaged by the arrival of Jean-François Coche of the legendary Domaine Coche-Dury, another superstar farmer who'd just stopped by with some friends to congratulate Johnnes. Hedge fund managers, investment bankers, and heirs to huge American fortunes—and yes, one novelist/wine columnist—almost squealed with excitement, like teenage girls who'd just been informed that Justin Bieber was in the house. And look, there's Eric Rousseau, the rumpled and taciturn proprietor of Domaine Armand Rousseau, besieged by a bellowing real estate mogul. To most in the room he's a huge celebrity, but he's clearly uncomfortable with all the attention. It would be easy to make fun of such star fucking—hey, wait, I think I just did—but I have to say that there's only one wine region in the world, as far as I know, that inspires this kind of passion, especially among an audience that can afford anything its pampered heart desires.

Sometime in the a.m. many of us repaired to the celebrity chef Tom Colicchio's latest restaurant, where the details become somewhat fuzzy, although I do remember taking bets with fellow Burgnuts on whether or not a certain sommelier's dress could continue to defy gravity. Then I realized I was defying gravity. As I was leaving, I saw Daniel Johnnes at a corner table, looking exhausted but not unhappy, and literally the only sober man in the room. For that reason alone, not to mention his great service to Burgundy, they should erect a statue of him in the center of Meursault, or Beaune, or Nuits St. Georges.

Off the Beaten Path

Way Down South:
The Great Whites, and Reds, of Hamilton Russell

The last time I visited Hamilton Russell Vineyards, I was still shivering after a morning spent in nearby Gansbaai Bay, submerged in a steel cage, which was periodically rammed by twelve-foot great white sharks crazed by chum. My friend Anthony Hamilton Russell, in the midst of preparing lunch for twelve, handed me a glass of his celebrated Chardonnay while I thawed out on the terrace of his Tuscan-style villa, looking out over the stark, pristine expanse of the Hemel-en-Aarde Valley. I remember thinking how convenient it would be for the visiting wine writer, analogy-wise, if Hamilton Russell's signature white were one of those big, strapping, take-no-prisoners New World Chardonnays. Alas, Hamilton Russell's elegant Chards, like its Pinot Noirs, are more suggestive of a brown trout rising to a dry fly than a great white slashing through a school of albacore.

If Hamilton Russell's wines are restrained and classical in demeanor, the same cannot necessarily be said for the dashing six-foot-four, forty-nine-year-old proprietor. An English wine writer, observing the vintner tearing around his rugged estate on his motorcycle, compared him to Steve McQueen. To American eyes, David Niven seems closer to the mark. Perhaps a combination of the two would be most accurate. Anthony is articulate and gregarious, his manner equal parts European sophistication and colonial exuberance, a guy who seems comfortable on horseback or on a dance floor. The wines made under his name are among the most convincing evidence of the potential of South African viticulture, although they are utterly singular in character.

South Africa's first vintage was harvested in 1659, and its sweet dessert wines were highly prized in eighteenth-century Europe; more recently, the combination of apartheid-era isolation and restrictive regulations hobbled the country's wine industry and delayed its entry into the world market.

When the wine enthusiast Tim Hamilton Russell, the director of J. Walter Thompson in South Africa, started looking for vineyard land in the mid-seventies, South African wine production was concentrated in warm Mediterranean climate zones north and east of Cape Town. A French wine enthusiast, Tim ended up buying a derelict farm at the southern tip of Africa, a mile from chilly Walker Bay. The vineyards he planted were farther south, and cooler, than any in Africa. His early vintages, crafted by the winemaker Peter Finlayson, drew favorable notice in South Africa and beyond. (Finlayson eventually bought land just up the road and is making fine Pinots of his own under the Bouchard Finlayson label.) Tim lobbied against crippling regulations and against the predominant dop system—which paid vineyard workers in wine. "He was a vocal opponent," Anthony recalls, "at a time when this attracted trouble for him within the industry. He also went on record criticizing apartheid and its expression within the industry at the time."

As a hobby farm, HRV worked fine, but after Tim quit his day job, he found it difficult to make the winery pay for itself. Tim asked his son Anthony, a Wharton Business School graduate then working for a consulting firm in London, to come home and save the farm.

Anthony admits that aside from his business training, his main credential was "helping my father drink down his collection of Bordeaux from the mid- to late-seventies," but he learned on the job. First off, he decided to specialize in Pinot and Chardonnay, the two varietals with which they'd had the most success. Clearly, the site had an affinity for these grapes. In 1995 it was rare to hear a

New World winemaker talking about *terroir*—the almost mystical French concept of "placeness"—but Anthony believed his father had found a special piece of ground, and he commissioned a thorough analysis of the soils on the 420-acre estate, finally concluding that 52 acres of clay-rich, shale-based soils were responsible for the best and most distinctive wines.

The Hamilton Russells were not the first to appreciate the qualities of the valley; the land is littered with prehistoric artifacts. Anthony, who is something of an obsessive collector, started accumulating them as a boy and now has a museum-quality collection of Acheulean hand axes made by *Homo erectus* dating from around 1.5 million years back to 250,000 years old. He's also found a more recent, late–Stone Age site in the vineyards. You don't have to be an anthropologist, or a mystic, to feel there's something incredibly special about this rugged valley.

What's special about the wines is that they bear an unmistakable signature of the place. "Vintage to vintage," he says, "it's like reading different books by a favorite author—the story changes, but the style remains, the style being the soul and character of the land." This proposition was verified at a recent tasting conducted at New York's Paris Commune: the five vintages of Pinot Noir poured by a bespoke-suited Anthony were each distinct, ranging on a scale of power versus elegance from the rich, tannic, dark-fruited 2006, which to my mind could benefit from a year or two in bottle and called to mind a ripe-year Gevrey-Chambertin Premier Cru, to the delicate, feminine 2008, which did a good imitation of a Village Volnay. The 2009 may be the vineyard's best vintage yet, although at two years old it was still too young to drink. The 2007 is a gorgeous medium-bodied Pinot that reminds Burg freaks of a Chambolle-Musigny. And yet, as I say, these wines, tasted together, have a family resemblance. The Chardonnays are equally distinct and superb, much leaner and stonier than most South African Chardonnays. While most South

African producers seem to look to the fruit bombers of Australia for inspiration, Hamilton Russell clearly has a French palate, and the 2010 Chardonnay reminded me and several sommeliers at the tasting of a Meursault. Unlike most New World wines, they are dominated more by earth (the Pinot) and mineral (the Chardonnay) notes than by pure fruit flavors. "Our wines are more expressive of site and soil," Anthony says, "than of the variety and the winemaker."

What's ironic about this, perhaps, is that South Africa's most internationally acclaimed winery is renowned for making what some call a European-style wine. "I love Burgundy, red and white," Anthony admits, and critics consistently liken the wines to those of Burgundy.

Hamilton Russell's latest venture is unmistakably South African in character. In 1994, he bought an adjacent estate—which he named Southern Right in honor of the whales that visit Walker Bay every year—devoted exclusively to Sauvignon Blanc and Pinotage. The latter is South Africa's signature red grape, a cross between Pinot Noir and Cinsault, and Anthony has cast his lot with those who believe in its potential. "I don't want my epitaph to read: 'He made great copies of Burgundy.' I want to add something to the world of wine. And there is a chance that South Africa can make something great with Pinotage." The early results are promising, full-bodied and powerful—any day now some wine writer will be comparing Southern Right Pinotage to its cetacean namesake.

Blending Their Way to an Identity:
Paso Robles

Stephan Asseo had never heard of Paso Robles when he set out for the New World. After twenty years in Bordeaux's Entre Deux Mers region, he was frustrated by the restrictions of the French Appellation d'Origine Contrôlée system and, to a lesser extent, by the weather. His quest for a viticultural Eden wound through South Africa, Chile, Napa, and Sonoma. "While I am visiting Santa Barbara," the ruddy, boyish vigneron says, pausing to light the stub of his cigar on a blowtorch, "I keep hearing about Paso Robles." Presumably, he heard this through a translator, since he spoke no English at the time. Even now, Asseo sticks strictly to the present tense, which suits his manic demeanor, and relies heavily on profanity, which he uses to express enthusiasm.

"I drive north, and I fall in love right away," he says. Standing in the middle of the rolling, hilly vineyards of his L'Aventure Winery, watching the condors circle overhead and the quail scuttling through the vines, I find it easy to understand this sentiment. "Fucking beautiful," is the proprietor's assessment. He clearly loves this land he's chosen, quite a bit of which is lodged under his fingernails.

Paso Robles is one of the most dramatic and unspoiled landscapes I've encountered in fifteen years of writing about wine, particularly in the spring, when the steep hillsides are green from the winter precipitation, sprinkled with purple lupine and yellow buttercups. Justin Vineyards' founder, Justin Baldwin, who arrived two decades before Asseo, says that the sleepy, prelapsarian vibe reminds him of Napa in the fifties and sixties. Driving along the winding, dusty back roads past grazing cattle, flocks of wild turkey, and Mennonite homesteads shaded by stands of towering live oaks, I feel as if I've stumbled onto one of the last undiscovered corners of the Golden State. The best of the wines have a special beauty of their own.

Beauty aside, Asseo's geological instincts proved astute; research showed that the soil composition on the eastern side of Paso Robles was incredibly complex and similar to Bordeaux, with lots of limestone, and the climate, with its fifty-degree daytime temperature swings, was pretty close to ideal for growing grapes with complex flavors. The Templeton Gap is a gash through the high coastal ridge that allows winds to funnel a cool oceanic influence and moisture into areas that would otherwise be sheltered.

Zinfandel was among the first grapes planted here early in the twentieth century, and these old vines eventually drew the Zin master Larry Turley of Napa's Turley Wine Cellars to establish a winery here among other Zin specialists like Dusi, Eberle, and Peachy Canyon. In the sixties and seventies Dr. Stanley Hoffman planted some of the first Cabernet, Pinot, and Chardonnay with the encouragement and guidance of the great André Tchelistcheff, one of the pioneers of the Napa Valley.

In the eighties, former banker Justin Baldwin and his wife, Deborah, focused on Cabernet and Chardonnay after they bought acreage from Mennonite farmers right across the ridge from the Hearst Castle. The glamorous couple met when he applied for a mortgage. She turned him down but eventually agreed to go on a date. Justin, who acquired a taste for wine when he was stationed in London, started out as a hobbyist, commuting from L.A. until finally moving to Paso Robles in 1991 to manage their growing estate, now one of the biggest in the area, with a production of forty thousand cases and twelve thousand wine club members, some of whom are always hanging around the special lounge adjacent to the barrel room in the new winery building. Justin Vineyards' Isosceles Cabernet Sauvignon has become a benchmark for the region, nailing big scores from the critics since the nineties—a rich, concentrated wine with a bright acidity that distinguishes it from the big Napa Valley cult Cabernets.

One of the most significant events in the development of Paso Robles was the arrival of the Perrin family, of Château de Beaucastel in Châteauneuf-du-Pape, which just happens to be my favorite southern Rhône domaine. After scouting the globe for a suitable spot with a Mediterranean climate and soils similar to those at home, they found a hilly site on the western side of Paso Robles and, in partnership with their American importer Robert Haas, began planting vines from France, producing their first vintage of Tablas Creek in 1997. Their excellent Esprit de Beaucastels, both red and white, mimic the blend of their great Châteauneuf-du-Papes—Mourvèdre, Grenache, Syrah, Counoise in the case of the red—but they seem more accessible and less earthy, possibly because of the youth of the vines. For whatever reason, they have a definite California accent, though they would never be mistaken for Chardonnays or Cabernets. At about the same time Tablas Creek went online, the winemakers Justin Smith and Matt Trevisan, of Linne Calodo, were starting to make some great wines with Rhône varietals, which they also blended with old-vine Zinfandel.

Faced with the choice of the Rhône model or the Bordeaux model, the intrepid interloper Stephan Asseo chose both. He now produces a Châteauneuf-style blend, Côte à Côte, that he calls "my prostitute wine," presumably because of its floozy sex appeal, as well as a straight Cabernet Sauvignon, which he frankly calls "a marketing concession." Cabernet being California's most recognizable varietal, he feels he needs one in the portfolio, but is far more proud of the estate cuvée, his most iconoclastic wine, a blend of Cabernet, Syrah, and Petit Verdot, which he considers the best representation of his *terroir* and his philosophy. Outside of Australia, Cab and Syrah, like crows and owls, are rarely seen together, although in fact there is a sub-rosa historical precedent: in the eighteenth century, weak vintages of Bordeaux were sometimes illegally beefed up with Syrah from the northern Rhône. Asseo thinks this combination is "pure Paso" and views the blend as his signature wine. Critics seem to agree. Robert Parker called the 2006 "a thrilling, nearly perfect effort." Other wineries, including the Cab specialists Justin Vineyards, are also producing Cab-Syrah blends.

Matt Trevisan, of Linne Calodo, is garnering praise with his quirky blends, bearing wacky names like Problem Child, Cherry Red, and Nemesis, as is his former partner, Justin Smith, with whom he parted ways. Smith has become a cult star at Saxum, where he specializes in small-production, Syrah-heavy blends, and helped to boost the profile of Paso Robles when Saxum's 2007 James Berry Vineyard was named *Wine Spectator*'s Wine of the Year in 2010. This wine is a blend of Grenache, Syrah, and Mourvèdre from a vineyard named after Smith's father. Blending seems to be the trend on both the drier west side and the east side of Paso Robles, with its proximity to the Salinas River. By contrast, in the Santa Barbara region to the south, single-varietal wines, especially Pinot Noir and Chardonnay, hold sway.

But Paso Robles is not so easily pigeonholed as a visitor might wish. Napa is inextricably identified with Cabernet, while *Sideways* has made Santa Ynez, an hour to the south, almost synonymous with Pinot Noir. When I comment on the lack of Pinot Noir in Paso Robles, Asseo tells me about his friend and neighbor Marc Goldberg, of Windward Vineyard, who makes "a great Pinot, very Burgundian, you must visit him. I give you his number."

By the time I leave Asseo's L'Aventure Winery, raising a cloud of dust along Live Oak Road in my borrowed Shelby, it's after six, and the Windward tasting room is closed, but I take a chance and bang on the door of the house beside it. The diminutive, goateed guy who eventually opens it, amid a pack of barking dogs, has all the signs of having been awakened from a nap and seems none too pleased, but he warms up when I tell him Stephan sent me and leads me over to his tasting room. Marc Goldberg pours me a glass of his 2005 Windward Pinot Noir, and when I express enthusiasm, he breaks out his 2005 Gold Barrel Select, which has the delicate complexity and earthy undertones of a Nuits St. Georges, although it finishes a little sweeter than a classic Burgundy, as do most New World Pinots.

Like many of the area's finest wineries, Windward produces a limited amount (two thousand cases) and is tough to find outside the region, although many, including L'Aventure, sell much of their wine via mailing list. The best and most enjoyable way to learn about the area's wines, and to acquire them, is to visit. If you do, be sure to bring a cigar for Stephan.

Kiwi Reds from Craggy Range

New Zealand is still best known for Sauvignon Blanc, but I predict we'll be hearing more and more about Kiwi reds in the near future. The Pinots, particularly those from the Otago region in the far south, are starting to attract international attention, and if Steve Smith has anything to say about it, New Zealand Syrahs and Merlots will, too.

For those of you who may have missed the first couple of chapters of Kiwi wine history, here's a short summary: in 1985 the Australian David Hohnen flew to New Zealand, convinced that the cool climate of that country's South Island could produce great Sauvignon Blanc. In fact Montana, a big wine company based on the North Island, had already planted Sauvignon in the Marlborough area, and the results were promising. Hohnen hired the winemaker Kevin Judd and bought land in Marlborough while producing his first vintage of Cloudy Bay Sauvignon Blanc from locally purchased grapes. The wine was soon creating a buzz and winning prizes in Australia and the United Kingdom. Within a decade Cloudy Bay had spawned numerous imitators and helped to create a new style of wine. For some reason, Sauvignon Blanc grown in cool, sunny Marlborough tastes like nothing else, certainly not the lean, grassy Sauvignons from Sancerre and Pouilly Fumé. They are brash fruit cocktails that put you in mind of grapefruit, lime, mango—just about everything you might find on Carmen Miranda's hat. The success of Sauvignon Blanc opened the door for Chardonnay, with almost twice as much acreage now devoted to the latter.

Craggy Range, founded in 1997 by Terry Peabody, yet another Aussie with deep pockets, staked out a stunningly beautiful patch of the southern part of the North Island, initially making its mark with a single-vineyard Sauvignon Blanc. For years now its Te Muna Road Vineyard has been my favorite Kiwi Sauvignon Blanc. But the winery has increasingly wagered its future on reds. While they are based in Hawkes Bay, the Craggy Range team has scoured both islands to find ideal vineyard sites for varietals we don't normally associate with New Zealand, including Syrah, Cabernet Franc, and Merlot.

The winemaker Steve Smith, a founding partner in the venture, recently visited New York and shook up my perceptions with some blind tasting over a dinner at Jean Georges, the flagship of the eponymous Vongerichten's international empire. I've known the towering and gregarious Smith for years, and he has pretty much single-handedly convinced me that New Zealand is capable of producing superb red wines. But that evening was the clincher, when he mixed his own wines in with some of the best from America, Australia, and France in a blind tasting. What was most surprising to me was that while I was usually able to identify the American and Aussie wines as New World and the French wines as Old World, I sometimes mistook the Craggy Range wines for their French counterparts. Which might have been the point. Smith certainly seemed rather pleased when I made this mistake.

We warmed up with the 2009 Te Muna Road Vineyard Sauvignon Blanc—as usual more restrained and nuanced than the typical Marlborough Sauvignon Blanc, the more extreme examples of which can taste like grapefruit juice filtered through a bed of fresh-mown grass—and moved on to a flight of Pinots. We were tasting blind, so I wasn't sure if the 2008 Craggy Range Te Muna Pinot was New or Old World, but I really liked it, much more so than I liked what turned out to be the 2006 Armand Rousseau Gevrey-Chambertin Lavaux St. Jacques, which was very lean, austere, and, at $170, expensive. Granted, it takes time for Burgundy to come around, and Rousseau is a great domaine, so I'll reserve judgment for the moment. If I'd been told which wines were in the lineup, I would have guessed that the 2005 Au Bon Climat Isabelle Pinot Noir was the Rousseau. Given that Au Bon Climat's Jim Clendenen likes to pick earlier than his California cronies, in part to achieve a Burgundian edge, maybe this wasn't so surprising. Meanwhile, Craggy Range's top bottling, the 2006 Aroha, was still young and closed up, but unlike the Rousseau it had masses of fruit in reserve. I picked this one as a Kiwi but was nevertheless surprised by how much structure, acid, and even tannin it had. This was no easy-drinking floozy by any means.

Smith is a firm believer that certain *terroirs* in New Zealand are ideal for Bordeaux varietals, with which he has been fascinated since he backpacked through that region in 1991. The experience of tasting 1990 Latour out of barrel was more or less his road-to-Damascus moment. The next flight pitted his 2007 Sophia, a blend of Merlot and Cab Franc from the right bank of the Ngaruroro River, against the 2007 Vieux Château Certan, from the right bank (what a coincidence!) of the Gironde, and the 2006 Duckhorn Three Palms Merlot. Not surprisingly, the latter, one of California's best Merlots, was the most open and opulent, being all Merlot and having an extra year of age. Merlot is generally less tannic and more flirtatious in its youth than Cabernet. The Sophia was much more restrained, yet still powerful and approachable, and I couldn't make up my mind whether it was Old or New World, whereas the Vieux Château Certan, which was wound up tighter than the inside of a golf ball, was definitely Old World.

The last flight, of Syrah/Shiraz (the former being the French nomenclature, the latter the Australian), presented a real challenge. All the wines were superb, but it was tough to make the New World/Old World calls, in part because the Rhône representative, the 2007 Chave Hermitage, came from a hot vintage and was uncharacteristically forward in style. Chave is generally acknowledged to be the greatest maker of Hermitage, though his wines usually take more than a decade to come around. The 2006 Torbreck RunRig is a New World classic—much more balanced and refined than the big jam bombs; it's one of Australia's greatest Shirazes, respected even by certain wine snobs who denigrate the Barossa Shiraz category in general. Suffice it to say that 2007 Craggy Range Le Sol Syrah was very much at home in this company, and it was tough to pick a winner.

Not hard to pick the best value, though. The Torbreck and the Chave both sell in the $200 range, while the Craggy Range is $70. Still, Steve Smith may have a tough time selling a $70 New Zealand Syrah in this market. California makers have failed in recent years to create much enthusiasm for the variety, while the market for the fruit-bombastic Barossa Shirazes, so popular just a decade ago, has been in serious decline. But I love guys who attack windmills, and I love restrained, aromatic Syrahs like Smith's Le Sol. Blind tasting, as Smith well knows, is hugely revealing, and this one suggested to me that New Zealand's wine story is well into its third chapter. If you missed the first, or rather the second, part of the story, try the Te Muna Road Vineyard Sauvignon Blanc, still under twenty bucks most everywhere—an absolute steal.

Spanish Olympian

Most American wine lovers are familiar with the Judgment of Paris, the 1976 tasting in which several Napa wines outscored the best from Bordeaux and Burgundy. The French wine establishment, including the tasters who'd participated in the blind tasting, were not amused. The spit buckets were still wet as they started to explain the results away. Patriotic French wine lovers must have been *really* pissed off three years later when a Spanish wine bested 1970 Château Latour and other top Bordeaux in another blind tasting sponsored by Gault Millau, the prestigious publisher of French food guides. The ringer was a 1970 Torres Gran Coronas, made from four-year-old Cabernet vines planted in Penedès, an area of gently rolling hills an hour west of Barcelona.

At the time of Gault Millau's so-called Wine Olympiad, Spain was best known for sherry and for the kind of rustic plonk that Sancho Panza and Ernest Hemingway's expats used to squirt out of wineskins. Torres itself was best known for a mass-produced red with a plastic bull attached to the neck. A few hard-core connoisseurs were aware of a winery called Vega-Sicilia, in Ribera del Duero, as a source of powerful, age-worthy reds, and Rioja produced some fine wines, but the general level of ambition and technical expertise was unimpressive. Thirty years later, Spain is the new Italy (which was, until recently, the new France, if you know what I mean). Every week, it seems, a new boutique wine from a previously obscure part of Spain lands here with a big noise. But no winery is more innovative, or emblematic of recent Spanish history, than Torres.

Soft-spoken, courtly Miguel Torres has light blue eyes and dresses in the tweedy style of the English country gentry, also favored by the chatelains of Bordeaux. At the age of sixty-eight, he seems to retain a youthful sense of curiosity; he has recently taken up Japanese and holds his own in a conversation with his Japanese importer, whose annual visit to the sprawling winery complex in Penedès coincides with my own. He drives a Prius, which seems as much a testament to his modest demeanor as to his passion for environmental issues. He stopped using pesticides in the early nineties, and he's committed to reducing CO_2 emissions at the winery 30 percent by 2020. He's also bought land in the cooler highlands near the Pyrenees, in case global warming makes the lowland vineyards in Penedès too hot for viticulture in the future.

The Torres family has been in the wine business for several hundred years—although the current company dates back to 1870, when Jaime Torres returned to his homeland after making a fortune in Cuba. Miguel A. Torres (who has two sons and a daughter working with him) took over from his autocratic father, Miguel Torres Carbó, who resisted many of his son's innovations but also managed to rescue the family business from the ashes of the Spanish Civil War. In the chaos leading up to the war, Torres Carbó was forced to flee the winery. "The anarchists took over in Catalonia," his son explains, over lunch at the winery, "and killed a lot of factory owners and vineyard owners. My father went to Barcelona and worked as a pharmacist and a chemist producing vaccines for the Republicans. The winery was confiscated, and the ownership went to the workers." Despite the poisonous atmosphere of class warfare, the workers apparently called the exiled boss on a regular basis to ask for advice. In January 1939, the winery was bombed and largely destroyed by Franco's air force. "Then at the end of the war," Torres says, "my father was taken prisoner and sent to a concentration camp. Fortunately, he had a cousin who was a colonel in Franco's army who managed to secure his release after a few weeks." Not surprisingly, he decided to get the hell out of Spain, moving initially to Cuba, where Miguel junior was conceived.

Torres Carbó happened to be in New York City when the news broke that the Germans had invaded France. He immediately set about courting anxious American wine importers, assuring them that he could supply Spanish "Chablis" and Spanish "Burgundy" to fill the demand for the French juice. Torres Carbó promptly returned to Spain to expand his negotiant business, buying grapes from local farmers and shipping faux French wine to the States. Miguel junior, who grew up in Barcelona, wanted to know more about the real thing; he studied oenology in Dijon and returned to Spain with a desire to make high-quality wine at home. He experimented with French varietals on a small family plot while buying and blending grapes from the local growers. Then, in 1965, an exceptional sixty-five-acre vineyard called Mas La Plana came up for sale, and Miguel convinced his father to buy it. "I knew we had to plant Cabernet there," he says. Just five years later, the infant vines produced the wine that would go on to win the Gault Millau tasting.

Not long after Franco died in 1975, Miguel senior dispatched his son to the New World. "There were strikes all over Spain and my father remembered the war. He said, 'I don't want to go through that again.'" The younger Torres, after touring California, eventually decided that Chile's Central Valley was a viticultural paradise, a conclusion that has been validated many times over in the succeeding years, though it was far from obvious at the time. In Chile as well as in Spain, they were the first to introduce new technology like temperature-controlled stainless steel fermentation tanks, at a time when locals were still stomping grapes with their feet. In 1984, some years before the area would become renowned for Pinot and Chardonnay, the family bought land in Sonoma's Russian River Valley, even as they continued to acquire vineyards in Spain, buying in emerging regions like Toro, Jumilla, and Priorat.

In the fine-wine world, of course, bigger is hardly better. Most wine geeks would say the reverse is true. Like teenage music fans who drop their favorite band at the first sign of popular acceptance, connoisseurs and critics—myself included—tend to seek out the newest and the rarest bottlings from boutique producers. I reflexively winced when I heard the production numbers—forty-four million bottles a year, 200 million euros in sales. But unlike his friend Robert Mondavi, who started out as a producer of premium wines and eventually moved down market in a way that many believed compromised the value of the brand, Torres has gone in almost the opposite direction, using the success of mass-market wines to finance the production of luxury single-vineyard cuvées. In 1984 he began a project to reclaim indigenous Spanish varietals, planting them in a beautiful walled vineyard called Grans Muralles, eventually producing one of the most intriguing new wines in Spain. The family's purchase of 250 acres in Priorat ten years later helped to seal the reputation of that area, and the early vintages are excellent—the 2007 Perpetual, for instance, made from old-vine Carignan and Grenache, is very lusty juice. Their Mas La Plana bottling, from the vineyard that produced that prizewinning Cabernet in 1970, has become a reference point for that varietal in Spain. And if you were to slip it into a blind tasting of cult Napa Cabernets, I suspect that their top Chilean Cabernet, Manso de Velasco, might upset expectations and slay some giants, just as their first Cabernet did back in the era when punk was trying to slay disco.

Location, Location, Location

Besides a little vineyard near Montmartre, in the heart of Paris, Moraga Bel Air may qualify as the unlikeliest patch of vines in the world. "A grapevine doesn't know its address," says Tom Jones, the former CEO of Northrop Aviation and current proprietor of Moraga. Which is a good thing, because vines need a hell of a lot of discipline, and if Jones's Cabernet Sauvignon and Sauvignon Blanc vines knew their address, there would probably be no dealing with them—they'd be getting agents. I almost hate to mention Moraga's location, because the wines speak for themselves—in very refined tones—and bear comparison with some of the best of Bordeaux. But the fact is these grapes are grown within sight of the Getty Museum on some of Los Angeles's most desirable real estate, which is, obviously, hugely expensive.

"I'm sick of that Hollywood and Vine stuff," says Jones, a handsome nonagenarian who would rather talk about his soils than his zip code. Moraga's wines show a subtle, complex Old World style; he himself has a quiet, patrician demeanor, and his bond with the land is palpable. "My wife and I are California born and raised," he says, standing at the base of his steep vineyard. Chickens are pecking at the dirt. It's hard to believe Rodeo Drive is fifteen minutes away. If not for the tennis court cantilevered out over the hillside on a neighboring property, or the Getty Museum across the canyon, you could easily imagine you were in an older, wilder California.

"I was born and raised in Pomona, where it was just agriculture, including vines," Jones says. "We bought this place because it was a piece of old California, and I saw it disappearing." It was formerly a horse ranch owned by Victor Fleming, the director of *Gone With the Wind* and *The Wizard of Oz*. The hard-boiled director Howard Hawks lived next door. "There used to be a lot of small horse ranches in the canyons. When we bought the property, it had chaparral and a lot of oak trees."

Jones and his wife are longtime Francophiles; as head of Northrop he regularly attended the Paris Air Show, and he used these occasions to visit some of the great vineyards of France, including Château Margaux, where he had lunch with the legendary French oenologist Émile Peynaud. "We noticed a similarity between our own soils and those of Bordeaux," he says. "We have calcareous sandstone from ancient ocean floors. The Los Angeles basin was under the ocean for millions of years." Jones scoops up a chalky fossilized snail shell to illustrate the point. Research also revealed that the canyon enjoyed a unique, grape-friendly microclimate with an average of nine inches more annual rainfall than arid downtown Los Angeles as well as cooler nighttime temperatures than in other parts of the city.

While much of Bordeaux is relatively flat, the steep hillside of Moraga Canyon is reminiscent of the best vineyards in Côte Rôtie or Chianti. In 1979, Jones succumbed to the temptation to plant grapes and eventually found that the lower-elevation canyon gravels were better suited to Sauvignon Blanc than to Cabernet Sauvignon. Early vintages were trucked up to Carneros and vinified by Tony Soter, the presiding genius of Etude (since replaced by Scott Rich). From the beginning, Jones was determined to make a world-class wine. "We knew we couldn't compete on price," he says. "We had to compete on quality. But some of the best wines in the world are made in small quantities. Look at Romanée-Conti, which is 4.3 acres."

His early vintages were praised by Jancis Robinson and Robert Parker, and Moraga became one of the first California wines featured on the list of Alain Ducasse's three-star restaurant in Paris. The former Ducasse sommelier Stéphane Colling calls Moraga his favorite California label. "The wines have so much more depth and character than most California wines," he says. "For me the white is incredibly refreshing, and the red is like a cross between Latour and Margaux." And they age well, like Bordeaux: The oldest I've tasted, from the early nineties, are wonderfully complex.

Despite his initial success, Jones knew that to get the best out of his grapes, he needed an on-site winery. Before he approached local authorities, he and his wife canvassed some two hundred neighbors to explain their plan. Construction was completed just in time for the 2005 harvest, when Moraga became the first commercial winery to be bonded in the city of Los Angeles since Prohibition.

As ambitious as he is about the quality of his wines, Jones is surprisingly demure about publicizing them, in part because he sells all he can make (about seven hundred cases of the red, even fewer of the white) to a loyal mailing-list clientele and a few select restaurants. "We try to keep a low profile," he says. When I showed up with Colling in 2006, Jones was taken aback when he learned I was a journalist and tried to discourage me from writing about the place. But after seeing the property, and tasting the 2003 red and the 2005 whites, I felt compelled to share the secret. The red reminded me in some ways of a Margaux, the latter of a fine white Graves. But in the end, as with all great wines, it is the singularity of Moraga—the voice of the land, unlikely as it might seem—that makes the story so compelling.

Swashbuckling Dandy: Talbott

You get the sense that Robb Talbott has always been a bit of a maverick, or perhaps "eccentric" is the right word. By the time he arrived at Colorado College, he'd already lost most of his hair, and the ascots and sport jackets he favored must have further distinguished him from his contemporaries. While his father had been a major in the air force, he registered as a conscientious objector; his federal court appeal succeeded just two weeks before he would have been sent to prison. Talbott's notion that great wine could be produced in Monterey County seemed pretty quixotic back in 1982, when he first planted Chardonnay vines from Corton-Charlemagne on the steep hillside where he was living in a log cabin of his own design. By now, Talbott's Chardonnays are among California's signature success stories.

When Robb was just two years old, his parents moved to Carmel to start a luxury tie company; his mother sewed the ties, and his father drove the length of California selling them from his station wagon. Young Robb accompanied them on silk-buying trips to Europe, during which the family frequently visited the vineyards of France and Italy. He remembers tasting his first Burgundy at the age of twelve. Monterey County at that time was known for the vegetables that grew in the fertile Salinas Valley. In the seventies grapes were planted, but they were inevitably sold in bulk to big producers from other areas.

The Talbott family founded their eponymous winery in 1982 with a much loftier ambition: to make wines comparable to those they'd fallen in love with in Burgundy. In 1985, while waiting for the vines at their Diamond T Ranch to mature, they bought grapes from the nearby Sleepy Hollow Vineyard, which had been planted in 1971 by a group of investors looking to cash in on the boom. Sleepy Hollow was planted on the Santa Lucia Highlands on steep benchland above the valley floor. Hillside land was much cheaper than the valley floor, and yet it soon became clear that the grapes it produced were superior to their low-lying neighbors'. (No big surprise to students of European viticulture, such as the Talbotts.)

Over the next few years, the Chardonnays fashioned by the winemaker Sam Balderas under the Talbott label became justly celebrated for their combination of intense tropical fruit and Burgundian minerality. I remember being knocked out by the first Talbott I encountered, in the late eighties, and the critics were equally impressed. Other producers were buying Sleepy Hollow grapes, but Talbott's were the standouts, which might be why the investors, when they decided to sell in 1994, offered Robb the first crack at their 450-acre vineyard. "I only had forty-eight hours to make up my mind," he says. "A major buyer was waiting in the wings." Standing at the lower edge of the property over a decade later, looking up at the rows of vines climbing up to the rugged peaks of the Santa Lucia Range above him, Talbott still clearly recalls the exhilaration and terror of that moment.

He comes across as a man of contradictions, his thick, neatly trimmed beard providing a stark contrast to his shining pate, his solid physique belying a refinement of manner. He's a kind of swashbuckling dandy, a motorcycle-racing aesthete. It's difficult to resist the temptation to compare the wines to their godfather: I can't help noting their combination of power and finesse is fairly seamless. Perhaps we should attribute that to the vineyard itself, its gravelly loam soil, its southeast-facing aspect soaking up the morning sun, dueling against the chilly influence of Monterey Bay to the west. In the end, who the hell knows?

While the Talbott Sleepy Hollow Chardonnay is undoubtedly

Talbott's signature wine, I sometimes find myself preferring its Diamond T Ranch bottling from the original hillside vineyard planted by Robb himself in 1982. Only twenty-two acres on a very steep slope, it usually yields less than a ton of grapes per acre, but that hard-earned juice makes some intense Chardonnay.

The Talbott empire includes several second labels, including Logan, named for Robb's son, which produces both Chardonnay and Pinot Noir from the Sleepy Hollow Vineyard. This Chard is more forward and easygoing than the Talbott Sleepy Hollow; the Pinot is often a very good value, although it doesn't have the potency of the small-production Diamond T Pinot Noir, nor of some of the neighboring Santa Lucia Highlands cult Pinots like those from Pisoni Vineyards. The lower-priced Kali Hart label is named for Talbott's daughter and uses grapes for its Chards and Pinots from the River Road Vineyards adjacent to Sleepy Hollow. The proliferation of names is confusing, but their labels share the same typography, the same stripped-down graphic design and coat of arms.

Other Santa Lucia Highlands producers worth seeking out include Mer Soleil, the Chardonnay estate of the Caymus producer Chuck Wagner. For bold Santa Lucia Pinots check out Morgan, Pisoni, and Roar. In the early eighties, no one believed that wines like these could come from a place best known for broccoli and lettuce, with the possible exception of the Talbott family.

Better Late Than Never: Ridge

> Monte Bello is the California Cabernet I admire above all others.
>
> —Jancis Robinson

I've been sitting here trying to figure out why it took me so long to get around to writing about Ridge, famous for its pioneering Zinfandels and for Monte Bello, widely acknowledged as one of the world's greatest Cabernets. Honestly, I think it's because ten or fifteen years ago my tastes ran a little more to flash and flesh. Like everyone else, I was impressed with the big ripe fruit bombs that literally exploded in your mouth—the super-concentrated cult wines that first appeared in the nineties, about the same time as Nirvana and Pearl Jam. The Ridge Zins of the nineties were more subtle than the new hypertrophied, high-octane versions, and the Monte Bello certainly wasn't made for instant gratification, taking years and even decades to really reveal its genius.

If the story of Ridge is hardly a new one, it's worth retelling every few years. In 2006, at the thirtieth-anniversary restaging of the famous 1976 Judgment of Paris tasting at which California wines bested some of the top French growths, judges on two continents picked the 1971 Ridge Monte Bello as the top red. (In 1976 it had placed fifth.) In a competition for new vintages at the same event, the 2000 Monte Bello also placed first. Shortly thereafter, Paul Draper, Ridge's longtime winemaker and presiding genius, quietly turned seventy and won the 2007 James Beard Foundation Award for wine making.

To find Ridge, you drive south from San Francisco toward San Jose and the congested sprawl of Silicon Valley, then turn right toward the ocean. Civilization has almost disappeared by the time you turn right on Monte Bello Road, a series of mad switchbacks that climb some two thousand feet in less than five miles. At this point you are a long way south of Napa and Sonoma. By the time you reach the lower vineyards of Monte Bello, you're wondering what kind of madman, or visionary, thought of planting grapes way the hell up here over a hundred years ago. In fact, several did, though it was a San Francisco physician named Oseo Perrone who planted and named the Monte Bello vineyard in the eighteen eighties. It has to be one of the most dramatically scenic vineyards on the planet, spilling down a wooded limestone ridge at the very edge of the San Andreas Fault, high above the Pacific and the fog line.

In 1959, four Stanford scientists bought the property as a retreat and made wine for their own consumption from the surviving vineyards. By 1969, seven years after their first commercial release, the original partners decided they needed a full-time winemaker and turned to the thirty-three-year-old Paul Draper, a Stanford grad who'd been making wine in Chile as a Peace Corps volunteer. (Don't ask.) Although he grew up on a farm in Illinois, by the time he arrived at Ridge, Draper was a multilingual epicurean. He'd attended Choate, the Connecticut prep school, before moving on to Stanford, where he majored in philosophy. After graduating, he joined the army and had the good fortune to be sent to Italy, where he spent all of his leaves touring the countryside on a motorcycle and becoming increasingly interested in food and wine. After he left the army, he went to Paris and studied at the Sorbonne. Not exactly a standard winemaker's résumé, and one can't help but wonder why the founders of Ridge chose him, but their judgment has been more than vindicated. He's become a dean of American wine making without sacrificing his broad portfolio of intellectual interests, a sophisticate who retains a youthful enthusiasm and curiosity and seems way more interested in *The New York Review of Books* than *Wine Spectator*.

While the north-coast California wine pioneers looked to UC Davis and high technology to reinvent the California wine-making tradition broken by Prohibition, Draper, who'd spent time in Bordeaux, was interested in traditional artisanal techniques, like fermenting with the natural yeasts found on the grape skins and avoiding flavor-stripping filtration in order to express the special character of the Monte Bello vineyard—what the French call *terroir*. The distance from the more established wine regions north of San Francisco probably helped to foster an independent vision. Forty years later, his peers in Napa and elsewhere have pretty much come around to his way of thinking. His trademark goatee, that Beat-era accessory, likewise made a comeback in recent years. Indeed, Eric Baugher, his wine-making colleague at Ridge, has one that's almost identical.

Draper's ambition for Monte Bello, he's often announced, was to make one of the greatest red wines in the world—in more emphatic moments he says *the* greatest—and it still is. On the basis of a 1984 and a 1991 tasted at the winery, I've concluded that he's succeeded. But along the way he and his partners realized this goal required cash flow, and they started making Zinfandel from old vines down the road and eventually, all over the state. Ridge almost single-handedly rehabilitated the reputation of that grape, creating spicy, accessible reds. While some of the early bottlings were blockbusters, the prevailing house style aims for balance over power, which has sometimes resulted in Ridge's getting over-shadowed in the numbers game of wine scores.

Though Draper remains the boss—the house palate, as it were—he runs a fairly democratic operation; I sat in on a blending committee session for the 2006 Geyserville, one of their bench-mark Zinfandels, where Draper presided over a lively debate about the merits of different vineyard lots and their worthiness to be included in the final blend. One lot Draper judged to be a little too hot, that is, overly alcoholic. "With Zin you want to be in the 14 to 15 percent alcohol range," he says, even though many of his peers are deliberately crafting fire-breathing dragons with as much as 17 percent alcohol.

His ideal Monte Bello, Draper says, is around 13 percent, a level far lower than today's average in Napa, if slightly higher than the classic pre-1982 Bordeaux. And in this quest he is aided by his relatively cool, high-altitude site. "I'm not trying to make a Bordeaux here," he says, although Monte Bello, like Latour and other top Bordeaux, takes years to reveal its greatness, which might be yet another reason he loves Zinfandel. Although they can last for decades—the 1985 Lytton Springs, tasted in 2010, was like a terrific twenty-five-year-old St. Émilion—these reds provide something close to instant gratification. The 2009 Lytton Springs was popping on its release in August 2011.

The 2003 Ridge Geyserville was the red wine I chose for my wedding dinner in 2006—and I doubt the judges of the Judgment of Paris rematch thought any longer or harder than I did before making a decision.

Old World Head, New World Body:
The Reds of Priorat

I'll never forget my first encounter with 1991 Clos Erasmus, which was pressed on me by the restaurant Daniel's sommelier Jean-Luc Le Dû in 1996. It was a curious and wonderful hippogriff of a wine with, it seemed to me, a New World body and an Old World head—a sort of thinking man's fruit bomb with lots of structure and a deep mineral undertone. It was a big wine with nuances. The next day I tried—to no avail—to track down a case or five. These wines were, and are, made in minuscule quantities; the hills are steep, the soils are poor and rocky, and the vines are stingy.

Even today the area feels isolated, though it's just ninety miles from Barcelona, the landscape primitive and almost lunar. In the twelfth century Carthusian monks planted the first grapes here, but by the middle of the last century many of these hard-to-work vineyards had been abandoned. Stately, plump René Barbier Sr., descendant of a wine-making family from France's Rhône Valley, was the guiding spirit for a band of five friends who resurrected the old terraced vineyards, planted new vines, and released their first wines in 1989. These five shared the same primitive winery until 1993. Within a few years of the first release, Priorat had become a destination for wine wonks (Gratallops, with a population of 224, now has at least five serious restaurants), and those five wines—Clos Mogador, Clos Martinet, Clos de l'Obac, Clos Erasmus, and L'Ermita—had become as sought after as almost any Grand Cru Burgundy or first-growth Bordeaux.

The lanky and garrulous Carles Pastrana was a childhood friend of Barbier's in the seaside town of Tarragona. Pastrana followed Barbier into these hills and made the first vintage of Clos de l'Obac in consultation with his friend. Pastrana waxes lyrical when he speaks of those early days, of restoring tumbledown Roman-era terraces by day and talking wine and poetry into the night. "When you're young," he says, "you have time to lose. Your capital is your time." They resuscitated the old Grenache and Carignan vineyards—which are still, especially the former, the heart and soul of the best Priorats—and planted French varietals like Syrah and Cabernet. They quoted Ortega y Gasset ("I am myself and my circumstances"). The harsh landscape and the isolation made them dependent on each other. This idyllic era culminated in the spring of 1992 when the French publisher Gault Millau touted Clos Mogador and Clos de l'Obac in a guidebook to the Catalonia area for the Barcelona Olympics, giving both wines 18 points out of 20. Robert Parker was close behind. Perhaps it's a mark of the success of their joint venture that Barbier and Pastrana no longer speak, although their wineries are literally next door to each other.

Alvaro Palacios, the fifth of nine brothers from a wine-making family in Rioja, was the last of the founding five to buy in. It wasn't until 1993 that he released what is arguably the most celebrated Priorat. Palacios's L'Ermita is made from centenarian Grenache vines in an insanely steep northeastern-facing amphitheater, which if it were a ski slope would be a Double Black Diamond. (Northeast exposure is ideal, southern exposure being apparently too much of a good thing in this torrid area.)

Scruffily good-looking and laid-back, René Barbier Jr. and his wife, Sara Pérez, both in their thirties, look as if they might be the proprietors of a surf shop in Laguna or a record store in Williamsburg, though in fact they are wine-world aristocrats, heirs to an unlikely success story. As he shows me around the cellars of Clos Mogador, René junior explains that he spent a good part of his youth living with "my hippie parents" in a trailer here near the tiny hilltop town of Gratallops while his father pursued his quixotic dream of reclaiming the moribund wine-making traditions of this rugged backwater of Catalonia.

What makes Priorat special, most local winemakers believe, is the soft blue slate and schist that underlie the vineyards. Though the degree to which decomposed minerals are absorbed by roots is a matter of some dispute, most experienced tasters would agree that the best Priorats, like the best Mosel Rieslings, exhibit a stony character that sets them apart. An earlier generation believed that the source of Priorat's distinction was divine; in the twelfth century a local man reported seeing angels carrying grapes up a stairway to heaven, after which a Carthusian monastery was established here. Priorat's wines enjoyed increasing renown until phylloxera wiped out the vineyards at the end of the nineteenth century. When Barbier and friends arrived in the eighties, the growers that remained sold their grapes to village cooperatives that produced inconsistent and often indifferent wine.

Now several of the cooperatives have been inspired by the success of the interlopers and are producing wines of character, notably Vinícola del Priorat (Ònix) and Cims de Porrera. And a second wave of ambitious outsiders is investing in the region, led by the Catalonian wine giant Torres, whose purchase of 250 acres in 1994 helped to confirm Priorat's reputation. The native son and former folksinger Lluís Llach launched his label Vall Llach in 1999.

Among the most promising of the newer estates is Mas d'en Gil, a starkly beautiful property with more than sixty acres of gnarled and wizened old vines that was purchased in 1998 by the wine broker Pere Rovira Rovira and that is managed by his daughters Marta and Pilar. The early vintages of their Clos Fontà are worthy of comparison with first-generation Priorats—and that's saying a lot.

Another second-generation property that's producing special wines is Gran Clos, purchased by the Irish-born, ginger-haired entrepreneur John Hunt in 2002, after he sold a software company he'd founded. Hunt's first big score came when he sold an English chain of coffee shops he'd founded to Starbucks, a neat trick considering that the buyer was the model he'd copied in the first place. As a child in Dublin, Hunt naturally first became interested in beer, which he started to brew when he was fourteen, but he soon turned to wine because the ingredients were cheaper. "Hops were expensive, but I discovered I could make wine out of elderflowers and oak leaves, which were free." Later, while attending the London School of Economics, he took a summer job on the ground crew for a ballooning company in Burgundy. His great epiphany came one night when he first sipped a glass of Chambertin. He can't remember the vintage or the maker, but from that moment forward wine became something of an obsession. "I started spending holidays visiting wine regions." Priorat was the one that finally stole his heart and convinced him to commit. He clearly picked good *terroir,* with some vines as much as a hundred years old; in 2005, the 1995 vintage from the property won the Priorat Wine Festival's first prize, beating out the wines of the founding five. Like their neighbors, these are wines that suggest paradoxes: rustic and sophisticated; powerful and nuanced; fruity and earthy.

Fortunately, Priorat is still far from a household word, and almost all these wines cost far less than second- or third-growth Bordeaux. You just have to look a little harder to find them.

Over the Top

His Magnum Is Bigger Than Yours

Big Boy is standing in the middle of the dining room at Cru, a three-star restaurant in Greenwich Village, waving a saber and demanding that everyone shut up and pay attention. It's not easy to shut this crowd up—they've been drinking really expensive wine for four hours and the adrenaline of big spending is in the air. But Big Boy, a.k.a. Rob Rosania, is more than capable of shouting down a roomful of buzzed alpha males. It's his party, and his magnum is bigger than anyone else's magnum. He didn't build a billion-dollar real estate empire by acting like a pussy. Signature sunglasses planted in his curly, dark mane, he's wearing a natty blue Kiton windowpane sport jacket over an open white shirt showing plenty of chest hair, and while he doesn't actually pound his chest, he often gives the impression that he's about to. He's in the process of selling off $7 million worth of his wine cellar to the assembled company—plus a few absentee bidders—and even though there are forty or fifty more lots to go, he wants to celebrate. After commanding the room's attention, Rosania hoists a jeroboam of 1945 Bollinger for all to see. Then he lowers the bottle and props it at a forty-five-degree angle as he prepares to saber it—the most dramatic and traditional method of opening Champagne, certainly no less than a $10,000 bottle deserves, and one that Rosania has perfected in the several years he's been collecting Champagne. For some reason this particular bottle is not cooperating, and it takes Big Boy a few whacks to decapitate it, but no matter. A cheer goes up as the top of the bottle goes flying, and within minutes we're all drinking a glass of Champagne made from grapes that were hanging on their vines when the Allies stormed Normandy Beach.

"Shut the fuck up and let's finish this," says John Kapon, standing a few feet above the crowd, pounding his gavel on the podium, like a judge addressing an unruly courtroom. Kapon is the thirty-six-year-old president of Acker Merrall & Condit, which bills itself as America's oldest wine store and under his watch has become the world's leading auctioneer of fine wine. It's not often that you hear an auctioneer address a roomful of well-heeled bidders this way—it's hard to imagine Sotheby's urbane, British-born Jamie Ritchie doing so—but Kapon knows most of these men personally, and the very few women in attendance are accustomed to the high-testosterone world of competitive oenophilia. The assembled company includes some of the most serious wine collectors on the planet, some of whom have flown from Europe and the West Coast for this particular auction. And none of them remind me of Frasier Crane. Raised pinkies and foppish horticultural analogies have been in short supply all night. Kapon tends to cheerfully mispronounce certain French names; "rock and roll" and "T and A" are among his highest vinous accolades. Unlike Rosania, Kapon doesn't come across as an alpha dog, at least initially . . . more like a slacker who borrowed his dad's suit for the occasion. Once he's sold off a few trophy lots, though, and downed a few glasses of Champagne, he starts to seem like the man in charge of the store.

Jeff Levy, an L.A.-based film and television director and philanthropist, who bankrolled his wife's company, Juicy Couture, and sold it a few years ago to Liz Claiborne, is in the process of dropping about $250,000 on vintage Champagne and Burgundy, including a case of 1962 Rousseau Chambertin Clos de Bèze for $80,000. Jeff has a distinctly Goth look—he's in his customary head-to-toe black, from his shades, formerly owned by Elvis, to his bespoke British crocodile shoes—and when he really wants an auction lot, he keeps his paddle in the air until Kapon tells him he's bidding against himself. Also in from L.A. is thirty-two-year-old Rudy Kurniawan, who vies with Rosania for the MDC title (Man with the Deepest Cellar) and who's alleged to spend more than $1 million a month on wine. Kurniawan is supposedly from a fabulously wealthy Chinese family, although his father gave him an Indonesian name in order to protect his privacy. Rudy is widely believed to have had a major impact on the escalating prices of the fine-wine market, and the Rosania auction includes some of his overstock, bottles of Rousseau, Ponsot, and Roumier Burgundies that would constitute the crown jewels of any other collection.

At one of the back booths sits a tall, almost gaunt, middle-aged man whose long hair is tied back in a ponytail and who seems conspicuously out of place, although a few of the cognoscenti recognize Laurent Ponsot, proprietor of one of the most revered domaines in Burgundy. Among the highlights of the auction are some twenty-two lots of old and rare Ponsot from Kurniawan's cellar. If Kapon were to announce his presence, the group would probably give him a boisterous ovation, but he remains relatively unnoticed and curiously subdued, not to say mournful, reminding at least one observer of Banquo's ghost. I forget about him until Kapon announces the withdrawal of all the Ponsot lots from the auction, at which point Jeff Levy says "Fuck!" and some of the company turn to observe the man whose grandfather founded the domaine, inscrutable in the back corner. The next time I look he's no longer in his seat.

While these kinds of multimillion-dollar auctions happen every other week in New York, what made this one unusual was the preponderance of old Champagne, a backwater category until Rosania began collecting with a vengeance after tasting a bottle of 1937 Krug he'd bought as part of a mixed-case auction lot. Tonight's climax came early, when two bottles of 1959 Dom Pérignon rosé—the never commercially released debut vintage—

provoked a telephone duel between two European bidders that quickly escalated from the opening price of $6,000. When Kapon slammed his hammer down three minutes and $64,000 later, a new record had been set for Champagne. With the so-called buyer's premium (which goes to the auction house) tacked onto the $70,000 hammer price, someone had just paid $84,000 for two forty-nine-year-old bottles of pink bubbly that very few people besides Rosania had ever tasted. The room erupted in cheers and applause. Bear Stearns had collapsed the month before, and the subprime crisis accelerated as the dollar continued its precipitous slide, but this, and several other spring auctions, proved that the market for fine vintage wine remained buoyant.

The celebration lasts until well after two, when the exhausted Kapon slips away. More wine is ordered from Cru's encyclopedic list, and Robert Bohr, the restaurant's manager, glides around the room like Jeeves, serenely presiding over the chaos. It has been five hours since we finished a three-course meal from the chef Shea Gallante, so Big Boy has six pizzas and six dozen hot dogs delivered, which are washed down with several bottles of 1990 Jaboulet Hermitage La Chapelle.

When Kapon joined the firm in 1996, after a brief foray into the music business, Acker was a somewhat sleepy operation grossing about four million a year. Sotheby's and Christie's pretty much had the fine-wine auction market to themselves, and Rob Rosania and Rudy Kurniawan had yet to become disciples of Bacchus. Like most wine geeks of his generation, Kapon's first love as a wine drinker was California Cabernets. The Napa Valley was undergoing a renaissance in the nineties, and the big ripe, voluptuous fruit-driven Cabs were easy to love, the vinous equivalent of *Seinfeld*-era Teri Hatcher. ("They're real and they're *spectacular*.") So-called cult Cabernets, small-production super-extracted wines like Harlan, Colgin, and Bryant Family, were garnering 100-point scores from über-critic Robert Parker and selling for as much as first-growth Bordeaux. Rosania and Kurniawan also cut their teeth on these Cabs—Kurniawan's epiphany wine being a 1995 Opus One Cabernet. For many serious collectors, Napa Cabs were the gateway drug that led them to the hard-core, super-addictive stuff, first Bordeaux, the motherland of Cabernet Sauvignon, which provided the inspiration for Napa, and then on to the secret kingdom known as Burgundy. (Kapon and his inner circle, like most true geeks, are Burgundy nuts; at the Rosania auction, several people booed when he announced the Bordeaux portion of the sale.)

In 1997, Acker sponsored an auction with Phillips de Pury. This and several subsequent auctions, according to Kapon, were disasters. But he persisted, even as his taste was beginning to shift toward older wines. Then, sometime in late 2000 or in 2001, Rob Rosania walked into the store on West Seventy-Second Street. Neither man can recall the moment very precisely, but their meeting would eventually prove to be a fine-wine milestone akin to Paul Allen meeting Bill Gates. Both were still in their twenties. Rosania was a partner in a real estate investment firm, a self-made mogul who was ready to spend some of his growing fortune.

Largely by cultivating young collectors like Rosania and Kurniawan—along with established collectors like the real estate baron Ed Milstein and Roy Welland, an options trader and bridge champ who also owns Cru—Kapon has made Acker Merrall the leading vendor of fine wines in America. "John has worked at it," says Peter Meltzer, author of *Keys to the Cellar*, who covers the auction scene for *Wine Spectator*. "I'm very impressed with him. He's really out there. The traditional houses have not been as aggressive." Kapon, Rosania, and Kurniawan, all in their thirties, have had a major impact on the international wine market. "You'd think they'd just be buying the best labels to show off," says Meltzer. "But they really know what they're doing. They've learned empirically. They will be able to tell you the best vintage of La Tâche tasted in the last five years."

A few years before the Rosania auction, I started receiving e-mails detailing bacchanalian gatherings with elaborate tasting notes about wines that most mortals could only dream about, sometimes dozens of them: 1959 Krugs washed down with 1945 Romanée-Contis. Wine-porn spam that had somehow escaped my spam filter, the notes were studded with references to Big Boy and King Angry and Hollywood Jef. Who the hell were these guys? I wondered. And why were they drinking so much better than I was? The author of the e-mails, I finally learned, was one John Kapon of Acker Merrall & Condit, and his fellow Dionysians were members of his tasting group, the Angry Men. The way they drink, you'd think they'd be the fucking Merry Men.

Having helped to fuel the collecting boom in this country as well as Europe, Kapon has set his sights on Asia. After selling off part of Rosania's Champagne collection, he presided over three more auctions in the space of five weeks, culminating with a May 31 auction at the Island Shangri-La Ballroom in Hong Kong that brought in $8.2 million, including $242,000 for a case of 1990 Romanée-Conti. That sale put Kapon in a good position to become a leader in the exploding Chinese market. (Acker has since become the top auction house for wine in Hong Kong.) A few years back the Chinese dropped the tax on wine sales from 80 percent to 0, and the center of the rare-wine trade, which shifted from London to New York in recent years, has moved to Hong Kong. In 2010, Acker's Hong Kong auctions outearned New York by $10 million.

Kapon scored another coup a few weeks after the rowdy Cru sale with an auction featuring wine from the cellar of Bipin Desai, a University of California particle physicist, who is one of the world's most famous collectors, in large part because of the elaborate tastings he organizes. Desai has been popping great corks since Kapon and his posse were in diapers, and he scooped up cases of Romanée-Conti and Petrus back when they were selling for the price of a room at the Ramada. Desai's sale of half of his cellar seems to be a case of acknowledging his own mortality. *So many wines, so little time.* As for the younger collectors who are selling, it's hard to say whether they are locking in profits, hedging against a possible decline, or just editing their holdings so they can buy even more. Probably all of the above. "All I can say is I've only seen prices go one way," says Kapon, as he noses a glass of 1971 Roumier Morey St. Denis Clos de la Bussière. (In fact, prices collapsed in 2009, but they've rebounded since, making the 2008 auctions look like bargain fests.)

"Tighter than a fourteen-year-old virgin," says Big Boy of one of the Champagnes he has brought to the table, and everybody seems to know what he means. By the standards of this group, a forty-four-year-old magnum like this 1964 Salon is still young and not yet fully developed. Most of these collectors are under forty themselves, but they like their wines older. It's the night before the auction, and we're seated in the private dining room at Cru, which has become the inner sanctum for New York's high-rolling wine community. Some of Kapon's biggest bidders have been invited to preview the wines at tomorrow's auction, along with select members of the Angry Men—the tasting group that he founded, which includes some of the biggest collectors in town. When I ask about the name, Kapon shrugs and says, "We're New York guys, and we don't tolerate bullshit. We're all busting balls and cracking on each other."

"Stinky as the crack of a ninety-year-old nun," says one of the Angry Men, nosing a red Burgundy that is exactly half that age. Curiously, this is intended as a compliment. There are murmurs of agreement and approval around the room. Old Burgundy is supposed to be funky, even fecal, but also elegant. Based on the following night's hammer price, the bottle in question, a 1962 Rousseau Chambertin Clos de Bèze, is worth $8,000, and it is by no means the most expensive of the wines we will taste that night, some forty in all. We follow it up with several from the Domaine de la Romanée-Conti, perhaps the single most resonant name in the world of wine worship, including a 1955 Romanée-Conti and a 1971 Richebourg, which is showing brilliantly. John Kapon's note on the wine, compiled at an earlier tasting, is a tad more formal than some of the Angry Men commentary: "incredible nose of sweet cherry, roses, wet earth, truffles, candied fruit . . . solid spice still . . . catnip, dognip—might as well call it whale bait (forgive me for that one)." He continues for another fifty words, finally concluding with the word "Stellar" and a score of 98 points. No one who tasted it that night was inclined to downgrade it.

Kapon can talk trash as well as the next guy, but he's also a serious taster who, at this point, has probably sampled—and written about—more rare old wines than almost anyone his age on the entire planet, with the possible exception of Kurniawan and Rosania, and he has the notes to prove it—thousands of them. He knows all the traditional terminology, but he's added some terms of his own, like "whips and chains," as he wrote recently of a powerful young Champagne. "T and A" is a frequently used term, and he often invokes the taste of vitamins. Robert Parker is widely considered the world's most influential wine critic, while Allen Meadows—author of the newsletter Burghound.com and a friend of Kapon's—is the Pope of Burgundy, but neither of them has tasted some of the rare and old bottles that the Angry Men routinely open at their gatherings.

Unlike some collectors, this group is drinking rather than hoarding. When I dined with the director Jeff Levy on a recent trip to Los Angeles, he invited four other friends along to Spago so we could open more bottles, seventeen in all, ranging from a

1937 Ausone to a 1999 La Tâche from Domaine de la Romanée-Conti, with a flight of Petrus—1955, 1971, and 1985—in between. The next night, at Cut, Wolfgang Puck's Beverly Hills steakhouse, we limited ourselves to a mere twelve bottles, going back to the 1929 Haut-Brion.

"The young collectors today are consumers of wine," Rosania tells me later over an alfresco lunch at San Pietro, the chic and expensive Upper East Side trattoria. He's clearly at home here, chatting in Italian with the waiter, and with the owner of the Kiton boutique next door. "Life is short," he says. "You've got to drink it." When I ask him how many bottles he has in his cellar, he says he has no idea. When I venture a guess of fifty thousand bottles, he says, "Hell, I have fifty thousand bottles of '96 Champagne." (The 1996 vintage was a great one, and by all accounts Rosania bought hundreds of cases of the rarest Champagnes as they were released, including most of the 1996 Salon that came to these shores.) When I tell him that one estimate places the value of his cellar at fifty million, he shrugs.

Having grown up in modest circumstances, Rosania clearly loves the good life, but his swaggering manner is tempered by frequent professions of noblesse oblige. "With privilege comes responsibility," he says. In fact, I've heard him say it four or five times. After his father died of prostate cancer, he helped found the Mount Sinai Hospital Wine Auction. And you can't swirl a glass at a Manhattan wine event without hearing testimonials to his generosity, not just from fellow collectors, but also from sommeliers and waiters and wine writers. "I have the privilege of owning these amazing wines," Rosania says. "To keep them to myself would be unimaginable. Wine is meant to be shared." It's a refreshing attitude, particularly if you are on the receiving end of it. The night before the auction I personally consumed, by my best estimate, over $20,000 worth of his wine—including the 1945 Mouton and the 1947 Cheval Blanc—and I was one of fourteen drinkers.

Having probably tasted more old Champagne than any of the alleged experts, Rosania has definitely formed his own opinions. Who else could tell you that the 1914 Pol Roger is one of the greatest ever made, much less prove it by pulling it from his cellar and serving it, as he did, the night before the auction? For once, the Angry Men seemed stunned nearly to silence.

Considering the age of these wines, it's amazing that most of them were brilliantly preserved, even as they acted their age. Poor storage can result in duds, Champagnes that have turned to sherry and red Burgs that have turned to vinegar. Then there are the fakes. No one likes to talk about them, any more than swingers like to talk about STDs. But just as hot art markets breed forgeries, the inexorable rise of the wine market has inevitably created a demand for counterfeit bottles. No one really knows how widespread the problem is, although anyone who has tasted enough will have come up against it. The first time I was aware of it was in 2002 when I tasted a suspiciously fruity magnum of the extremely rare and prized 1947 Petrus while dining at the home of Jancis Robinson, one of the world's leading wine critics. After the wealthy friend who'd brought the bottle went home, I asked Jancis if she really thought the wine, which tasted remarkably young and fresh to me, was either a 1947 or a Petrus. "It certainly didn't seem to be," she said diplomatically. I've since heard of a lot of dubious mags of 1947 Petrus, and in fact, given the tiny production of the vineyard and the unusual nature of the magnum format, there shouldn't be more than a couple floating around these days. Needless to say, it's generally the most legendary wines that are being faked. During my marathon with Jeff Levy in Los Angeles we encountered at least one bottle that was obviously an impostor. (Sent to our table by another collector.) One reason that Rosania's Champagne auction attracted such interest was its aura of authenticity: Big Boy had purchased most of the stuff from the original buyers in Europe, and the market for vintage Champagne is a relatively new one that hasn't really attracted the counterfeiters yet, although reports of suspicious bottles of Dom Pérignon are starting to circulate. As for Bordeaux and Burgundy, no one knows how many fake bottles are residing in multimillion-dollar cellars around the world, though sometimes we get a clue.

The billionaire collector William Koch has filed a string of lawsuits against dealers and vendors who sold him bottles that were allegedly fakes (see *The Billionaire's Vinegar,* by Benjamin Wallace), including Eric Greenberg, an Internet consulting billionaire, who allegedly sold some seventeen thousand bottles in an October 2005 Zachys auction. According to the suit, Koch alleges that before he went to Zachys, Greenberg's collection was first rejected by Sotheby's Serena Sutcliffe on the grounds that too many bottles were fakes. Acker Merrall subsequently held a major auction from the so-called Golden Cellar (as opposed to Kurniawan's, which is referred to as "*The* Cellar"). For the Golden Cellar auction Kapon rejected lots that he found suspect and attached an unprecedented eighty pages of documentation to the catalog for this auction. "All the great collections in this country have lemons," he says. "You've got to navigate around them."

Kapon's navigational skills seem to have temporarily deserted him when he accepted twenty-two lots of alleged Domaine Ponsot Burgundy from Rudy Kurniawan for the Rosania sale. When Laurent Ponsot saw the catalog, he immediately called Kapon to express his doubts about the authenticity of the lots and later attended the auction in order to make sure that the disputed wines had indeen been withdrawn. Seeing photographs of the purported Ponsots in the Acker catalog, Laurent found problems with all of them, including the alleged 1929 Clos de la Roche; his grandfather didn't start estate bottling until 1934, a fact that was clearly stated in the catalog. Also problematic, the 1945, 1949, 1959, 1962, 1966, and 1971 Clos St. Denis. All great vintages, but Laurent's father produced his first vintage of this wine in 1982.

A few weeks after the Big Boy auction, Kapon agrees to meet me at Veritas, the Flatiron District restaurant that vies with Cru for the title of Wine Geek Central. (Veritas was opened in 1998 by the collectors Park B. Smith and Steve Verlin in part because of the surpluses in their massive cellars.) Although Cru is his headquarters, he's clearly a regular here and treated as a visiting dignitary. He arrived with his girlfriend, Dasha Vlasenko, a statuesque, Estonian-born former model. (They married in 2009.) They met at a party, and she took a while to warm up to him. "He was incredibly persistent," she says.

Kapon looks a little ragged tonight, pale and puffy faced, with a three-day growth. He quickly orders a 1996 Drouhin Marquis de Laguiche Montrachet, a Grand Cru white Burgundy, then fills me in on his schedule. Less than three weeks after the Rosania auction he's busy preparing for three more to take place within the month. Fans of his wine porn have bemoaned the fact that he's weeks behind posting his tasting notes, but it doesn't seem as if he'll catch up anytime soon. Not with a trip to Hong Kong and a barrage of dinners, at one of which he will be inducted into the Commanderie de Bordeaux, and others devoted to the wines of Pichon Lalande and Romanée-Conti, all of which sounds daunting, particularly for his liver.

This counts as a down night for Kapon. After we polish off the Montrachet, he orders a 1998 JF Mugnier Musigny, a rare bottle from another legendary Burgundy vineyard that we both liked a great deal, and that should have been the wine of the night except that by the time our second course arrived, we'd finished it. So John ordered a 1971 Roumier Morey St. Denis Clos de la Bussière, which, as a Premier Cru, is lower in the hierarchy than the Grand Cru Musigny. But it blew the youngster away. John later observed of the wine, "Autumnal aromas were inviting like football season, and meat dripped from its bones like parking lot cookouts."

Halfway through the bottle John spotted Danny DeVito across the room and asked the sommelier to send him a glass. We could see that he was drinking a Colgin Cabernet, very serious juice, if not quite Burgundy. "I don't know if he's a Burgundy man," I said.

"Hey, just open up and say ah," John said. "You don't have to know it to love it." And sure enough, a few minutes later DeVito hoisted the glass aloft and waved Kapon over to his table. They were still talking twenty minutes later.

Aged Effervescence: 1996 Champagne

Most Champagne is consumed soon after its release; until fairly recently, the belief that it could improve and develop with age was a heresy restricted to the English upper classes and the Champenois themselves. But in fact its high acidity acts as a natural preservative, and certain years are particularly conducive to making long-lived bubblies. Like the great reds of Bordeaux and Burgundy, Champagne can develop tremendous complexity as it ages. The rise of aged Champagne as a collectible category is a recent phenomenon, and it really gained momentum with the 1996 vintage.

The year was being hailed, even as the grapes were being picked, as one of the greatest ever, and its reputation has only grown ever since. What was remarkable was that the almost unprecedented level of ripeness was accompanied by very high acidity. Ripeness without acidity is a recipe for flabby, short-lived Champagne; the 1996s on the other hand seemed destined for a long and happy life, although the high acidity meant that they would take a long time to really integrate and show their true colors.

I decided to revisit them on the occasion of their fifteenth birthday to see how they were coming along and to that end invited some of New York's best sommeliers to join me in a tasting of the top cuvées, most of which I'd bought on release. The restaurateur Ken Friedman offered to host us at the Monkey Bar; he's been hired to sex up the food and beverages at Graydon Carter's celebrity watering hole and has engaged the services of the super sommelier Belinda Chang, who in 2011 won the James Beard Foundation Award for wine service.

Under the eyes of the Edward Sorel caricatures on the walls—Zelda and Scott, Dorothy Parker, and others—we started off with four Blanc de Blancs: 100 percent Chardonnay Champagnes, most from the prosperous, Mercedes-infested Grand Cru village of Mesnil: the Pol Roger Blanc de Chardonnay, the Guy Charlemagne Mesnillésime, the Taittinger Comtes de Champagne, and Salon, the holy grail of B de B. The Pol was delicious and toasty but a little advanced—probably not a perfect bottle. The Guy Charlemagne, a small-grower Champagne, was a surprise hit, lively, fresh, and dry. Most controversial was the Taittinger. Bernard Sun of the Jean Georges group called it "lively and opulent," and Belinda liked "the brioche on the nose," whereas Raj Vaidya of Daniel, serving as the class clown, thought it smelled "like the air coming out of the subway on a hot day" or "a decaying dishrag." The Salon, we decided reluctantly, was slightly corked. Aldo Sohm of Le Bernardin, named Best Sommelier in the World in 2008, and probably our most technical taster, was the first to identify the problem.

From there we moved on to Pinot Noir–dominated wines, starting with the sensational Pol Roger Cuvée Sir Winston Churchill, which the former prime minister's favorite Champagne house created in his honor after his death. The soms were shouting their approval, drowning one another out with praise. It was more like a wine than a Champagne, so complete it was hard to dissect. The Dom Ruinart that followed didn't stand a chance. Aldo felt it was too sweet, and Raj pretty much spoiled it for everyone when he detected petroleum jelly on the nose. The Bollinger Grande Année on the other hand was wonderfully austere and dry, beloved by all, though Carla "Downtown" Rzeszewski of the Breslin claimed she'd had a better bottle this past Christmas, to which John Slover of Ciano retorted, "Yeah—it was *Christmas.*" These tastings can get feisty.

The next flight was a clash of the titans—Cristal, Dom Pérignon, and Dom Pérignon Oenothèque, the latter from Raj's cellar. The Cristal was extremely ripe and rich, a little sweet for some tastes, including Aldo's; our youngest som, Jerusha Frost of the Lion, who looks as if she were painted by Dante Rossetti, admitted that she was prejudiced against Cristal on principle, but said she really loved the wine. Belinda was also a fan. The Dom Pérignon, which we have all loved in the past, wasn't showing well, but the Oenothèque, a late release that was disgorged in 2008, some four years after the regular bottling, was absolutely stellar, though it was a bit out of context, seeming both fresher and younger than the earlier-disgorged wines.

Everyone loved the 1996 Philipponnat Clos des Goisses. Never heard of it? Clos des Goisses has always been an insider's fave—as opposed to the kind of Champagne a Russian oligarch would order to impress his young date. Raj felt it was basically a red wine in character. Carla Rzeszewski, whose dark hair was frosted with white highlights that night, said, "This wine makes me want to flip the table over it's so beautiful." (That's my kind of wine note, though my thought was to leave the table upright and ravish someone on top of it.) Keri Levens of Aquavit said she loved the "sexy roasted-pineapple notes. I just can't stop drinking this." We also loved the next one, the Billecart-Salmon Clos St. Hilaire, a single-vineyard, 100 percent Pinot Noir Champers that was very powerful, rich, and complete—though it didn't inspire any acrobatic feats. Bernie, who provided a steady note of decorum, said it was "like a great Burgundy." (This was a theme—when the soms really love a Champagne, they always compare it to a great still wine.) Raj said it was one of the greatest he'd ever had. The 1996 Krug, often heralded as the wine of the vintage, was searingly tart and acidic. John said he'd had a similar bottle in the past month, with Raj, so caveat emptor. (The 1995 we threw in for comparison was terrific.) If it develops like the 1990 and the 1988, all will be well in the end.

The final flight was composed of rosés. Foolishly, someone had decided to pour the Dom Pérignon first, which was hardly fair because it was so regal, pure and precise and dense, that it was an almost impossible act to follow. Incredibly young and tight, though. By contrast, the Dom Ruinart, provided by Jerusha, was very showy and friendly, as was the Comtes de Champagne rosé, but both ultimately seemed a little floozy compared with the DP.

I asked everyone to rank their top three wines, and the Clos des Goisses was the clear winner. Damon Wise, the Monkey Bar's new head chef, claimed to be a wine novice but ranked it number one, as did five of the sommeliers, including Shin Tseng of Lupa, the least voluble member of a fairly noisy group. The Cuvée Sir Winston Churchill ranked just slightly ahead of the Bollinger Grande Année and the Billecart-Salmon Clos St. Hilaire. Two of the soms chose the DP rosé as their champion, while Belinda broke ranks by choosing the Cristal as number one.

We were blown away by many of these 1996s and disappointed in a few. Of course, bottle variation and cork problems are facts of the wine lover's life. Bernie considered the results reflective of a "very good but not great year." John thought the 1996s lived up to their billing, with "firm structure, complexity, and great longevity." Richard Geoffroy, the winemaker of Dom Pérignon, told me later that it was "a puzzling vintage, made of the winds" (September winds dehydrated some later-picked grapes). He thinks some Pinot-based wines may disappoint in the long run.

I'd like to repeat this tasting a few years down the road. Two things we all agreed on: that many of these wines were truly great and are just barely coming into their maturity; and that mature-vintage Champagne is a treat worthy of a much wider audience. Well, at least most of us agreed on this—Raj at one point suggesting that we keep the secret to ourselves.

A Towering Red: Château Latour

When Frédéric Engerer was a university student in Paris, he would drive once a month to Burgundy. "For a young man in his twenties, Burgundy was less intimidating," he told me, "and you can get appointments more easily." Bordeaux, with its grand châteaus and wealthy absentee owners, is much more formal and daunting. The first time Engerer ever set foot on the hallowed ground of Bordeaux's first-growth Château Latour was after François Pinault had offered him the job of managing the place. "Latour had always been a mystical estate for me, but I honestly didn't dare ask for an appointment at Latour in those days."

The appointment of Engerer to run this fabled domaine caused almost as much comment as Pinault's purchase of the property in 1993. One of Europe's most successful and wealthy businessmen, he acquired Latour from Allied Lyons. At the time he was hired, Engerer was working as a management consultant in Paris, after a previous stint in advertising; the Bordelais were understandably baffled by the appointment, which had been recommended by Pinault's son François-Henri, who'd gone to university with Engerer, who, in fact, grew up in a family of wine merchants from the Languedoc Roussillon and spent his summers working in his grandfather's cellar. Even as his business career flourished, most of his free time revolved around his love of wine. He visited Burgundy on weekends and opened a wine bar in Paris. Getting the call from Pinault was basically the equivalent of an aspiring rapper getting tapped to record a track with Jay-Z. Latour is, by anyone's reckoning, one of the greatest domaines on the planet.

The wines of Latour were already highly regarded when Alexandre de Ségur, a.k.a the Prince des Vignes, a big Bordeaux landowner, married Marie-Thérèse de Clauzel in the late sixteenth century, thereby adding Latour to his holdings. He also owned Château Lafite (which would become beloved of Chinese collectors four centuries later) at the northern end of the commune of Pauillac. Both Latour and Lafite were anointed as first growths in the 1855 classification of Bordeaux estates—along with Châteaux Margaux and Haut-Brion—although by then they were separate entities. Latour remained in the de Ségur family, but Lafite was sold to a Dutch group, from which it was purchased by Baron James Mayer Rothschild in 1868.

Latour was named for a tower, or castle, built on the property in the fourteenth century and razed more than a century later at the end of the Hundred Years War (the catchy title by which that 116-year-long conflict is remembered). The three-story "tower" that stands on the property today is actually a *pigeonnier,* or dovecote, built in 1625 and is not, as is commonly imagined, the structure that gave the estate its name. The wine would presumably be called Latour even if it was a dainty and delicate wine, but this is not the case: Latour is a huge wine that can seem entirely unassailable in its youth and seems to measure its age in geologic time. A Latour from a good year can take thirty years to show its charms, and when it does so, its virtues are almost inevitably described with adjectives that skew toward the masculine end of the spectrum: robust, powerful, massive. I've never seen the word "pretty" in any tasting notes. (Lafite, by contrast, has always been characterized as lighter and more ethereal, though the wine-making style has become more robust in recent years. I'm sure it's not fair to think of Lafite as rhyming with "effete," but it's a useful mnemonic.)

"Latour is not an easy woman," Engerer told me when we first met. (Indeed, I don't think it's a woman at all—I think it's a man.)

"It requires patience. It doesn't give much up at an early age. It's a long runner. It often surprises you, even when you think the wine is—theoretically—ready for drinking." There is, in other words, something terribly anachronistic about Latour; it's the antithesis of instant gratification. If that doesn't scare you, consider how forbiddingly expensive it is, as are all of the first-growth Bordeaux. New levels of insanity—over $1,000 a bottle—were reached with the release of futures for all the 2009 and 2010 vintages.

Even Engerer—whose boss can't be all that sad about this situation—seems a little chastened by what has happened to the price. "My first *en primeur* campaign was with the '94 vintage, which we sold for 28 euros a bottle." (This is the ex-cellar or wholesale price.) "Now we sell the wines at 500 euros a bottle." As a young man, Engerer and his friends would enjoy the occasional first growth. Now, he admits, they've become inaccessible for most wine lovers—a depressing situation for those, like me, who love Latour. True, massive capital investment has been made since Pinault took over. The new winery is spectacular, and production of the *grand vin* has been cut drastically in order to improve quality. None of this would matter if not for the situation and composition of the land itself.

The main vineyard occupies a rise above the Gironde estuary and is composed of a thick layer of gravel, providing excellent drainage, over a bed of clay. Lafite and Mouton sit on sand. I can't begin to explain the interaction of roots and soil—and I don't know that anyone can, except to say that the superb drainage means Latour is good even in rainy vintages—but I can assert with confidence that Latour's unique *terroir* creates a unique wine. Over the years it has retained its signature character no matter who has made it, with an unparalleled ability to age and to develop. The 1961, which I tasted for the third time with Engerer, is one of the greatest I've ever encountered, a Beethoven's Ninth of a wine, and is still on its way up. The 1982, for me the wine of the vintage, is still a baby. But they are clearly siblings, remarkably similar in their aromatics and their flavor profiles, despite being made by different teams, twenty years apart. They're incredibly powerful but nuanced; every sip or sniff yields something new. Even in a poor vintage, like 1964, which I also tasted with Engerer, Latour is similarly complex, just not as powerful or concentrated. I think if Latour were an actor it would be Gregory Peck; the 1961 would be Peck in *To Kill a Mockingbird*, the 1964 would be that actor in *Beloved Infidel*. He has many of the same qualities in the latter movie, though he doesn't quite leap off the screen into archetype as he does in the former.

Is any of this relevant to the average wine lover, as opposed to the wealthy collector? It is, I think, in several ways. Just as developments in Formula One race cars eventually inform the engineering of the cars the rest of us drive every day, the no-expense-spared aesthetic of Latour under François Pinault serves as an inspiration for winemakers in Bordeaux and the world over. Unlike, say, Screaming Eagle, a Napa Valley cult Cabernet that costs more in most vintages, Latour has a proven history; you know that the 2010 vintage, when you or your heirs pop the cork thirty years from now, will be spectacular. It is the ultimate exemplar of the notion of wine improving with age. Interestingly enough, mature vintages of Latour are available at auction for less than later vintages like 2003 and 2005, a market anomaly that reflects the rapid escalation of prices in the first decade of the twenty-first century. It's generally conceded that Latour went through a bit of a slump between 1983 and 1990, but the latter vintage was a triumph, and the Pinault-Engerer era has produced a string of trophies, notably the 1995 and 1996, the 2000, 2003, and 2005.

There is only one Latour, but happily Pinault and Engerer have extended their vinous empire, together and separately. The man who owns Gucci, Christie's, and Yves Saint Laurent has very good taste in wine *terroir*. In 2006, Pinault bought the Domaine

René Engel in Vosne-Romanée, much to the delight of Latour's Burgundy-loving president. Engel owned choice vineyards in Vosne, notably in Grand Cru Clos-Vougeot. Pinault and Engerer rechristened the property Domaine d'Eugénie, and beginning with the 2007 vintage the results have been exciting. In the spring of 2010, Pinault rocked the wine world once more with the purchase of Chateau-Grillet, a spectacular property in the northern Rhône adjacent to Condrieu, which is an appellation unto itself. Long renowned for its unique, long-lived Viognier-based white wines, it has been badly underperforming for two decades, and I know I'm not the only one who's thrilled that the estate is finally in the hands of the Latour team.

Engerer, meanwhile, has a couple of side projects in his native southwest. In 1996 he and his friend Jérôme Malet acquired a vineyard in the Pyrenees that they planted with Cabernet vines sourced from the heart of Latour. The wine, Marius, has received stellar reviews in the French wine press and sells for about a thirtieth of its genetic parent. Later they bought a property in the southern Rhône called Fontbonau, where the wines are made from old-vine Grenache and Syrah. Both places are already producing very good wine, though Engerer would be the last to compare them with Latour.

Latour is Latour is Latour. In the opinion of some it's easily the world's greatest red wine. If you really love wine, you owe it to yourself to find a way to taste a mature example and decide for yourself.

What to Drink with Thirty-Seven Courses:
El Bulli

It begins with a glistening, olive-colored sphere, wobbling on a spoon as you raise it toward your lips, exploding in the mouth to unleash a bath of intense olive-flavored liquid. Then, as the waiter has instructed, you raise the silver atomizer to your mouth and spray the gin-and-vermouth mixture on your tongue. In your case three sprays for good measure. Or seven. (The waiter didn't specify how many.) This is your martini, as deconstructed by Ferran Adrià. The meal ends some thirty-four courses later—just after the penultimate frozen foam of Parmigiano Reggiano—with another trembling sphere, which turns out to be a reconstituted lychee. You've made your way here to El Bulli, Adrià's remote beachside restaurant in Cala Montjoi, some two hours north of Barcelona, to check off a prominent entry on your list of Things to Do Before You Die, and to try to find out why the world's greatest chef is shutting down the world's most celebrated restaurant at the height of its fame.

At a ceremony in his honor at the Madrid Fusión food festival in January 2010, Adrià announced that in 2011 he would close El Bulli for two years. The closing of El Bulli made headlines around the world, including the front page of London's *Financial Times*. "It reminds me of how I felt when I heard the Beatles were breaking up," a gourmand of your acquaintance confessed. Less than two weeks later, as the international fraternity of foodies was absorbing the news and trying to think of how to score a reservation before the hiatus, the forty-seven-year-old chef explained that in fact he would be closing the restaurant permanently. Then he seemed to disappear for several months. Meanwhile, two million people tried to book reservations in El Bulli's few remaining months.

Assuming that you defied the astronomical odds and were granted one of the forty-eight seats available nightly, five nights a week, in season, possibly because your girlfriend used to date a chef who had once done a stage in El Bulli's kitchen or you were writing for a well-known publication that had called in a lot of chits, you would probably fly to Barcelona, where if you were unlucky—or just absentminded and careless—your new Prada carry-on bag would be stolen from behind your chair while you paused to eat a sandwich in an airport café. After a fruitless discussion with a policeman, you would proceed to the Avis counter to collect the keys to your rental car and ask the clerk to write down the directions and then proceed with great trepidation into the labyrinth of freeways encircling Barcelona.

Allowing for one wrong turn and twenty minutes of panic— God damn it! How can *both* directions lead to Gironde?—you arrive in the town of Roses, a scruffy resort on the Costa Brava, only to realize that your itinerary was in the stolen bag and you don't remember the name of your hotel, of which Roses has dozens. You have to remind yourself at this point how lucky you are to be one of approximately seven thousand people who got a reservation at the greatest restaurant in the world this year, even as your wife begins to express her skepticism about the whole cost-benefit equation of this quest.

You tell her what Mario Batali said when you asked his opinion of Adrià: "Dudeski, he's simply the most influential chef for chefs in our time. He has provoked more interest—both good and angry—in food and restaurants than anyone ever. True to his Catalonian roots—like Dalí, Casals, and Miró—he's created a new way to work with raw materials that challenges a lot of what had previously been considered 'the rules' about eating and cooking."

When Hans Schilling and his wife, Marketta, discovered the cove called Cala Montjoi in the nineteen fifties, the hills and the shoreline were untouched except for a small house from which the Civil Guard watched for smugglers. Schilling was a German doctor who fell in love with the rugged Costa Brava and eventually bought five and a half acres above the beach. They built their home above the treacherous road from Roses and constructed a mini golf course to attract tourists as well as a beachside snack bar. The golf course was a failure, but the Schillings, who were prototypes of the species known as foodies, decided to turn the snack bar into a real restaurant, the kind that might someday attract people like themselves to the remote cove. The restaurant was named after Marketta Schilling's beloved French bulldogs, *bulli* being a French slang term for that bat-eared breed. Meanwhile, Hans Schilling took up with his German housekeeper, but he continued to visit his wife and subsidize the restaurant.

In 1975, the year that Franco's death signaled the beginning of the end of Spain's cultural isolation, the Schillings hired Jean Louis Neichel, an Alsatian-born French chef with an impressive résumé. In 1976 he won El Bulli its first Michelin star, although how the inspectors found the place is a bit of a mystery. There was no telephone, and the road from Roses was so bad that vendors from the town, seven miles away, refused to deliver supplies. One early customer—the British pop artist Richard Hamilton, who first visited El Bulli with his neighbor Marcel Duchamp—used to pilot his Zodiac from nearby Cadaqués and land on the beach.

In 1981 the Schillings hired Juli Soler, who would later become Adrià's business brain, to manage the restaurant. A Rolling Stones fanatic, he'd previously run a discotheque and enjoyed a brief career as a concert promoter. El Bulli got a new French chef, Jean-Paul Vinay, in 1982, and the next year his nouvelle-cuisine menu won a second Michelin star. That same year, a young naval recruit named Ferran Adrià decided to spend his summer leave in the kitchen at El Bulli. Adrià, who'd had some restaurant experience before being called up for his military service, had been assigned to work in the admiral's kitchen, where he eventually met Fermí Puig, another young chef, who would become his best friend. When Puig arrived in the admiral's kitchen with a collection of French cookbooks, they set about teaching themselves the techniques therein. It was Fermí who suggested they try a stint at El Bulli.

"He told me it was one of the best in Spain and that it had two Michelin stars," Adrià wrote in his book *A Day at El Bulli*. "At that time I had no idea what that meant." Ferran was more interested in the restaurant's proximity to the beach and the nearby resort town of Roses, which attracted Swedish and German tourists. A high school dropout who had hoped to play professional soccer, Adrià had taken his first restaurant job as a dishwasher at the seaside Hotel Playafels so that he could finance a summer in Ibiza. He would often show up at the chef Miguel Moy's kitchen only an hour or two after he left the bars and discos, but he demonstrated a remarkable aptitude for cooking. In his biography *Ferran: The Inside Story of El Bulli and the Man Who Reinvented Food*, Colman Andrews reports that one day Moy called Adrià's father, who had arranged for his job, and said, "Please take your son back, because now this boy knows more than me."

When he finished his military service in 1984, Adrià returned to El Bulli and, when Vinay left to start his own restaurant, became the *chef de cuisine*. Adrià was joined by his younger brother the following year, and Albert would go on to become the pâtissier, responsible for most of the exotic and bizarre desserts that were an important part of the menu. Ironically, it was a traditional French chef who provided Adrià with his road-to-Damascus moment, his conversion to the avant-garde. In the early days El Bulli's menu reflected French traditions as well as the innovations of nouvelle cuisine, but in 1987 Adrià decided to try to invent his own style after listening to a lecture by the Chantecler chef Jacques Maximin. "Creativity means not copying," Maximin had declared in answer to a question. "This simple sentence was what brought about a change in approach to our cooking," Adrià wrote later, "and was the cut-off point between 're-creation' and a firm decision to become involved in creativity." That year he decided to close the restaurant for five months in the winter—a period later extended to six months—and devote the hiatus to experimentation. One early innovation, created with the help of a whipped-cream siphon, was the famous "foam"—essentially a superlight mousse—that has since become something of a gastronomic cliché, imitated from Toulouse to Topeka. Adrià's first foam, made of white beans and served on a sea urchin, appeared in 1994. He even made a foam infused with wood smoke. At about this time he began his "deconstructions" of traditional recipes such as his "chicken curry"—chicken sauce over curry ice cream. This new cuisine would eventually be tagged with the label "molecular gastronomy," a phrase Adrià is weary of, though he may never escape it. He prefers "avant-garde cuisine."

El Bulli gained a third Michelin star in 1997, but perhaps even more significant was the declaration by Joël Robuchon the previous year that Ferran Adrià was the best cook on the planet. Widely regarded as the best chef in the world, Robuchon ostensibly retired in 1996 and identified Ferran Adrià as his "heir" in a French television interview. That the grand master of the French culinary tradition passed the baton to a Spaniard provoked howls of indignation in France. In fact, *l'affaire* Adrià was only one of many signs that classical French cooking had stagnated and that Spain now represented cuisine's creative cutting edge, a perception that was endorsed by a 2003 cover story in *The New York Times Magazine* headlined "The Nueva Nouvelle Cuisine: How Spain Became the New France." The Chicago chef Charlie Trotter was quoted in it as saying, "Spain is where the zeitgeist has shifted." At the center of this shift was Adrià. "Like Elvis or Miles," wrote Arthur Lubow, the author of the piece, "he is usually known by his first name alone: Ferran."

Adrià himself acknowledges that the *Times* article was seminal in the history of El Bulli. "It was the consolidation of our reputation," he says. "The beginning of the myth." In 2006, *Restaurant* magazine named it the World's Best Restaurant, a title maintained for the next four years. Suddenly Adrià was an international celebrity, and every single gastronome wanted a seat at his table, along with countless heat seekers who didn't know the difference between a puree and a foam. One can only imagine the frenzy of sharp elbows and conspicuous displays of entitlement that might have resulted if El Bulli had been located in New York, or even Barcelona, which is on everyone's New Europe itinerary.

Like many before her, my wife couldn't help wondering why El Bulli was located so far from civilization, a question Adrià answered in the course of a two-hour monologue without my even having to ask it. "We wanted to create a discourse with our diners, to create an experience," he said, when we met him at the restaurant a few days after the commencement of its final season. We were sitting on the terrace, overlooking the beach at Cala Montjoi and the Mediterranean, the view framed by pines. I had just driven some twenty-five minutes over the still treacherous road—in fact passing an accident scene, where two police cars with flashing lights were perched at the edge of the road, a banged-up Audi at the bottom of the hillside fifty yards below. By all accounts the road was much improved since the early days. The rugged countryside was extraordinarily beautiful, the steep hillsides covered in olive trees and pines. "The road coming here, getting a reservation, it's all part of the experience." But more than that, he added, "this project would only be possible outside a city. For many years almost nobody came, so we had time to grow and experiment. The environment, the peace and tranquillity here, make our work possible."

The landscape may have been tranquil, but Adrià is anything but. For two hours he talked, answering my first question, waving his arms for emphasis, pausing only when our translator touched his arm to remind him that she needed to do her job, listening intently to her translation, and sometimes repeating a word or nodding in agreement. His plastic, wildly expressive face reminded me a lot of Jackie Gleason's. I started with a simple question, the one that everyone was asking: Was El Bulli really closing for good?

"A lot of people talk about this, but no one really understands it," he said. He admitted that even he was taken aback by the international hue and cry occasioned by his announcement at Madrid Fusión that he was closing the restaurant for two years. At the time, his vision of the future was somewhat inchoate, but in the intervening months his plans have become more concrete.

"If you look at the history of El Bulli, you will see that it's exceptional. This is a logical stage of the evolution of the restaurant. In 1987 we decided to close for six months of the year." In 1998 he founded the Taller, a kitchen/laboratory in Barcelona where the El Bulli team experimented and created new dishes in the off-season. "In 2001, when El Bulli was becoming very well-known, the logical thing would have been to stay open year-round. But for us the most important thing was creativity. So instead we decided to close for lunch, and the level of creativity kept getting higher. But at some point I realized we wouldn't be able to continue to evolve as a restaurant." In other words, in order to save El Bulli, he would have to close it to the public.

As El Bulli evolved and became more and more successful, it became less and less accessible. At each stage, pushing the boundaries of cuisine required a respite from the demands of running a restaurant. Viewed from this perspective, closing the restaurant is the final stage in its creative evolution. The pressure of customers, the spectacular disparity between the supply of seats and the hordes of people who wanted them, seemed to have reached a kind of tipping point. Ferran's a friendly and gregarious man who travels extensively in the off-season, and everyone he meets, sooner or later, will ask for a reservation for himself or a friend or a friend of a friend. And Ferran hates to say no, though he claims to have no problem turning away celebrities. "Only if it's somebody I really admire," he said. "I don't really care about movie stars. I want this to be a democratic place." For this reason he refused to charge what the market would bear; 250 euros a head isn't cheap, but he could charge triple that and still fill the place ten times over. "It's an affordable luxury." But he realized the result wasn't so much a democracy as a nepotocracy; chefs seemed to form no small part of the clientele, plus friends of friends. When I ran into a Williams classmate in the dining room, I asked how he'd gotten in, and he explained that his girlfriend worked in a museum whose director was a friend of Ferran's.

In 2014, El Bulli will reopen under a different format, one that probably won't accommodate paying customers. "It will be kind of a think tank," Adrià said. "Not a school exactly, but a foundation. A private nonprofit foundation." He still seemed to be improvising, refining the concept. "We'll have twenty-five people here, chefs, two or three journalists, tech people. At the end of the day our work will be posted on the Internet. We will collaborate with the world of art and design. It will not be a restaurant. No Michelin, no customers, no pressure. Every year will be different."

"There aren't enough professionals dedicated to analysis and research," he said, drumming the table in front of us. "This is work that people are doing at universities. Cuisine is entering a new phase. There will be cooking at Harvard." I would have scoffed at this notion if I hadn't already read that Adrià was going to teach at Harvard that fall, presiding over a course called Science and Cooking: From Haute Cuisine to the Science of Soft Matter. The course would bring together Harvard science profs and top chefs like Adrià, his friend Jose Andrés, Wylie Dufresne of wd~50, and Dan Barber of Blue Hill.

"Cooking provides an ideal framework to study a variety of complex phenomena—from basic chemistry to materials science to applied physics," according to the physics professor David A. Weitz, one of the organizers of the course. "Much of what we do in the lab is what chefs like Ferran Adrià are now doing in their kitchens." (In fact, El Bulli's kitchen looked like a lab, with thirty-odd chefs and stagiaires in pristine whites lined up on either side of several spotless stainless steel cooking surfaces. There wasn't a flame in sight, and just three hours before the first seating the atmosphere was strangely calm and focused.) The Harvard course grew out of a hugely popular one-night stand in 2008, when Adrià spoke to an overflow Harvard audience about such subjects as the use of hydrocolloids that allow delicate fruit or vegetable purees to be transformed into a dense gel, and techniques like spherification, creating a resistant skin of liquid—like my spherical martini olive.

Having never finished high school, Adrià seemed tremendously proud of the Harvard connection—and of the honorary degrees from several Spanish universities. He also seemed to value his invitation to participate in the 2007 Documenta, the quinquennial art fair in Kassel, Germany. Rather than performing or speaking at the fair, Adrià decided to make El Bulli a pavilion, albeit one some eight hundred miles away from Kassel. Every day two festivalgoers were invited to travel to Cala Montjoi, have dinner, and write about the experience; these collected essays, along with assorted photographs and documents, were published as *Food for Thought, Thought for Food*. The selection of Adrià was not without controversy, some doubting that cooking and art were coextensive. But he himself is proud that the question's been raised. "The word 'artist' can't and shouldn't be used in respect to chefs," said Tony Bourdain, "with very few exceptions. Ferran Adrià is, without a doubt, an artist. I always find myself comparing Ferran to musicians—rather than other chefs. People like Jimi Hendrix . . . or Charlie Parker, who heard notes, heard music, where others heard nothing. Who made noises come out of their instruments that no one else had ever dreamed possible. I don't know—but suspect—that Ferran, like Hendrix, like Parker, might find it a burden year after year to be that far out in front of everybody else. I can't imagine what that pressure might be like."

I'm not entirely certain whether what Adrià creates is art, but I can say that dining at El Bulli was a truly extraordinary aesthetic experience. I felt more than a little like Keats on first looking into Chapman's Homer. I'd worried that the meal would be too intellectual to be genuinely enjoyable—a rap that one hears against Adrià, especially from those who have never eaten here—but in fact it was a hedonistic revel, at once a feast and a mind game, Dionysus and Apollo wrestling on the plate, the senses ultimately triumphing over the brain in the end. At each stage it seemed hard to imagine how the kitchen could follow up on some particularly exquisite creation; yet the rhythm of the dinner felt perfect, the individual courses seeming to add up to something like a narrative, although it was definitely postmodern, rather than linear. There was a Japanese chapter of about seven courses, including the best miso soup I've ever tasted and ten iterations of soy on a single plate; another chapter focused on strictly local ingredients, including sea anemone and pine nuts. Sweet and savory elements alternated throughout. We sometimes couldn't help laughing— beetroot cookie? Gorgonzola with chocolate?—though at other times we felt more like stout Cortés as described by Keats, stricken silent with wonder at the spectacle. And for brief moments I actually felt high, as if I'd ingested some fast-acting THC or psilocybin.

It would be interesting, if utterly improbable, to imagine the diner who arrived with neither preconceptions nor expectations. The unfussy, rustic Mediterranean decor of the dining room certainly couldn't prepare you for what was about to come. Your fellow diners are a mixed bunch: two well-dressed young newlyweds from France; a middle-aged New York couple in black; a Spanish couple in jeans and T-shirts; two glamorous women accompanying much older men, both in white jeans and skimpy tops, speaking English, one blonde with a French accent, the other brunette with an Italian. You might sense a certain giddiness in the air. Many of the diners are brandishing cameras, and Juli Soler, the maître d'hôtel, volunteers to take pictures. There is no silverware on the table, only a white linen tablecloth.

And then that deconstructed martini arrives, followed by four more "cocktails," including what looks like a strawberry made from frozen Campari, a gin fizz "snow," and a hot-and-cold gin fizz. At some point a piece of sculpture appears, a wavy blond convoluted ribbon that looks like a model of a deconstructed Eames chair, which the waiter insists is corn bread—without doubt the most delicious I've ever tasted, crunchy, salty, and slightly sweet. That's followed by something resembling a softball. The waiter cracks it open, the substance in question about as thick as a Christmas tree ornament, and sprinkles it with nutmeg. It's a sphere of semi-frozen Gorgonzola.

My wife's two favorite foods are bone marrow and oysters, but she never thought she'd eat them together, out of an oyster shell, or that the combination would be brilliant. Only a fanatic would try to match a wine to every course—though it's apparently been done. Instead, we drink Champagne, which is what the chef has recommended, or rather we drink one bottle of Champagne, another of Cava, the sparkling wine associated with Catalonia. The latter is the 2004 Kripta Brut Nature Gran Reserva, a toasty, rich bubbly that reminded me more than a little of the slightly oxidative Krug style. It came in a great bottle with a rounded bottom and needed to be kept upright in an ice bucket. The Champagne is one of my favorites, the VO from Anselme Selosse, the leading light of the small-grower movement. Although he recommends sparkling wine, Adrià himself favors beer. He consults for one of Spain's biggest breweries and came up with the idea for a beer in an attractive wine-like bottle for the fine-restaurant trade. (Adrià consults for several major Spanish food and beverage corporations, which helps subsidize El Bulli.)

At some point we're given a single honeysuckle blossom on a small plate and are instructed to pull off the stem and suck it. Again, we can't help laughing. In fact we laugh through much of the meal. The honeysuckle teases forth memories of childhood; the nectar of the blossom, almost certainly enhanced, is far more intense than I remember it from those long-ago summers, though when I ask Ferran about it later, he is uncharacteristically cagey about what was actually in it. The marinated rose petals with artichoke foam are not a complete success; they tasted exactly the way roses smell, but I discovered that I don't really like rose petals, and perhaps that's a good thing to know. The sprig of marinated pine, on the other hand, is delicious. Since my last unpleasant experience eating a sprig of pine some forty-five years ago, back in the days when I tasted almost everything I encountered in a spirit of childish open-mindedness, I didn't think I'd ever want to have one again, but I was wrong.

In the nights that followed my evening at El Bulli, I dined at two Michelin one-star restaurants in Barcelona, including one run by a disciple of Ferran's, and I found myself disappointed to be back in the realm of conventional cuisine. It's like climbing behind the wheel of a Camry after spending the day driving Ferraris at the company test track in Maranello. Or perhaps it would be more accurate to say it's like returning to the present day after spending a few hours in some utopian future complete with antigravity and previously unimagined erogenous zones. This feeling gradually fades, thank God, and I'm able to enjoy retro food once again. But I can't help hoping that Adrià changes his mind and that I get another chance to try whatever he's up to. In the meantime, I comfort myself with the thought that much of what I otherwise eat will be greatly influenced by his work, past and future.

Epilogue

Travels with Lora

Sharing food with another human being is an intimate act that should not be indulged in lightly.

—M. F. K. Fisher

When I first met Lora Zarubin, I could never have imagined that we'd find ourselves locked in adjacent cells in the police station of a provincial French town at three in the morning. In fact I never thought I'd see her again after our disastrous first encounter, which took place in 1995 at the Grill Room of the Four Seasons. My friend Dominique Browning had recently been appointed editor in chief of *House & Garden,* and she'd decided to ramp up the magazine's coverage of food and wine. She'd already hired Lora as food editor, and Lora was quite adamant that there should be a regular wine column. Dominique, a longtime friend, knew this was a passion of mine and thought it would be interesting to have someone outside the field write about it. When she proposed me, Lora and some of the other editors were aghast. I was known, among other things, for writing about people who abused controlled substances, and I was written about in the New York gossip press as one of those very individuals, a monster of ego and excess. Lora found it hard to believe I knew much about wine. Certainly I had a reputation as a party animal; no one had ever accused me of being a connoisseur.

When we got together for lunch with Dominique, I confirmed all of her worst suspicions. The night before I'd been out until the wee hours with Bret Easton Ellis, and I was not, as we say of certain wines, showing very well. There in the Grill Room, surrounded by moguls sipping mineral water, I felt seriously misplaced and miscast. Mort Zuckerman, Mort Janklow, Martha Stewart, Henry Kissinger, and a downtown fuckup brat-pack novelist. Even on the best of days this wouldn't have been my scene, or my hour to shine. I wasn't really in the mood to talk about wine, much less drink it. My olfactory acuity was at a low point. However, I was eventually able to impress Lora a little, despite my condition, correctly guessing the provenance of a glass that was given to me blind, surprising myself perhaps even more than Lora. One would have to say her admiration was grudging at best, and I believe Dominique gave me the job over her protests, but suddenly we were colleagues. Neither one of us could have predicted how intimate that association would become.

It was strange we hadn't met earlier; for an all too brief spell in the late eighties her eponymous restaurant in the West Village was one of my favorite dinner destinations, although I don't recall that I ever met the proprietress. At the time downtown restaurants were divided into those places where you went to see and be seen and those places where you went for the food. Although Lora's had a surfeit of celebrity patrons—Madonna was a regular—the food was the real draw; it was a homey place, the menu startlingly simple and refreshing at a time when chefs were competing to see how many diverse and incompatible ingredients they could cram into one dish, when every meal seemed to be topped with something along the lines of raspberry chili cilantro vinaigrette with green tea anchovy sorbet. Ah, yes, the eighties. Who can remember them? Strangely enough, I do remember a sublime grilled chicken I had upstairs at Lora's. When I first saw the menu, I didn't know what to make of it, so devoid of frills, flourishes, and furbelows. Where the hell was the chipotle mango pesto, the raspberry mole? (When I later learned she was from San Francisco, and was friends with Alice Waters of Chez Panisse fame, the whole thing made a little more sense.) Over the course of a few visits I noticed that the menu changed almost daily and was based on seasonally available ingredients—much less common then than it is today.

Some six years after Lora shuttered her restaurant and shouldered debts she'd be paying off for years to come, I was hired to write the wine column for *House & Garden*. Her other reservations aside, Lora was appalled to discover my lack of knowledge and enthusiasm for California wine, and she dispatched me there to begin my education, the first and last trip I made by myself for the magazine. It's possible she was trying to sabotage me by arranging my first-ever professional appointment with the winemaker Helen Turley, a.k.a the Wine Goddess, a notorious perfectionist and curmudgeon, but, scary as it was, I somehow managed to survive that tasting without entirely revealing my vast reserves of ignorance. In subsequent years I learned a great deal from Turley and her husband, John Wetlaufer—not only about tasting and viticulture, but also about the importance of taking milk thistle to protect the liver and how to sauté fresh foie gras. That first trip Lora also sent me to a little place in Yountville called the French Laundry. I'd eaten at Rakel, the chef's short-lived venture in downtown New York, but I was totally unprepared for the wildly inventive, multicourse orgy Thomas Keller was conjuring nightly at his new West Coast post. Later, I shared many feasts with Lora there, after days spent at wineries in Napa and Sonoma. Although she usually objected to overly elaborate cuisine, she was one of Keller's earliest and most enthusiastic fans.

From the start our respective roles in the Condé Nast hierarchy were ill defined. As food editor and full-time employee, she had a kind of supervisory role over my column, although she had no editorial background, and my columns were in fact edited by a literary intellectual named Elizabeth Pochoda, friend of Philip Roth's, late of *The Nation*. I guess Lora thought of herself as my boss, whereas I thought of her as my assistant. Luckily, I knew more about wine than she did. Not much more, but enough. On the other hand, she had an extraordinary palate; she was a great blind taster and could parse out the scent and flavor components of wine better than anyone I've ever known. She was also a great cook and utterly passionate about food; I didn't know all that much about food, wine's alleged boon companion, and Lora was to become my tutor in the joys of cooking and eating, although not without a fight, or rather many fights, along the way.

I'm still not sure how Lora became my travel companion or convinced Dominique to pay for her to accompany me on all wine-related trips. She must have suggested that I couldn't be trusted on my own, and it's true that I'm very absentminded and badly organized. Lora is the opposite. I don't want to say she's anal-retentive, but I can't think of a better phrase at the moment. She organized the trips, made the calls, held the tickets until the gate, and drove the rental car. She hated my driving and early on banned me from the driver's seat. Apparently, I bounce up and down on the accelerator in a way that's conducive to nausea. I was happy enough to be the navigator and happy to have everything taken care of. For the next twelve years we logged tens of thousands of miles across Europe, the States, and South America. We visited the best winemakers in the world: Angelo Gaja, Robert Mondavi, Richard Geoffroy of Dom Pérignon, Bruno Borie of Ducru-Beaucaillou, Marcel Guigal, Helen Turley, and Baroness Philippine Rothschild. We became friends with many of these people, some of them early in their careers. We dined with them at some of the best restaurants in the world, drank too much with them, and even flirted with some of them. At least I did and would have gotten lucky on occasion if not for Lora's interference. Determined not to see me sleep with anyone I shouldn't be sleeping with, she claimed it wasn't professional, but her own vehemence seemed strangely personal, her ostensible jealousy all the more interesting since she's gay.

Lora somehow must have thought that she was in the closet when we first met, or else that I was too much of a heterosexual clod to notice alternative sexual bents. About two years after we started working together, we were on a wine trip in the Napa Valley, and she made me sit down and watch the two-hour "coming out" episode of *Ellen,* Ellen DeGeneres's nineties sitcom. "Well, hon," she said afterward—she called everyone "hon"—"can you guess what I'm trying to say?" I pretended to be surprised, and we had a weepy, huggy scene, then opened a bottle of Champagne. I became the confidant of her love life, and she of mine. My third marriage was starting to unravel during our early years on the road, and Lora listened to the whole story. And I, in my turn, heard the story of the breakdown of the great love of her life, a few years before.

Food was an important part of our bond, almost as important as wine, though we didn't always agree on what, or how, to eat. Lora believes in simplicity of preparation and presentation. She loves to grill over an open fire and has often told me that our most memorable meal was an *asado,* a cookout of virtually every part of a recently living cow, washed down with some now forgotten Malbec, on the slopes of the Andes in Argentina. And indeed, as soon as she reminded me, I remembered eating beef liver on a stick, looking up at the snowcapped Andes after a vigorous horseback ride in the foothills, wondering how it was that the most romantic moments of my life seemed to be shared with my prickly lesbian friend.

Our quasi marriage had a surrogate daughter named Bessie, Lora's high-strung fox terrier, who usually traveled with us and barked incessantly at everyone she encountered along the way. I'd visited the new puppy the day Lora brought her home, and she subsequently greeted me with hysterical displays of affection, but she didn't seem to have much use for most other humans. Grateful as I was to be singled out, I was also frequently embarrassed by the way she treated the rest of my species, and more than a few hang-overs were exacerbated by that high-pitched bark echoing through the confines of a wine cellar. One winemaker expressed a wish, sotto voce, to toss her into a bubbling fermentation tank.

Bessie was happiest when it was just the three of us, on the road, or in a French restaurant where she could lie under the table and collect scraps. When it comes to restaurants, Bessie is defi-nitely a Francophile. Lora also likes French cuisine, up to a point: she believes that some of the best restaurants in France have no Michelin stars, that these are the places most likely to serve hon-est, regional food, whereas I also love the haute cuisine and drama of the two- and even three-star establishments. We were always struggling and clashing on this front. As she told a friend recently, "Jay believed in treating himself well, very well. We might have had four hours of wine tasting along with eating the food that gra-cious vintners always offer, but Jay had to end the day with a two-star meal. Often Jay ended up eating alone or inviting a stranger to join him, even if that stranger spoke a language he didn't in a country we knew little about."

One night we agreed to go to a famous two-star restaurant in Avignon, and though as I recall it was initially her idea, in the end it was hard to know whom she was madder at—me or the chef. "This food's so phony," she said, loud enough for everyone in the restaurant to hear. "It has no soul. It has no sense of place." She was right about that one, though she grudgingly came to admire Alain Ducasse's three-star restaurant in Paris, one of my favorites, even as I came to see the point of her no-star crusade. One of the best meals we ever had was a lunch at a place she somehow knew about, Elisabeth Bourgeois's starless restaurant in Provence, sit-ting out in the courtyard surrounded by birdcages and trees laden with cherries. We started out with the best tomato soup I've ever had, accompanied by a local Viognier, and later, after one of the best meals I've ever had in my life, we drove a few miles up the road to visit the man who'd made the Viognier and taste more of his wine.

Our split on the Michelin issue might have partly reflected the fact that she was the keeper of the expense account, the one who had to go back to New York and try to justify the $900 meal at Taillevent. In a way we both became prisoners of our roles, me playing the part of the spoiled epicure, Lora taking the part of the disciplinarian, although we were sometimes able to see the humor in the clash. Not infrequently we would drop the roles and collaborate, for example when we saw a particularly amazing bottle of wine on a list, calculating how much Condé Nast would be willing to bear and how much we would thereafter chip in together to get what we wanted. Such was the case when we were dining at Beaugravière in the Rhône Valley, which is famous for its wine list and for its way with black truffles in season, when, naturally, we arranged to arrive. (Or I should say, Lora arranged to arrive, since I was incapable of this kind of forward planning.) We knew that the 1989 Château Rayas on the list was a relative bargain at around $200, knew also the magazine would never spring for that *and* the truffles, so we asked the proprietor to divide the bill, half for *House & Garden* and a quarter for each of its trusted employees.

Memorably, there was no argument about the bill or about anything else when in 1999 we shared Easter lunch at La Tour d'Argent, looking out the window at Notre Dame and listening to the bells. The venue was her idea, even though at the time it had two Michelin stars. I wasn't even annoyed when Lora told me I didn't know what it was like to be raised a Christian. I had to remind her that Catholics were Christians, since she'd been raised in a strict, born-again household, a source of much guilt and torment for her later in life. I told her that I was feeling guilty myself for not having attended Easter Mass, although not so bad that I was unable to enjoy our lunch about as much as I've ever enjoyed a meal, guilt perhaps giving an edge to my appetite. The duck à la presse—served in a sauce made in part from its own blood and marrow—wasn't necessarily the greatest dish we'd ever eaten together, but we agreed it was absolutely superb that day, washed down with a bottle of 1990 d'Angerville Volnay Clos des Ducs—and then, for good measure, a 1989 Beaucastel, which lasted us through the cheese course—but it had been absolutely essential that we order it, the restaurant's signature dish.

As with so many other foods, Lora had introduced me to black truffles and decided that we should make a pilgrimage to the source, Périgord, also noted for its gut-busting cuisine, much of which involves ducks, geese, and their livers. Lora had somehow befriended the Pebeyre family, black truffle dealers extraordinaire, and we had an exquisite dinner at their home in Périgueux during which we stood beside the stove with Babeth Pebeyre and learned seventeen uses for black truffles while drinking copious amounts of Cahors, the inky Malbec of the region.

I'd discovered white truffles on my own, more or less by accident, when I was on a date shortly after I arrived in Manhattan and a waiter offered to shave some onto our pasta, and nearly had a heart attack when the bill arrived. But I craved them from that day forth—a passion Lora shared with me. We discovered Piedmont, the homeland of tartufi, together, and it became our favorite region. About the Langhe and its down-home cuisine we were in total agreement, and we both remember the Carne Cruda all'Albese at Da Cesare in Albaretto—the signature veal tartare dish, very delicately rendered here with some nice herbs, lemon, and olive oil. It was our first experience of this dish, and our first visit with the motormouth Angelo Gaja, the baron of Barbaresco, who terrified us with his driving on the way to the restaurant and with whom we would share many meals. Gaja taught us how to cut tagliatelle—or *tajarin,* in the local dialect—in the kitchen of a restaurant next to his winery in Barbaresco. We had the same dish at the Trattoria Della Posta in Monforte, a nineteenth-century restaurant overlooking some of the best vineyards in Barolo, with Luca Currado of Vietti. The menu wherever we went in Piedmont was reassuringly familiar after our first few visits—inevitably including Agnolotti del Plin, a little envelope stuffed with whatever, in this case, rabbit and veal. At Guido da Costigliole in Santo Stefano Belbo, at another dinner with Angelo Gaja, the agnolotti were served with a meat sauce and also plain, to be eaten by hand, preceded by a wonderful vitello tonnato, another Piedmontese standard, rendered more wonderful by the 2000 Gaja Sauvignon Blanc, an incredibly crisp and pure white made in tiny quantities. Neither one of us can remember the name of the restaurant where we first enjoyed the ultimate Piedmontese dish, but we'll never forget the taste of the almost transparent shavings from that huge, pink-hued white truffle showered over a sunny-side-up egg.

Typically, somewhere around the fifth or sixth day of travel, after we'd eaten two big meals and consumed a bottle and a half each a day, Lora's liver would give out, and she'd have a meltdown, screaming at me, threatening to go home, threatening to quit her job. Sometimes it happened when I failed in my navigational duties and we found ourselves stranded on a dirt road in Tuscany with no clue as to our whereabouts. Sometimes it was a disagreement about a particular wine. Sometimes it was the matter of the hotel room. She was convinced that sexism was at work whenever I got a better room than she did. A simpler explanation, possibly, was that I had a day job and my novels happened to be very popular in France and Italy, our most frequent destinations. But when I tried to suggest this to Lora, she told me I was being self-important. Her conflicted feeling about my books was one of the more curious aspects of our relationship. At times she would brag on me, and at other times she seemed convinced it was impossible that anyone had ever heard of them. In Milan, on our way to the Piedmont, I once made the mistake of pointing out one of my books on display in the window of a bookstore. She turned away and stalked up the street without a word, and I had to run to catch up with her. I think it's possible she was jealous of this other career, the one in which she wasn't my partner.

Lora was a witness to the slow disintegration of my marriage; and when I finally sold the four-bedroom apartment uptown that I'd shared with my wife and kids, she found me an apartment in her own building, the London Terrace in west Chelsea. I never really bothered to decorate my own place, and I loved being in hers, which was paradoxically exquisite *and* homey, with its beautifully curated collection of important photography, its antique cooking implements, vintage fabrics and light fixtures, and the fireplace that seemed always to be blazing. It was like the lair of an art director/homebody. Lora had a better eye than most set designers and had a bit of a second career as a designer for wealthy friends like Julianne Moore, her art tending to the illusion of artlessness. Whenever I got lonely, I hung out with Lora and Bessie downstairs. We liked being neighbors, although she came to regret that I was directly upstairs; she claimed to be able to distinguish various mating cries she heard and insisted that even when I was alone, I thumped and stomped on her ceiling. At least once or twice a week I would go downstairs with a bottle of good wine, and she would cook for me, a ritual we repeated on September 11, 2001. She ran upstairs to wake me, but I was already up, earlier than usual, and I'd seen the first plane hit while I was standing on a chair in front of the window trying to fix the chain on my blackout shade. And then, with a growing sense of shock and horror, we watched the towers fall from my picture window.

That night she cooked a pot-au-feu, and we opened the best stuff we had handy, a bottle of 1982 Lynch Bages from my stash, a bottle of 1990 Jaboulet Hermitage La Chapelle from hers. We figured we'd better seize the day, the future suddenly being entirely uncertain. It's a principle I have tried to continue to observe ever since. In the following weeks, when I worked at a soup kitchen near Ground Zero, Lora helped me connect with sources for food donations.

That spring, on a trip to Alsace, we had lunch with the wine-maker Olivier Humbrecht and his beautiful English wife, drinking old wines and eating the first white asparagus of the season. I think we were both pretty hot on Olivier's wife. We had some of the best white asparagus I have ever had, washed down with a spectacular 1990 Zind Humbrecht Muscat. That afternoon, at Lora's insistence, we drove two hours south to visit Bernard Antony, an acclaimed *affineur*. I had no idea what an *affineur* was, or does, but it turned out to be a man, or possibly a woman, who "raised" cheese to its proper state of maturity after it has left its maker. Alain Ducasse apparently discovered Antony, who in addition to provisioning the great restaurants of Paris served all-cheese dinners at his home in rural France for perhaps a dozen guests a few nights a week, and Lora was determined to be one of them, distance be damned. We had a hell of a time finding the unmarked house in the little town of Vieux-Ferrette but eventually found Antony, who took us on a tour of the caves under his house and later served us some forty or fifty cheeses and a great deal of wine. Antony kept opening special bottles for us once he learned that we were wine buffs. I remember him serving a perfect farmhouse Muenster with a Riesling from Boxler, and a soft, creamy Brie de Meaux with a Trimbach Pinot Noir. After a three-hour cheese bacchanal Lora once again insisted on driving us back to Strasbourg. For once she considered letting me drive but then judged me to be too intoxicated. An hour later we were pulled over at a roadblock, and the cops had no choice but to arrest Lora when they got a rough blood-alcohol reading from her Breathalyzer test.

"What about your husband?" asked one of the cops hopefully. "Maybe he can drive." The last thing they wanted was the headache of dealing with foreigners, of processing our arrest. Unfortunately, my blood alcohol was even higher than Lora's. So we spent the next few hours at the police station, talking with the cops and periodically blowing a new test. We spent our first hour in adjacent cells, but eventually they deemed us harmless and let us hang around the office. None of them seemed to speak English, and we both have pretty poor French, but I recall a lively and intricate conversation with the gendarmes that night. (One of the things that I always admired about Lora, even sober, was that she was never afraid to blunder forth *en français* and somehow managed to get her point across.) Lora kept saying I was a very famous writer, which seemed to impress them, France being one of the few countries in the world where writers rank high on the social ladder. Finally, close to dawn, they dropped us off near our car and told us to get out of their jurisdiction. I promised I'd get my French publisher to send them some books, but somehow I never got around to it.

Every year one of us would threaten to quit the magazine after suffering some slight at the hand of the other. I once missed a flight to Paris, where Lora was waiting to help me with a column about wine stores, because the fax the magazine's travel department had sent me had been blurry and I read six thirty as eight thirty. When I arrived at JFK at six thirty-five, having just missed the flight, I found that the cheap ticket they'd bought me wouldn't get me out on any other flight. Of course, no one, especially Lora, seemed to believe me. I couldn't reach her that night, and she went absolutely ballistic when I got her on the phone the next morning. Indignant at this lack of trust, I threatened to quit. When she finally returned, Dominique prescribed—no, insisted on—couples counseling for the two of us and got the magazine to pay for it (presumably a first in Condé Nast history). We did three or four sessions, and they helped me to understand Lora, and to realize what a difficult childhood she'd experienced, though we still had one or two breakdowns to go.

In October 2007, I was staying in the Beverly Hills Hotel when I got an e-mail from Lora with an alarming subject line. When I reached her, she told me Dominique had called the staff in to her office that morning to convey the news that *House & Garden* had been shut down. We'd been hearing the rumors for years and were almost inured to them. Almost from the moment Dominique resurrected the magazine, her rivals had been predicting its failure, but she'd lasted for twelve years, as had I, which, when I thought about it, surprised me. Doing a wine column seemed like a lark, and I certainly hadn't intended to stretch it out this long. I didn't know until long after it was over that it had been one of the great adventures of my life.

I was fortunate in having a parallel career, but I worried about my colleagues and Lora in particular. Eventually, she found a job with the *L.A. Times* as a food editor, which included commissioning wine pieces and complaining to me about the quality of the writing. I saw her a couple of times on trips to Los Angeles, where we went to the opening of Thomas Keller's Bouchon, but it only served to make us nostalgic for the feasts we'd enjoyed at the French Laundry in Napa. I'd made the mistake of inviting a group of high-strung and neurotic individuals—not that hard to do in L.A., actually—and no one really seemed to click. Lora seemed to be in a bad mood; she eventually told me the newspaper was bankrupt, hemorrhaging cash, and that her salary had been cut in half. In 2010 she moved back to New York to work part-time for her old friend Annie Leibovitz as a personal chef while she figured out her next move. I'm still using the Tuscan grill she gave me for my forty-fifth birthday to cook steaks and chops in my fireplace. She's been working hard at creating the perfect loaf of sourdough bread, and judging by samples she dropped off at my house in the Hamptons, I'd say she's getting close. We talk about doing a project together, and in fact a director who was at the dinner at Bouchon later expressed an interest in developing a screenplay about our travels together, but that idea seems to have gone the way of most Hollywood pitches.

Now, when I visit a wine region, I manage my own itinerary; there are no fights about driving, or choosing a restaurant, or expenses, no jealousy about rooms or waitresses. I still love discovering new wines and meeting the people who make them, eating meals with them, and walking their vineyards, although now and then on these journeys I feel something—or rather someone—is missing.

Acknowledgments

I'd like to raise a glass to Eben Shapiro, Emily Gitter, John Edwards, and Monika Anderson at *The Wall Street Journal* for their gentle and enlightened assistance.

One last time, hearty thanks to Dominique Browning, Lora Zarubin, and Elizabeth Pochoda for their friendship and support during my tenure at *House & Garden,* where some of these pieces were first published. Thanks also to James Truman, who lorded over all as Condé Nast's editorial director, and who in a later incarnation commissioned several of these pieces for *The Ritz-Carlton Magazine.*

Once again I must thank Gary Fisketjon for his meticulous scrutiny of my prose, and for his skeptical queries when things got too geeky. Thanks to his assistant Ruthie Reisner for keeping us both on track.

Special thanks to Binky Urban and Liz Farrell for making sure that I got well paid for these labors of love.

Many thanks to Jeanine Pepler for connecting me to the web and to Alana Tobacco for keeping me organized.

I'd also like to thank my drinking buddies, gentlemen and scholars all. And thanks to Anne, for putting up with us.

A Note on the Type

This book was set in Minion, a typeface produced by the Adobe Corporation specifically for the Macintosh personal computer, and released in 1990. Designed by Robert Slimbach, Minion combines the classic characteristics of old-style faces with the full complement of weights required for modern typesetting.

Typeset by Scribe, Philadelphia, Pennsylvania

Printed and bound by R. R. Donnelley, Harrisonburg, Virginia

Designed by M. Kristen Bearse

—